ARCTIC CIRCLE

60

NORTH ATLANTIC DRIFT

NORTH

Europe

40

Azores

Madeira

Canaries

CANARY CURRENT

Africa

TROPIC OF CANCER

20

ATLANTIC
Currents

Cape Verde Isl.

20

GUINEA CURRENT

20   0   20

METZIG

FAIR GODS
AND STONE FACES

FAIR GODS
AND
STONE FACES

Constance Irwin

St Martin's Press, New York

To my husband
W. R. IRWIN
for his invaluable assistance
and enormous patience

SECOND PRINTING

Copyright © 1963 by Constance Irwin
All rights reserved
Library of Congress Catalog Card Number 62-14158
MANUFACTURED IN THE UNITED STATES OF AMERICA
Designed by Joan Wall

FOREWORD

EACH YEAR archaeologists slog through the jungles of Mexico, cut away trees and tangled vines, and peel back the layers of history. Strange and perplexing things lie revealed. Each year archaeologists in Peru strike spades into desert or valley or mountain and summon forth cultures interred and forgotten. There too the dead, recalled from oblivion, bear mutely disturbing witness.

Running miles of books have described the Aztecs, the Mayas, the Incas. These publicized peoples, however, are only the uppermost layer of the refuse of history, comparable in their sphere to the Romans in theirs; for all were latecomers. Behind the Aztecs, Mayas, and Incas lie older, unexplained cultures and baffling hints of pre-Columbian, even pre-Christian contact between the New World and the Old.

The very mention of transoceanic pre-Columbian contact is anathema to many an archaeologist, abhorrent of hasty conclusions. He has seen a visitor gaze a moment on a Mexican pyramid and come away proclaiming that Egyptians themselves surely built it. And yet, now that the secretive earth is reluctantly yielding a few of the clues she long ago buried, this question of transoceanic contact within times that were somewhere historic has become enormously rich, enormously stirring.

Much still is unknown, but even that which is known is shared by too few. The finds have been duly reported in technical journals, but the intellectually agile reader who wishes to keep abreast of events in this age of specialization rarely turns to professional journals in fields outside his own. Moreover, only a few scattered efforts have been made to sort and assess the findings of recent research pertinent to this intriguing question.

I propose, therefore, to examine the evidence, fragmentary and moot though it is, of possible precursors of Columbus.

I am aware that every reader was educated in the belief that the American Indian existed for aeons in a hemisphere totally isolated, a belief that is slowly dissolving but still, like a shrinking glacier, looms large. Nor am I unaware that our national pride in the Genoese Christopher Columbus is sometimes perverted into prejudice, that many deem it an act of near sacrilege to place any name before his. In suggesting that nameless others may have found their way to these shores before him I do not for one instant propose to disparage the man whose achievement remains unique: he guided the world to our doorstep.

My purpose, furthermore, is not to persuade but to present—with as much detachment as the subject and human frailty permit—those elements found in early America suggestive of outside influence. It was perhaps inevitable that, becoming steeped in the subject, I should draw from these implications certain inferences. Failure to set them forth would have been sheer timidity and, in a sense, defection from duty: for if one believes that some New World artifacts seem to carry the mark of a certain Old World people, he must then investigate further, attempting to ascertain whether those people *could* have come, and how and when and why. He must lay out these findings for examination, that others may look them over and freely accept or reject them. History itself is inferential and interpretative, prehistory certainly more so. One who works without written records can be neither dogmatic nor doctrinaire.

Although this presentation is unrepentantly popularized, it is, within the limits of my ability, factually correct. I have drawn the material from several specialized fields of knowledge and from many sources: from the latest reports on research and from the writings of ancients, from learned journals and also from sound popularizations. It gnaws at my mind that this sprawling subject offers materials still unexamined; that errors have doubtless crept in, here and there; and that archaeological or botanical discoveries being made even as these lines are written may invalidate an opinion here set forth or confirm another beyond all doubt, thus rendering an intricately constructed hypothesis only a useless superstructure on fact.

As an amateur archaeologist I derive reassurance from the fact that nonprofessionals have sometimes served this field with distinction. Some of the world's great archaeological discoveries have been the achievements of amateurs: Heinrich Schliemann, merchant; John Lloyd Stephens, lawyer; Paul Émile Botta, physician; and George Smith, banknote-engraver, to mention a few. Obviously I pretend to no such original contribution but rather acknowledge with deepest gratitude the spade and trowel, the learning and insights, the bookish labors of many others.

For the inferences however I can blame no one: many or most are strictly my own. Those who reject my interpretation will nevertheless lay aside this book with a heightened awareness that shining pages of the American story were inscribed before 1492 as well as after, before the Mayas erected pyramids in the jungles of Mexico, before the Roman legions tramped across Europe, and even before the Golden Age of Greece.

CONSTANCE IRWIN

ACKNOWLEDGMENTS

The author wishes to express her thanks to the following persons and publishers for permission to excerpt from the books and articles listed below.

R. J. C. Atkinson, *Stonehenge*, Hamish Hamilton, Ltd., London. G. Bibby, *The Testimony of the Spade*, Alfred A. Knopf, Inc., New York, and William Collins Sons & Co., London. F. Blom, *The Conquest of Yucatan*, Houghton Mifflin Co., Boston. P. H. Buck, *Vikings of the Sunrise*, J. B. Lippincott Co., Philadelphia. C. A. Burland, "Postscript" to G. C. Vaillant, *The Aztecs of Mexico*, Penguin Books, Ltd., Harmondsworth, Middlesex. C. W. Ceram, *Gods, Graves, and Scholars*, translated by E. B. Garside, Alfred A. Knopf, Inc., New York, and Victor Gollancz, Ltd., London. Cieza, *The Travels of Pedro de Cieza de León, A.D. 1532-1550*, edited and translated by C. R. Markham, Hakluyt Society, London. H. Cortés, *Five Letters, 1519-1526*, translated by J. B. Morris, Routledge & Kegan Paul, Ltd., London. A. Cortesão, *The Nautical Chart of 1424*, University of Coimbra, Portugal. Bernal Díaz del Castillo, *The True History of the Conquest of New Spain*, translated by A. P. Maudslay. Hakluyt Society, London. *Diodorus of Sicily*, translated by C. H. Oldfather, Harvard University Press, Cambridge, Mass., and William Heinemann, Ltd., London. D. Diringer, *The Alphabet*, The Philosophical Library, New York. P. Drucker and R. F.

Heizer, "Gifts for the Jaguar Gods," *National Geographic,* National Geographic Society, Washington, D.C. P. Drucker, R. F. Heizer, and R. J. Squier, "Radiocarbon Dates from La Venta, Tabasco," *Science,* Washington, D.C. W. E. Gates, "Commentary upon the Maya-Tzental Perez Codex," *Papers of the Peabody Museum of American Archaeology and Ethnology,* Peabody Museum, Harvard University, Cambridge, Mass. H. S. Gladwin, *Men Out of Asia,* McGraw-Hill Book Co., New York. Hanno, *The Periplus of Hanno,* translated by W. H. Schoff, The Commercial Museum, Philadelphia. T. Heyerdahl, *Kon-Tiki,* Rand McNally & Co., Chicago, and George Allen & Unwin, Ltd., London. E. A. Hooton, *Up from the Ape,* The Macmillan Co., New York, E. E. Kisch, *Entdeckungen in Mexiko,* Aufbau-Verlag, Berlin. K. Macgowan, *Early Man in the New World,* The Macmillan Co., New York. J. A. Mason, *The Ancient Civilizations of Peru,* Penguin Books, Ltd., Harmondsworth, Middlesex. P. A. Means, *Ancient Civilizations of the Andes,* Charles Scribner's Sons, New York. S. G. Morley and G. W. Brainerd, *The Ancient Maya,* Stanford University Press, Stanford. E. Nordenskiöld, "Origin of the Indian Civilizations in South America," *The American Aborigines, Their Origin and Antiquity,* edited by D. Jenness, University of Toronto Press, Toronto. A. T. Olmstead, *History of Palestine and Syria,* Charles Scribner's Sons, New York. R. L. Olson, "Old Empires of the Andes," *Natural History,* The American Museum of Natural History, New York, G. Perrot and C. Chipiez, *History of Art in Phoenicia and Its Dependencies,* translated by W. Armstrong, Chapman & Hall, Ltd., London. I. B. Richman, *The Spanish Conquerors,* from The Chronicles of America Series, Yale University Press, New Haven. *The Song of Quetzalcoatl,* translated by J. H. Cornyn, Antioch Press, Yellow Springs. V. Stefansson, *Great Adventures and Explorations,* The Dial Press, New York. M. W. Stirling, "Discovering the New World's Oldest Dated Work of Man," and "Great Stone Faces of the Mexican Jungle," *National Geographic,* National Geographic Society, Washington, D.C. Strabo, *The Geography of Strabo,* translated by H. L. Jones, The Loeb Classical Library, William Heinemann, Ltd., London, and G. P. Putnam's Sons, New York. E. R. G. Taylor, *The Haven-Finding Art,* Hollis & Carter, Ltd., London. G. C. Vaillant, *The Aztecs of Mexico,* Doubleday, Doran, New York. G. C. Vaillant, "A Bearded Mystery," *Natural History,* The American Museum of Natural History, New York. A. Villiers, *Wild Ocean,* McGraw-Hill Book Co., New York. R. Wauchope, "Implications of Radiocarbon Dates from Middle and South America," *Middle American Research Records,* Tulane University, New Orleans. C. L. Woolley, *The Sumerians,* The Clarendon Press, Oxford. H. M. Wormington, *Ancient Man in North America,* Denver Museum of Natural History, Denver.

CONTENTS

ILLUSTRATIONS

MAPS

ENDPAPERS

FAIR GODS
AND STONE FACES

I

MONTEZUMA'S DILEMMA

ONE DROWSY MORNING in 1519, natives who dwelt along Mexico's eastern seaboard glanced out across the "waters of heaven" and noted with casual interest several peculiar objects out to sea. Slowly the queer craft grew larger, their sails glinting white against the indigo Gulf. The Indians' curiosity, mounting apace, passed from wonder into awe, for these were no long, low native canoes heaped high with pottery, feathers, or similar goods for the market. Instead, they were "floating towers"; tall tublike vessels with bellying sails, vessels that glided less than they bobbed, dipped deep, rose, nodded majestically, and moved inexorably closer.

The floating towers grew larger and larger, swept in toward shore, and anchored. Soon they were spewing forth strange-looking men—men with white faces, white hands, and bristling black beards. To the beardless yellow-brown Indians the newcomers seemed as alien as creatures from space. And yet not utterly alien, for legend told that once long ago another such personage, white and bearded, had come to this land from out of the east, bringing the gift of knowledge. In time the Fair God had de-

3

parted, promising that others like him would come "from the sea where the sun rises."

Now promptly the natives dispatched a runner to report the arrival to Montezuma, the Aztec *tlacatecuhtli,* or Chief-of-Men, who lived far inland over the mountains.

FIGURE 1. The Spanish landing near the site of Veracruz in 1519. *Codex Florentino.*

Off in the Valley of Mexico, the high plateau on which Mexico City even then stood, Montezuma duly received the report. It was probably the most disquieting news he had ever received in a reign that was rife with dissension. If these fair strangers were would-be conquerors, Montezuma as head war chief of the Aztecs must annihilate or expel them. If, however, they were sent by the Fair God Quetzalcoatl, then Montezuma as Aztec high priest must welcome and honor them. And well they might be, for this was the year Ce Acatl, year of the morning star, associated in legend with the God of the Planet Venus, the long-vanished Quetzalcoatl.

Montezuma pondered the situation.

Feeling his way in approved diplomatic fashion, he first dispatched emissaries to call on the leader of the fair-skinned strangers, with instructions to ascertain who he might be and why he had come. The emissaries returned bearing gifts. One article in particular must have shaken the Aztec ruler: a gilt helmet of a style that was widely asserted to have been worn by the gods of Mexico. Orders from the white leader came with the helmet: "Fill it with gold dust!" The helmet was filled with grains of gold and returned to its owner. With it went other gifts great and small—objects wrought from silver and gold, their value possibly three hundred thousand dollars. This was scarcely the way to deter a gold-hungry Spaniard, had Montezuma but known.

Soon came word that the white men—or white gods—were heading west. They were coming on swift-striding creatures who "swallowed the ground with fierceness and rage"—great animals "clothed with thunder." The Indians lacked even a name for these unbelievable creatures, for horses—like camels and mammoths—had disappeared from this hemisphere countless centuries earlier.

FIGURE 2. Spanish cavalry and crossbows. *Codex Florentino.*

Word came again. The white men were moving closer. Soon they would reach the gates of the Aztec capital city, Mexico-Tenochtitlán. Montezuma waited and wondered.

While Montezuma was vacillating, shuttling unhappily back and forth between two potentially fatal courses, Hernán Cortés and the hour of decision were fast approaching.

Having anchored his fleet near the site of the present-day Veracruz, Cortés and his four hundred Spanish conquistadors were at that moment marching proudly behind the banner of the cross farther and ever farther inland. Plodding across territory never before penetrated by Europeans, the Spaniards were jolted time and again by glimpses of a culture far higher than any they had seen in the West Indies. In Mexico, they noted, the natives were "richly and tastefully" clothed in shirts and cloaks of white and colored cotton. Here people wore jeweled earrings fashioned from gold and silver. And here, above all, were cities.

Resting for a time at Tlaxcala, still almost seventy miles east of his goal, Cortés wrote to his emperor, Charles V, the grandson of Ferdinand and Isabella: "The city [Tlaxcala] is . . . almost incredible. It is much larger than Granada and much better fortified. Its houses are as fine and its inhabitants far more numerous than those of Granada when that city was captured."

Spanish Granada, when Ferdinand and Isabella wrested it from the Moors, was a city of some 200,000. Archaeologists have questioned whether Mexican Tlaxcala, which since has dwindled to a mere 5,000, was ever as large as Granada. Some scholars, suspecting gross exaggeration, prefer to believe that the Tlaxcala seen by Cortés was about as large as its neighbor Cholula, which Las Casas in his *Destruccion de las Indias* estimated at approximately 30,000. Even at that, these were no mean cities to have been built by "savages," as too often all preconquest American natives are labeled by those whose concept of Indians was shaped and hardened in early youth in the image of the Stone Age people who harassed the English colonists in the eastern United States.

"There is a market in this city," Cortés continued his description of Tlaxcala, "in which more than thirty thousand people daily are occupied in buying and selling, and this in addition to other similar shops which there are in all parts of the city. Nothing is lacking in this market of what they are wont to use, whether utensils, garments, footwear or the like. . . . There are also public baths. Finally, good order and an efficient police system are maintained among them, and they behave as people of sense and reason."[1]

From Tlaxcala the Spaniards continued westward and soon were nearing their destination, the halls of Montezuma in Mexico-Tenochtitlán, which today we call Mexico City.

FIGURE 3. Cortés and conquistadors ask directions to Mexico City; in the background: Popocatepetl. *Codex Florentino.*

Came the eighth of November, 1519. In the morning the conquistadors arrived at a causeway that would lead them across a lake, a causeway so broad and strong, wrote Cortés, "that eight horsemen could ride along it abreast." But broad as it was, his honest and doughty soldier Bernal Díaz added, "it was so crowded with people . . . that we were hardly able to pass." The lake itself swarmed with canoes, all of them filled with people. And four miles out in the lake lay the city Cortés was seeking.

The Spaniards came on, marveling, drawing closer with every step to "the most romantic moment in all history," as one historian terms it, when Europeans first gazed on the living city of wonders. "Gazing on such wonderful sights," said Bernal Díaz, "we did not know . . . whether what appeared before us was real, for on one side, on the land, there were great cities, and in the lake ever so many more . . . and in the Causeway were many bridges at intervals, and in front of us stood the great City of Mexico, and we—we did not even number four hundred soldiers!"[2]

Within a mile of the city and still on the causeway, the conquistadors saw a large group of Aztecs advancing toward them, clad in rich and colorful mantles. Approaching Cortés, each Aztec subchief in turn placed his hand on the ground and kissed it. "For nearly an hour," Cortés relates querulously, "I stood while they performed this ceremony." Then, with four subchiefs clearing the causeway before them, the Spaniards continued their march to conquest.

Close to the city they crossed a bridge and noted uneasily that certain beams were removable: the bridge could serve as a drawbridge, cutting off their escape from the island city. Bernal Díaz and many another "remembered the words and the warnings given us . . . that we should beware of entering Mexico, where they would kill us as soon as they had us inside." The Spaniards had four hundred men, fifteen horses, and seven light guns, sixteenth-century model. At the command of Montezuma—should he elect to use them—were untold thousands of skillful and tested warriors, their weapons the bow and arrow and the murderous *macquaitl,* a wooden broadsword edged with volcanic glass which could lop off a man's head with a single stroke.

But now the escorted invaders had almost reached the city. Far down the street they could see Montezuma himself approaching, borne on a sumptuous litter, followed by two hundred nobles. "They came forward in two long lines," wrote Cortés, "keeping close to the walls of the street, which is very broad and fine and so straight that one can see from one end of it to the other, though it is some two-thirds of a league in length and lined on

both sides with very beautiful, large houses. . . ."³ Here in Tenochtitlán were white temples, official buildings, and communal
dwellings built of stone; and everywhere roses were growing. Here
were canals as in Venice, drawbridges, sluice dikes, a double
aqueduct made of concrete, fountains and baths—and down the
middle of the street the ruler himself now fully in view.

The litter bearers halted, and Montezuma stepped down. A
slender man of approximately forty, he was wearing a robe of
azure and gold, and golden sandals studded with precious stones.
Before him, nobles and chieftains were sweeping the ground
and spreading fine cloths for the great Montezuma to tread on.
Slowly he walked forward, attendants holding over him a canopy
made of green feathers embroidered with gold and silver and
bordered with pearls. Along the avenue hundreds of barefoot
natives, afire with curiosity, struggled to keep their eyes on the
ground, for no one was permitted to gaze on the glory of
Montezuma.

Cortés, dismounting from his horse, strode forward with armor
clanking. Simultaneously the two leaders greeted each other,
and Cortés removed a necklace of pearls and crystals which he
was wearing and hung it about Montezuma's neck. When the
high-level diplomatic exchanges had been concluded, the Aztec
nobles came forward and greeted Cortés by kissing the earth.
This done, Montezuma turned and led the way into the city
(Figure 4). His nobles followed in two long lines, eyes focused
reverently on the ground.

"They took us to lodge in some large houses," Bernal Díaz
continued his eyewitness account, "where there were apartments
for all of us, for they had belonged to the father of the Great
Montezuma. . . . They took us to lodge in that house because
they called us Teules [gods], and took us for such."⁴

So the Spaniards moved in—into palaces that were coated
"with shining cement and swept and garlanded," into "great
halls and chambers canopied with the cloth of the country." The
wary conquistadors, however, "placed the artillery pointing in a
convenient direction."

And then they waited.

Much later Montezuma arrived with a company of kinsmen
and chieftains. He indicated a low bench richly embroidered in

FIGURE 4. Mexico-Tenochtitlán in 1519. To the left of the great temple stands the palace of Axayacatl, father of Montezuma, where Cortés and his men were housed. To the right of the great temple stands the palace of Montezuma. Reconstruction by Ignacio Marquina.

gold, and asked Cortés to be seated. Nearby stood the interpreter Cortés had acquired shortly after landing: the beauteous and intelligent Marina, who spoke both Maya and Aztec and who, as Cortés' mistress, had quickly learned Spanish. Montezuma seated himself near Cortés and began to speak:

"Long time have we been informed by the writings of our ancestors," said Montezuma, "that neither myself nor any of those who inhabit this land are natives of it, but rather strangers who have come to it from foreign parts. We likewise know that from those parts our nation was led by a certain lord (to whom all were subject), and who then went back to his native land, where he remained so long delaying his return that at his coming those whom he had left had married the women of the land and had many children by them and had built themselves cities in which they lived, so that they would in no wise return to their own land nor acknowledge him as lord; upon which he left them.

FIGURE 5.   Montezuma, Cortés, and his interpreter Marina. Lienzo de Tlaxcala.

And we have always believed that among his descendants one would surely come to subject this land and us as rightful vassals. Now seeing the regions from which you say you come, which is from where the sun rises, and the news you tell us of this great king and ruler who sent you hither, we believe and hold it certain that he is our natural lord: especially in that you say he has long had knowledge of us.

"Wherefore," Montezuma concluded, "be certain that we will obey you and hold you as lord in place of that great lord of whom you speak, in which service there shall be neither slackness nor deceit: and throughout all the land, that is to say all that I rule, you may command anything you desire, and it shall be obeyed and done, and all that we have is at your will and pleasure."[5]

This is the note on which the account should end. But history has a sly way of being anticlimactic. Not all of the warlike Aztecs shared Montezuma's views—views that he literally stood up for, was stoned by his own people and died for. The trail of Cortés was long and bloody before the nobles of Tenochtitlán again bent a knee to the strangers who—despite their white faces and bristling beards—were not the emissaries of Quetzalcoatl.

It is one of fate's poorer ironies that Quetzalcoatl, to whom the Mexicans attributed their culture, was even for an hour confused with Cortés who destroyed it—"beheaded a culture as the passer-by sweeps off the head of a sunflower."

2

COLUMBUS CAME LATE

THE ENDURING LEGEND of a bearded Fair God who came out of the east in the misty past and departed again into the sunrise is only one of the myriad mysteries of Middle America. Old statues, old murals, old maps, and old manuscripts reveal that the history of early America is immensely richer than most of us ever have dreamed; but interpretation of this snarl of evidence has long been the problem. Now in the twentieth century the probing spade, as it lays bare the moldering bones and stones of vanished peoples, heaps riddle upon riddle—and perhaps here and there a clue to the answer.

The Spanish conquistadors and missionaries who came on the heels of Columbus and swarmed across the New World's wasp waist in the sixteenth century noted—in areas presumably never before visited by Europeans—hundreds of cultural similarities which bespoke, to them, an Old World origin. Presently, out of their observations and their reports to a startled Europe, there evolved a dozen different theories attributing these amazing American islands of higher culture to contact with the Phoenicians, the Egyptians, the Hittites, the Babylonians, or the Greeks, or even to the lost tribes of Israel, to Atlantis, or the lost continent of Mu.

But positive proof was not forthcoming. And in the nineteenth century the new broom of science swept all of these theories out like so much rubbish.

Today the most widely known "fact" of American history, as tests have shown, is this: in 1492 Columbus discovered America. Generations of Americans have been drilled to believe that for aeons the Western Hemisphere, isolated by two great oceans, lay totally unheard of—till scarlet-clad Christopher Columbus stepped ashore and planted the Spanish standard on the beach of an island he named San Salvador. This theory, in turn, has since been exploded, gently and respectfully, with so timid a *poof* as to be scarcely audible. For the achievements of Christopher Columbus are many, and our debt to him can never be lightly dismissed. From 1492 on, the line of development is essentially unbroken. The inscription on his tomb is the literal truth: "To Castile and León Columbus gave a new world"; and Castile and León then staked out the unclaimed hemisphere.

Nevertheless, Columbus came late. The eyes of other Europeans had gazed upon the New World long before Columbus first saw it.

Public acceptance of this flat statement has moved at a snail's pace, in part perhaps because little of what is now known has found its way into textbooks. In the bristling polemical world of the academics, the reputable scholar armors himself with conservatism; anticipating attack, he is loath to stand on vulnerable ground. The Columbus cult still holds the fort, and authentication of the precursors of Columbus is rarely easy. Documentary proof of earlier discoveries is scanty or often nonexistent. At least one such discovery antedated writing in the homeland of the explorers. Some of the claims are patently false; thus others are charged unwarrantedly with guilt by association. And even though some are true and are proved so, the detractors can ask: Do they really matter?

By and large this is the tone of twentieth-century scholarship: that discoveries of the New World before the year 1492 contributed nothing of permanent value and hence are without historical significance. To this point of view the late A. W. Brøgger took strong exception. "No," he replied in his presidential address before the second International Congress of Archaeologists in Oslo in 1934, "not if you imagine 'the historical process' as a deliberate progress from prehistoric times to the present day, and every phase of it as of necessity fitting into the preparations for our modern civilization. But it is precisely the logical conclusion of my argument that this view of 'the historical process' is wrong. There is no steady progress; there are ups and downs, jumps and mutations."[1]

One such deviation is suggested by a time-faded map bearing the date 1424, which was rediscovered in 1946. For a century this sea chart had lain buried among the thousands of manuscripts in the awesome miscellany collected by Sir Thomas Phillipps, an eccentric English antiquarian who died in 1872. Falling at last into other hands, the map was dug out, dusted, and studied. Four red and blue blotches in the western Atlantic mark four islands, one of them clearly labeled Antilia. The importance of the chart was deemed to be such that Armando Cortesão, a world-acknowledged authority on fifteenth-century maps, was asked to study it and render judgment. After exhaustive scrutiny Cortesão concluded that the map is authentic and that the island group which includes Antilia definitely lies in the New World. In other words, here is a map of New World islands charted almost seven decades before Columbus set out for the Indies.

In this connection it is interesting to note that Ferdinand Columbus wrote that his father, before undertaking his first trans-Atlantic voyage, had "diligently gathered information" about a mysterious island called Antilia, which was said to lie far to the west in the Atlantic. "There are those who affirm," wrote Ferdinand Columbus, "that some Portuguese mariners have been to the island but could never find their way back to it again."[2]

Every schoolchild knows that a Portuguese junta, a committee of men well versed in geography and navigation, rejected Columbus' proposal to sail westward to obtain the wealth of the Orient. Less widely known is the fact that this much-maligned junta knew full well that the earth was round and doubtless knew also that the Genoese mariner had grossly underestimated the girth of the globe and hence the length of a voyage westward from Portugal to the Orient. It is of especial significance that within the same year the well-advised, canny King John II of Portugal granted permission to two other mariners, Dulmo and Estreito (the former a Dutchman whose name was really Van Ulm), to sail westward in search of Antilia with the promise of certain privileges in that "island or continental land."

This was the pattern: each man seeking what had once been found and then lost again.

A favorite device of modern authors is to refer to Antilia as a "mythical" island. We need scarcely embroil ourselves here, however, in the controversy of Antilia, for although ships were roaming the dark Atlantic during much of the fifteenth century, they were by no means the first to do so.

Moving backward through time, we note that before the dawn of the year 1000, white colonists had landed and built their homes on New World soil.

The Norsemen—or vikings, if you prefer—settled in Greenland in about 985 A.D., and there in the shadow of the growing glacier their descendants dwelt as civilized Christian Europeans for almost five hundred years, even down to the lifetime of Columbus. In far-off Rome the pope was aware of his wandering sheep and saw fit to send out a Bishop of Greenland early in the twelfth century. It was, by strange coincidence, in the year 1492 that Pope Alexander VI expressed concern in a letter still extant as to the fate of his children in Greenland, "which is at the end of the world." This letter was first made public from Vatican files in the twentieth century. Also in the twentieth century the ruins of twelve pre-Columbian Christian churches have been discovered in Greenland. Archaeologist Poul Nørlund, digging in the graveyard of one of these churches, exhumed bodies that had been remarkably well preserved by the frozen subsoil— bodies still clothed in garments that represented the height of fashion in Europe in 1450.[3] Here is positive proof that not only life but also contact continued at least till that date. In other words, ships were plying between the Old and the New World within the lifetime of Columbus.

Geographically Greenland lies in the New World and therefore warrants acclaim as the site of the earliest fully authenticated

European colony in the Western Hemisphere. But politically and spiritually Greenland was rather a distant segment of Europe. Thus our major interest in Greenland focuses on those stout-hearted Greenlanders who left their misty white mountains behind them and sailed southwest to Vinland.

There can no longer be any doubt that Leif Ericsson reached —if he did not discover—the North American continent. The Greenlanders themselves in their written records accord the honor of that discovery to another Greenlander, Bjarni Herjulfsson, in the year 985 or 986 A.D.; and Bjarni in turn, one infers, told Leif the Lucky what route to follow. Bjarni's discovery is still controversial, but Leif Ericsson's voyage to Vinland must be accepted as fact and is recorded as such in the soberest records of Greenland and Iceland. The discovery of America by the Norsemen was, moreover, set down in writing outside of Scandinavian lands when the Vinland voyages were yet within living memory. In about 1070 a German scholar, Adam of Bremen, described the new land in his *Descriptio Insularum Aquilonis.*

One of the strangest gaps in the knowledge of Americans today concerns the deeds of Thorfinn Karlsefni, an Icelander who led two or three ships to the North American continent in about 1011—ships that rode low with their heavy lading of cattle and colonists, for these people planned to settle in the new land if they could. Karlsefni's expedition and the birth of his son Snorri, the first white child of written record born on the American continent, are accepted as facts without a whisper of doubt by those who know the material best. Details of topography and thumbnail descriptions of the natives we know as Indians were reported, repeated, and recorded in Iceland; and the vellum was darkening with age before Columbus was born.

To their greater glory but ultimate failure, these early American colonists lived too soon—before the invention of gunpowder, compass, and quadrant; before the construction of tall-masted, high-sided vessels; and most of all before Europe itself was ready. And yet, like Miniver Cheevy, they also were born too late. "At the end of a seafaring epoch," Brøgger observed, "it is no use making 'discoveries'; they disappear in the general ruins." When the gusty wind of adventure dies, when the seafarer folds his sails and the whole people turn to tilling the home fields, who then will follow in the explorer's gossamer wake? The land he has found is swallowed again by the sea, as it were; centuries pass, and its very existence is all but forgotten.

These, then, were white men who looked on the New World before Columbus. But fair as they were and bearded, they were not the bearded Fair Gods of Middle America. There is nothing in any Norse record which suggests that those sea rovers ranged as far south as Mexico or Central or South America. The undated legends of Fair Gods are, moreover, found in association with baffling ruins of higher cultures—ruins older than a mere thousand years.

And so once again we move backward in time.

Beyond the Norsemen we enter the nebulous realm of legend, where fact is blended with fiction into a strange and heady concoction not to be trusted, and yet to be tasted and tested and analyzed. To reject these ancient legends *in toto* is surely the easiest course—but scarcely the course of one who would hope to determine the component of truth which once was the legends' basic ingredient.

From southern Europe comes the legend of the seven Portuguese bishops who fled with their people in seven ships—ostensibly to the New World—when the Moors invaded and conquered Spain early in the eighth century. It would be difficult indeed to make a case for their safe arrival, though admittedly stranger things have happened.

From Ireland come the *Imrama* or Irish sea legends, fantastic tales of the seagoing monk St. Brendan and his long, mysterious voyages upon the Atlantic during the sixth century, including a voyage to an unknown land or island where he tarried, traditionally, from 565 till 573 A.D. Some students stoutly believe that St. Brendan was the first European to discover the New World. And perhaps he was, but proof of the feat is lacking. On the other hand, it is hard to forget that the vanguard of Spaniards who entered Mexico and Central America saw several things (including the rites of baptism and penance as practiced by the Mayas) which suggested to them that other Christians had passed this way before.

Whether St. Brendan reached the New World, however, or only one of the long-lost islands which lie off the Old (islands discovered once by Phoenicians and long since forgotten), he is scarcely our man, for legends of Fair Gods are older still.

Going back, therefore, yet deeper into the past, we come to one of the strangest finds that American soil has yielded. A hoard of several hundred Roman coins, the latest from about 350 A.D., was dug up near the shore in Venezuela a few years ago. Here indeed is an early American mystery!

And yet not the earliest. For archaeologists hacking their way through Middle American jungles have latterly come upon great stone faces and faces tiny, hook-nosed, and bearded carefully carved from jade, faces on pottery, faces on buildings—faces which bear little resemblance to those of Indians but much to a certain Old World type. These faces were found where higher cultures had flourished not only before the Christian era but back in the days when "the Eternal City" was little more than a village.

If one reconsiders the possibility that ancient seafarers found their way to these shores, then several stray pieces that have long perplexed the literate world fall suddenly into place. One such stray piece is the knowledge which ancient Greek writers displayed of a land that lay far out in the Atlantic. In the fourth century B.C., for example, the Greek Theopompus could write that beyond the known world there was "an island of immense extent inhabited by strange people quite different from ours." There are, to be sure, islands in the eastern Atlantic, and hence Old World islands, but none of immense extent. Other ancients too, recording legends out of a past dim and distant even to them, wrote of lands beyond the Pillars of Hercules—far beyond. This baffling tradition possessed a vitality that kept it alive through the ages.

I therefore propose, later in this investigation, to look at the ancient maritime nations and delve somewhat into their nautical past in an attempt to ascertain the why and how of any such voyage.

Of the myriad questions surrounding this thorny problem of transoceanic contact, one above all persists. It is asked most often by the "dirt" archaeologists themselves, who quickly acquire a proprietary air toward the people whose buildings and baubles they daily uncover: Why must one feel that *anyone* came? What hemispheric inferiority complex compels the belief that American natives could not themselves by their labors and theirs alone have produced the marvels of Middle America?

The answer is simply that, having turned early to agriculture, they could have—and perhaps they did. But this answer in turn leaves many questions dangling unanswered—legends of bearded Fair Gods, for example, and bearded stone faces and innumerable other puzzlers—and leaves them among those ruins of higher cultures that shine like a few bright torches in this vast half-world of savagery.

Thus, willy-nilly, we find ourselves set down in the midst of a seething battle: the war of the archaeologists. The issue here is whether those orchidaceous pre-Columbian Indian cultures were strictly home-grown or largely imported. On the battlefield of the archaeologists the waving banners are labeled Diffusion and Independent Invention.

Man, the independent inventionist argues, is a creative animal. If man can invent in one place, he can invent in another. Facing a similar need and having arrived at a given cultural level, he might well invent something previously invented elsewhere, even halfway around the world. Similarity, this faction maintains, is no proof of imitation. And it certainly cannot prove that somebody sailed an ocean transporting the great invention inside his hull or his skull. The independent inventionist doubts that anyone ever did—before Columbus.

The diffusionist might go along with this line of thought at the start—but not very far. He insists that *identity* in *complex* inventions can never be coincidental. Also, he asks, if nobody came, why did complex inventions which duplicate those of the Old World appear in the *early*, the infant years of each of the Indian centers of culture? Why was so little of real importance added later?

One might assume that somewhere there must be a middle ground, a granting of certain concessions to both. Traditionally, however, the middle ground on a battlefield is no man's land;

in the war of the archaeologists too, the middle ground is sparsely populated.

On one point all will agree. Columbus was not the first to set eyes on the New World; nor were the Norsemen; nor, if they came at all, were the Irish, the Romans, or the roving Phoenicians. Others had traveled this way before them. Who came first? That tireless traveler, Stone Age man, who managed to precede historic man to every continent except the seventh, grim Antarctica. We call the first Americans "Indians," but where did the Indians come from?

It is not my purpose to dwell at length on the peregrinations of prototypal Indians, but this discussion of early Americans would be incomplete without a brief chapter on the first and the staunchest, those immigrant pioneers from whom the red Indian himself evolved. For the ancestors of the Indians came from another continent, even as once our own forefathers came, but with this difference: the Indians traveled on foot.

ACROSS THE TOP
OF THE WORLD

TIME WAS, the Americas lay fair and fertile with fish and fowl and game and waving grass, but not one human being. Then came the true discoverer, unknown and forever nameless.

The peopling of the Western Hemisphere is one of the great dramas of all time, twenty-five thousand years or more in the making, and one of the great mysteries too. It is a pageant enacted by many men from many places—black, brown, yellow, and probably white men—for the so-called red man evolved from all of these; the American Indian is not of one race but a mixture of many.

Having gone backward in time beyond all written records, beyond the earliest surviving legend, we must piece together the shards of evidence like a jigsaw puzzle. In the ashes of ancient campfires and among the time-buried fragments of old bones and stone weapons we seek the answers to such fundamental questions as these: How do we know that the Americas lay unpeopled long after men were roaming about in Asia, Africa, and Europe? Where did the first American come from, and why and when? How did he get here, what did he look like, where did he go? And who came after?

It is generally conceded that this hemisphere was not the cradle of human life because here there were no great apes. Anthropologists believe with Darwin that man and the great apes—gorilla, chimpanzee, orangutan—evolved from a common primate ancestor. Where the great apes were found, there too was early man; but the Western Hemisphere seems to have had neither. Kenneth Macgowan puts it succinctly: "Its monkeys are quite out of the running. They have four too many teeth, their nose is flat, and they are cursed with a prehensile tail."[1]

About 1,750,000 years ago—a mere flicker of time in the life of this spinning globe—earth's earliest manlike creature emerged. The remains of *Zinjanthropus,* discovered in East Africa in 1959, were recently submitted to a potassium-argon isotope test, and his age was calculated with a probable error of less than 2%—which is closer than we can estimate the age of some of our daily associates. Then there was *Homo erectus,* whose age is generally estimated at almost a million years. *Homo erectus* had a smallish brain and virtually no forehead or chin, but he walked erect like a man. Hundreds of millennia later a brutish-looking fellow appeared, long-jawed and burly, stooped and shambling, behind whose low brow lay a large brain. Neanderthal Man exemplifies this species. Meanwhile—no one knows where or when—the first modern man had come into being, perhaps 300,000 years ago, though theories vary widely. Tall, handsome, intelligent, he existed contemporaneously with the anatomically more primitive types, and eventually annihilated, assimilated, or merely survived them. We modestly call this modern man (and ourselves) *Homo sapiens.* Given a shave, a haircut, and suitable clothes, he could pass unnoticed on the street today.

Early man grappled with a fearsome world, his nimble fingers and growing brain his only distinctive equipment. Food was the first necessity, and he sampled whatever came to hand. He chomped on roots and fruits and nuts; he nibbled on berries and insects. Presently—perhaps about 650,000 years ago, though dating is hazardous—his fingers began to shape crude tools, and the Paleolithic or Old Stone Age began. Of all earth's creatures only man has created tools. First with a club and a chopper (a cracked stone

clumsily sharpened) and later with a spear, a hand ax, a scraper—
but most of all with guile and cunning—man became a great
hunter. As the first rude tool was the indispensable precursor of
the space ship, so too the first man to quit the ancestral forest was
the spiritual progenitor of the man who will one day visit the
moon.

Pursuing the migrant beasts, early man wandered far afield—
wandered for thousands of centuries. He meandered across three
continents, leaving his eoliths or "dawn stones," the crudest of
human implements, and sometimes leaving his skull. While he was
wandering, aeons rolled by. The human mind can scarcely cope
with time so vast and tends to telescope millennia. Little enough
there was to show for those aeons, but these were the critical years
of the species, corresponding to the first few months of the human
embryo or the first few days of the germinating seed beneath the
warm topsoil. In 50,000 B.C., man was still in the Stone Age,
living by hunting and fishing and gathering food: he had not
yet learned to grow it.

And still the Americas lay unpeopled—till, finally, man came.

Our first discoverers came from the west, on foot. They
walked the weary miles across Asia, ever northward and eastward. At night they rested by campfires and talked of what
tomorrow might bring. Old men died on the way, babies were
born, and still the people moved on. As the years sloughed away,
innumerable generations lived out their span and died; and
still the people moved on, ever northward and eastward. They
came by the great-circle route, crossing into the New World
where Siberia and Alaska, reaching out, almost touch fingertips
—and once did. Probably our first discoverers were hunters, pursuing the wandering beasts on which their existence was based.
They could also, however, have been the hunted.

Only a few anthropologists believe that the first Americans
may have been Pygmies, but the reasons merit a passing glance,
stemming as they do from the ways of stick-and-stone culture,
when men ate men. "Pygmies must have seemed particularly
luscious," writes Harold S. Gladwin, "and the poor little devils
were chased literally to the ends of the earth." Gladwin suggests
that we follow Griffith Taylor's advice and imagine ourselves

poised above the North Pole. Looking down, we see that the
land masses form three long peninsulas—African, Asian, and
American. "From your vantage point, the people down near the
tips will all appear to be small and undersized, and, strangely
enough, they are." Off the southernmost tip of South America
on Tierra del Fuego, he notes, are the Yahgan, who even today
stand only about five feet tall; nearby are the Alikuluf, who average a couple of inches taller. Were these the first Americans?
"Nothing can be pinned down," Gladwin concludes, "but just
enough to make one wonder if there may not have been a few
Pygmy groups who strayed over here long, long ago and who
were pushed off to the edges and ends when the Australoid tide
flowed in."[2]

Bolstering the Pygmy theory, I might add, is the widely held
belief that the earliest comers to a new land frequently meet this
fate: their descendants are "pushed off to the edges and ends,"
farthest from the point of entry, by the tide of latecomers. Witness
the westward push of American Indians when Europeans swept
in from the eastern shore. Perhaps the stunted and backward
Yahgan, huddling on lonely Tierra del Fuego and staring out
over the South Polar Sea, are indeed the descendants of early
Pygmies who had traveled the length of three continents on their
short Pygmy legs, only to arrive at the end of the earth.

No scientist has yet proposed that the Pygmies constituted
a major migration. For the earliest major migration—if occasional
small bands of wanderers can be formalized by the phrase—we
must look elsewhere: we must examine the oldest skulls found
in the Western Hemisphere. These skulls, though strikingly
similar one to another, are quite unlike those of American Indians. The earliest skulls are dolichocephalic (long-headed, as
measured from front to back), with a low brain vault and a flat
nose. Anthropologists group such skulls and the people who
wore them under a single convenient term, Australoid, which
means merely *like* the Australian aborigines.

On the basis of these earliest skulls, some scientists now
visualize the first migration into primeval America as having
occurred somewhat like this:

A group of Australoids rambled northward from tropical
southeastern Asia. They were beetle-browed fellows with bony

ridges above their eyes; their noses were broad and flat, their foreheads low and receding, their mouths and jaws protruding (the better to eat one another). Their skin color—which the skulls do not reveal—may have been brown, though Earnest A. Hooton, physical anthropologist, called the Australoid "an archaic form of modern White man."[3] (While these early Asiatic emigrants were meandering northward, some of their relatives were on their way to Australia, where their descendants, not the most enterprising of men, still live in much the same fashion today.) Meanwhile the northbound contingent made their way slowly up the eastern littoral of Asia. They were traveling light, carrying only a few weapons and tools, including the curved throwing-stick now known as the Australian boomerang, a spear thrower such as the Australians still use (this was before the invention of the bow and arrow), and some chipped stone darts. Examples of all of these have been found in western Texas.

With their women and children, the reconstruction continues, the Australoids crossed to the American continent and then began moving southward. From what is now Vancouver south they followed the coast. This surmise is based on the fact that even these ancient Americans were typical picnickers; after feasting on oysters, abalones, and clams, they moved along, leaving huge heaps of shells. Such heaps have been found from Vancouver to Mexico and particularly along the California coast. The lower layers of shell heaps on Santa Catalina and San Clemente islands off the coast of California have yielded Australoid skulls. Some of these people settled down in California, Texas, Arizona, and elsewhere throughout the Southwest, often in caves. A few broke off and turned eastward across the continent; Roland B. Dixon, cultural anthropologist, sees their stamp on the Iroquois and southern Algonquin Indians.[4] Still others seem to have kept going—down into Lower California, on into Mexico, and deep into South America, where very old skulls of this type have been found.

The beetle-browed Australoids were not the only men out of Asia who came. Then as now, Asia mothered all kinds and colors of men, even those commonly associated with other continents. Some students theorize that the second major migration into the New World was Negroid. Ethnologists and anthropolo-

gists see distinct signs of Negroid ancestry in many a New World
skull—skulls that antedate by untold centuries the first African
slaves brought in by the post-Columbian Europeans. The list
of others who may have followed is long, and varies with each
compiler.

At this point we begin to visualize wave after wave of immigrants seeking these shores, each group—though different—racially
pure. This is doubtless an oversimplification. Most anthropologists now believe that some racial blending occurred on the long
trek through Asia, if not before. As Hooton observed, "When
different races of man come into contact wth each other they
sometimes fight, but they always breed."[5]

Thus far we have sidestepped an important question: when
did the first American come?

There is no easy answer to this question, as the excavations
of Frank C. Hibben illustrate. In 1936 Hibben was digging in
a large, tunnel-like cave in the Sandia Mountains in New Mexico.
Near the mouth of the cave he found indications that Pueblo
Indians had once dwelt there briefly. Below these remains was
a six-inch layer of stalagmitic calcium carbonate, and every
amateur speleologist knows how slowly stalagmites form in caves
from the ceaseless, steady dripping of water. Hibben kept digging. Under this stony crust he found Folsom spearpoints, fluted
and delicate points identified readily by their distinctive shape.
The makers of Folsom points lived when the shaggy elephantine
mammoth, the long-jawed mastodon, and the little American
horse—all extinct thousands of years ago—roamed the prairies.
Folsom points have been found between the ribs of an extinct
species of bison, and Folsom man himself is believed to have
arrived here 10,000 or 15,000 years ago, many millennia before
the invention of writing and even thousands of years before the
world's first agriculturalist planted his first seed. Some geologists
and paleontologists date the arrival of Folsom man as early as
25,000 B.C. Once he was thought to have been the first American.
. . . But Hibben kept digging.

After removing the Folsom points, he came to another layer:
a crust of yellow ocher that varied in thickness from two inches
to two feet, formed during a period of cold and moisture such

as geologists generally associate with glaciers. Beneath that layer Hibben found nineteen more points. These were entirely different from Folsom points but equally distinctive and certainly older, perhaps by many thousands of years. Assigning a date to these nineteen points and to the craftsmen who shaped them has proved exceedingly difficult. Some have estimated them to be more than 25,000 years old. What kind of people left these points in a cave in New Mexico? The answer is not forthcoming: the craftsmen neglected to leave their skulls.

Though science is still probing to establish the earliest date of man in the Western Hemisphere (for America lags far behind Europe in uncovering its prehistoric past), great strides have been made within the last decade by means of Carbon 14 or radiocarbon dating. So much has been written concerning radiocarbon dating that one sometimes forgets that this exciting temporal yardstick was only first put to use in 1946.

Its simple principle, stripped of details, is this. Every living organism—animal or vegetable—constantly ingests carbon from the atmosphere. All carbon in atmosphere everywhere contains an infinitesimal but standard percentage of the isotope Carbon 14, an unstable radioactive substance which disintegrates at a regular rate. When the organism dies, it can no longer replace its supply of Carbon 14, but the disintegration continues at the same set pace—50 per cent in 5,568 years, half of the remainder in the next 5,568 years, and so on. Thus by measuring the radioactivity of any organic material—a skeleton, for example, or wood or cloth—a qualified scientist can calculate how many years have elapsed since the death of the living organism. The test is not without limitations, even beyond the need for organic substances to test. There is always a margin of error; contamination will alter results by *reducing* the apparent age of the object tested; a large quantity of material is required for each test and is destroyed in the process. Nevertheless, given time for adequate testing and checking by means of numerous samples from the same site, radiocarbon dating promises to impose order where guesswork and chaos now gambol.[6]

Other means of dating objects are just now becoming available to archaeologists. By thermoluminescence, for example, a scientist reheats a piece of pottery, measures the electron emissions, and determines thus when the pot was first fired. The age of *Zinjanthropus* was computed by the potassium-argon isotope system, in which the scientist measures the amount of potassium 40 and its decay product, argon 40.

Some surprising results have emanated from testing laboratories. Charcoal from what appeared to be ancient campfires "of human origin" uncovered at La Jolla, California, and Tule Springs, Nevada, for example, was tested and reported to be 21,500 years old and "older than 23,800 years" respectively. Remains from a camp site in Denton County, Texas, were found to be 37,000 years old, an age which raised eyebrows, questions, and doubts.

As evidence mounts, fewer scientists now believe that man's first arrival in the New World occurred as late as postglacial times, formerly the favored view and probably still the most generally held as recently as ten years ago. An increasing number of scientists now date man's arrival in North America as during the Pleistocene (glacial period). And a few contend that man found his way here as long as 70,000 or 100,000 years ago, before the last great Ice Age set in.

Thus with quiet cold malignancy, ice and the Ice Age creep inevitably into consideration. No picture of the earliest Americans struggling south is complete if it lacks a backdrop of glaciers, for glaciers alternately created, blocked, and—retreating—opened the route.

Our sole concern here is the last great period of glaciation, which began very roughly about 70,000 B.C. When the temperature dropped, perhaps no more than an average of seven degrees, ice started to form, touching off a cumulative process. It cooled the surface and the air above it, causing more snowfall, less melting, more ice. Slowly, inexorably, the perennial ice built to mountainous heights, burying all of Canada under a blanket estimated to have averaged 9,000 feet in thickness, and also pushing below the Canadian border to bury some of our northern states. Significantly, however, much of Alaska and probably eastern Asia were relatively ice-free except in mountainous areas. Geological evidence indicates that Bering Strait and the Mackenzie River Valley were unglaciated.

Equally important, the Ice Age brought lower sea levels. Vast quantities of sea water were drawn up, precipitated on land in the form of rain or snow, and locked there in glaciers. Land once submerged rose from the shallower oceans, and a man could walk from Siberia to Alaska over a land bridge at what is now Bering Strait, then an isthmus some three hundred miles in width from north to south.

A wayfaring stranger who entered Alaska from Asia via this land bridge could traverse Alaska and then attempt to cross the Canadian glaciers; or he could dig in and wait for a warm spell. One such "false dawn," which came along about 40,000 years ago, melted and parted the ice at its thinnest point, just east of the Rockies, and opened a corridor that led from the Arctic down to the ice-free land to the south. It is entirely possible that the men who left nineteen spearpoints in Sandia Cave in New Mexico near the southern tip of the Rockies had come through this glacial corridor. After a few thousand years the warm spell passed, the glaciers grew, and the corridor closed.

Not until about 25,000 years ago did the glaciers again begin to shrink. Even this date is approximate, for while glaciers waned in one place they waxed in another. The last great icecap in northern Wisconsin is believed to have melted about 11,000 years ago. At first the rate of glacial retreat was so slow as to be imperceptible in a human lifetime. But gradually the earth became warmer, the ice melted, the oceans rose, and the land bridge between Siberia and Alaska narrowed and disappeared. If our wayfarer came late, say roughly 15,000 years ago, he may have got his feet wet.

The gradual disappearance of the land bridge did not necessarily terminate traffic from Asia, although it may well have interrupted it. Much has been made of the isolation of the American Indian, and yet—on a clear day a man can stand on the easternmost tip of Siberia and see the misty coast of Alaska. As Chief Alaskan Geologist Philip S. Smith pointed out, "The longest stretch of open water is only twenty-five miles."[7] Natives today, he added, make the trip in small boats of animal skins.

In what age the construction of skin boats began is problematical. They are said to have been used in these parts "from time immemorial," a difficult date to transmute into figures. Rock carvings depicting skin boats of the umiak type have been found in Norway and assigned to the early northern hunters of about 7000 B.C. No later than 3000 B.C. the woodland hunters of Siberia traversed Bering Strait in their skin boats. Not many centuries after that date, when triangular shadows of Pharaonic pyramids already lay black on the yellow sands of Egypt, hunters from the Asiatic pine forests were spreading rapidly through the forests of North America. They could have come only by boat, as the Eskimos came some two thousand years later. The skin boats thus serve to bring us another picture, this one likewise conjectural but enacted perhaps while, far off, blind Homer was telling grandly of a lesser odyssey.

An Asiatic with his wife and children and this time his dog, but not even yet a bow and arrow, is paddling his frail craft over the chill green water off Siberia, pointing for that dim eastern shore where the hunting is said to be better. He island-hops to Alaska. In time he crosses Alaska by river (the Yukon and the Porcupine), then portages to the Mackenzie and paddles his groping way southward into a vast new land. Keeping the mountains ever in view, he follows the rivers south across Canada, nameless then, moving from stream to stream till he comes at length to the headwaters of the Missouri and to the Great Plains. There he finds bewildering networks of rivers to lead him in every direction.

There were many routes, as we know from the trail of points, and many migrations. Funneling in through Alaska, these early colonists flowed down and across two continents.

When our European ancestors arrived in the late fifteenth century, they found the New World inhabited by a strange people unlike any they had ever seen. Columbus called them Indians; others called them red men and agreed that they were a race quite apart: "the one great American red race." Nineteenth-century historians wrote that this red race had been "cut off and isolated from the Old World for probably more than fifty thousand years."[8] But the fifty thousand years have shrunk like the glaciers, and now we know too that the red race is neither a race nor red. In fact, the American Indian has been classified as mixed Mongoloid, basically of the yellow race.

You scan the gallery of Indian portraits deep in your memory. These Indians resemble no Chinaman you ever saw. What, indeed, are the marks of a Mongoloid?

When Mongoloids mix with another race, four Mongoloid

physical characteristics are likely to be passed on to the children. These four "dominant" traits are shovel-shaped upper incisors (front teeth), brown eyes, straight coarse black hair, and prominent cheekbones. Most American Indians exhibit these Mongoloid traits.[9] They also have other Mongoloid traits: yellow or yellowish-brown skin and sparse hair on the body and face, with less beard than any other race. Who can recall having seen a Chinese or an Indian wearing a bushy beard?

Even so, most American Indians lack certain important Mongoloid traits. Their eyes do not slant. The "Mongoloid fold," a fold of skin that covers all or part of the rim of the upper eyelid, reappears only occasionally. And the hawklike nose of the Plains Indians scarcely mirrors the Mongoloid's flat one. In short, as H. Marie Wormington summarized neatly, "Most anthropologists believe that, although American aborigines must be placed in the generally Mongoloid division of mankind, they represent a composite race."[10] This heresy against "the sacred unity of the American Indian race," that old and cherished misapprehension, is substantiated by the wide diversity among the Indians. From tribe to tribe, from coast to coast, from continent to continent, as the ingredients varied so the Indians varied in physical characteristics. But considering the diversity of early American immigrants (if ancestors of aborigines may be so labeled), the wonder is rather that the product presents as much homogeneity as it does.

Physical characteristics aside, a claim to unity must also be granted a people whose ancestors shared a journey "unthinkably long in both time and space," a people whose forebears possessed the stamina, the tough tenacity, to cross the top of the world and travel on foot or by flimsy skin boat from the frozen North through thousands of miles of tangled wilderness, some of them down to the steaming jungles and on beyond, without a map, a compass, a rifle, or a known destination in an alien world.

These were the people, then, whose descendants watched from the shore of the Gulf of Mexico while the billowing towers grew larger and larger and presently spewed forth pale, bearded creatures who looked like men.

MEXICO'S FAIR GOD
QUETZALCOATL

W HEN THE ILL-STARRED Montezuma sat facing Hernán Cortés in a garlanded Mexican palace and told of "a certain lord" who had led his people from foreign parts to the land of Mexico and then returned to his native land "which is where the sun rises," Montezuma assuredly was speaking of Quetzalcoatl.

In all of America's past no figure is more exciting, more tantalizing, or more frustrating than that of the Fair God Quetzalcoatl. A stranger, a bearded white man dressed in a flowing robe, he is said to have come from afar and from the east. According to the many legends that surround his name, he appeared in Mexico of a sudden and lingered long in several places, dispensing a vastness of information, for which he was called the bringer of knowledge, "the traditional master-builder of American civilization." He disappeared as mysteriously as he had come, with the promise that he would return.

No one can say with certainty who Quetzalcoatl might have

been or whence he had come. Some archaeologists flatly declare
that he never existed—except in the minds of the myriad Indians
who worshiped him through the centuries. Others believe that
there must have been several flesh-and-blood culture heroes who
were given this name, one very early and another or others some
centuries later, and that in time their various deeds came to be
attributed to a single Quetzalcoatl. Confusing the matter further,
the Toltec high priests assumed the name with the office. As for
the military conqueror named Quetzalcoatl, a few archaeologists
recite with assurance the dates of the major events of his life and
hold that the worship of Quetzalcoatl stemmed from his triumphs.

"Long time have we been informed by the writings of our
ancestors . . ." With these words Montezuma opened his speech
to Cortés. It would be altogether too easy to say that the answer
to the mystery of Quetzalcoatl vanished in smoke when the conquering Spaniards, intent on destroying all pagan evils, made
bonfires of Mayan and Mexican manuscripts while the native
priests cried out in anguish and some committed suicide. For
the Mayas and Aztecs had written records, including records of
ages past, believed to have been largely the work of their priests.

The Aztec writing was pictographic, and Diringer calls it
"probably nothing but a degenerative derivative of the Maya
script." Mayan writing, on the other hand, was a sort of bastard
hieroglyphic, "partly pictorial and partly conventionalized, partly
ideographic and partly in all probability phonetic."[1] When
Christopher Columbus visited Nicaragua in 1502, he wrote to
King Ferdinand and Queen Isabella saying that in that province
he had seen "some large sheets of cotton very elaborately and
cleverly worked, and others delicately painted in colors."[2] Archaeologists now surmise that the sheets Columbus saw "painted
in colors" may have been codices, some of which were on cotton.
But whether the legend of Quetzalcoatl could have been traced
to its source through the masses of pre-Columbian manuscripts
which fanatical Spaniards reduced to ashes is at best a dubious
surmise.

The hasty destruction was soon regretted. A few years later
other Spaniards, known to us now as the Spanish chroniclers—
churchmen, soldiers, administrators—commenced a diligent search
for just such records in the hope that some had escaped their
compatriots' zeal Less than a score were ever recovered. The

chroniclers had to turn, therefore, to oral sources. Men of intelligence and compassion, they sometimes "lent a too willing ear"
to peripheral lore. We honor them, nevertheless, as the patient
preservers of all that remains to us now of pre-Columbian Mexican literature.

One of the first of the Spanish historians was Father Bernardino de Sahagún, a Franciscan missionary. Father Sahagún
sought out the most learned and often the oldest natives, gathered
them about him, and asked each to paint in his Aztec picture
writing as much as he could clearly remember of Aztec history,
religion, and legend. Next Sahagún called in other Aztecs who
had attended the Spanish mission schools established in Mexico
and had been taught the Roman alphabet. Sahagún set these
natives to work transcribing into Roman characters, though still
in the Aztec language, the Aztec picture writing produced by his
learned recruits. Then, having himself learned the Aztec language, he compared the results in the hope of detecting errors
and fabrications. These labors over the years produced many
volumes of Mexican lore, among them the epic *Song of Quetzalcoatl*.[3]

Here I can quote only a small part, translated into English
almost four centuries after Sahagún by John Hubert Cornyn,
who has tried to retain its trochaic meter, the meter of so many
of the Aztecs' treasured legends.

THE PROPHET

All the glory of the godhead
Had the prophet Quétzalcóatl;
All the honor of the people.
Sanctified his name and holy;
And their prayers they offered to him
In the days of ancient Tula.
There in grandeur rose his temple;
Reared aloft its mighty ramparts,
Reaching upward to the heavens.

. . . .

See, his beard is very lengthy;
See, exceeding long his beard is;
Yellow as the straw his beard is!

And his people, they the Toltecs,
Wondrous skilled in all the trades were,
All the arts and artifices,
So that naught there was they knew not;
And as master workmen worked they.
Fashioned they the sacred emeralds;
Fashioned they the precious turquoise;
Smelted they both gold and silver.
Other arts and trades they mastered;
In all crafts and artifices
Skilled were they as wondrous workmen.
And in Quétzalcóatl all these
Arts and crafts had their beginning;
In him all were manifested.
He the master workman taught them
All their trades and artifices.

. . . .

Very rich was Quétzalcóatl.
Nothing pleasing to the palate,
Nothing helpful to the body
Ever lacked they there in Tula.
Very large there grew the squashes;
Wondrous big and stout the squashes
So that one could scarcely span them
With the outstretched arms embracing.
Very long and thick the corn ears,
So that in their arms they bore them.

. . . .

Wondrous rich were all the Toltecs;
Masters they of wealth uncounted;
Every need was satisfied them;
Nothing lacked they in their households;
Hunger never dwelt among them;
And the small corn never used they
Save to heat their thermal baths with.

Quétzalcóatl offered penance
And with thorns his legs he punctured
Till the blood came oozing outward.
Even bathed he in the night-time;
Bathed he in the Xippacóyan,
In the bathing place of Xípe.

And this custom imitated
They the sacred fire expenders;
They the priests officiating
Kept the mode of Quétzalcóatl,
Master of their organization
And creator of their being;
Kept the usages of Tula,
Even as today we keep them;
Here in Mexico observe them.[4]

One can picture the good Franciscan friar frowning in puzzlement over this epic of Quetzalcoatl, for, despite the stirring avowal of Montezuma, this poem reveals that Quetzalcoatl was only by adoption a god of the Aztecs. He belonged to the Toltecs: "And his people, they the Toltecs." But who were the Toltecs?

Other chroniclers meanwhile were likewise gathering data, and the shadowy image of Quetzalcoatl was beginning to take on more detail. Juan de Torquemada, a late sixteenth-century Spanish chronicler, summarized thus the information he was able to glean:

"Certain people came from the north by way of Pánuco. These were men of good carriage, well-dressed in long robes of black linen, open in front, and without capes, cut low at the neck, with short sleeves that did not come to the elbow; the same, in fact, as the natives use to this day in their dances. From Pánuco they passed on very peaceably by degrees to Tulla, where they were well received by the inhabitants. The country there, however, was already too thickly populated to sustain the new-comers, so these passed on to Cholula where they had an excellent reception. They brought with them as their chief and head, a personage called Quetzalcoatl, a fair and ruddy complexioned man, with a long beard. In Cholula these people remained and multiplied, and sent colonists to Upper and Lower Mizteca and the Zapotecan country; and these it is said raised the grand edifices whose remains are still to be seen at Mictlan. These followers of Quetzalcoatl were men of great knowledge and cunning artists in all kinds of fine work; not so good at masonry and the use of the hammer, as in casting and in the engraving and setting of precious stones, and in all kinds of artistic sculpture, and in agriculture."[5]

Torquemada commented elsewhere that Quetzalcoatl was a white man: *era Hombre blanco*; a large man, broad-browed, with huge eyes, long black hair, and a great, rounded beard: *la barba grande y redonda*.[6]

In this description, particularly the black hair, most of the early writers concur. The line quoted previously from *The Song of Quetzalcoatl*—"Yellow as the straw his beard is"—is in flat contradiction to other descriptions of Quetzalcoatl that refer specifically to his black hair or black beard; from which several scholars have inferred that the nameless Aztec poet, employing poetic license, bleached the black beard of Quetzalcoatl to present him as a sun symbol. As for Torquemada's two descriptions of Quetzalcoatl, the apparent contradiction between the "fair and ruddy complexioned man" and the "long black hair" puts me in mind of our Mexican guide Alfredo, a full-blooded Spaniard with black hair, flashing dark eyes, and olive skin; yet I have heard Alfredo described as "fair" by other Mexicans.

Concerning the robe of Quetzalcoatl, a few reports indicate that it was white rather than black, and Gomara in his *Crónica* adds that it was decorated with crosses; but all agree that the Fair God was garbed in a long robe.

Torquemada's statement that Quetzalcoatl "came from the north by way of Pánuco" might be misconstrued unless one consults a map. Although north-northeast of Mexico City, Pánuco lies near the eastern shore, a few miles inland from the Gulf of Mexico on the Pánuco River, close to modern Tampico. Most of the early writers held that Quetzalcoatl had come from the east. One version records that he lived "in a distant East, beyond immense seas and lands." Others say that this stranger simply appeared, that one day the natives noticed "the sudden presence among them of persons differing from themselves in appearance and descent."

Legends grow like the snowball, gathering fragments to them. Legends change, like the chrysalis into the butterfly. Archaeologists know that uncovering ancient bones with a trowel is rarely as arduous as sifting the truth from an ancient legend.

The early Spaniards soon learned that Quetzalcoatl was more than "the bringer of civilization." He was also the god of learning and culture, the wind god, and god of the air. If they went to his temple hoping to find his statue, they were disappointed, for they found instead his symbol sculptured in stone: a feathered serpent.

FIGURE 6.   Quetzalcoatl. Drawing by Miguel Covarrubias from a relief at Xochicalco.

Culture gods are not rare. Primitive man gropes to explain how everything happened, everything since and including creation. Legends spring up. One legend absorbs another; the old and the new are blended; the lesser hero becomes a part of the greater. Men become gods, and gods become men who walk on the earth. The mingled legend lives on. A thousand or thousands of years go by, and scholars arrive to try to untangle the snarl. Understandably, many are tempted to say, "This is a myth; this is sheer fable." But other and equally serious scholars profoundly believe there was never a myth without a meaning, never a fable without a basis of fact.

One could wander for years in the maze of the legend of Quetzalcoatl, and many have done so. We need to emerge for a moment into the tropical sunshine and walk with resounding tread across the silent stone ruins, tangible, measurable, and in their way more eloquent than the deathless legend of Quetzalcoatl that had kept the Indians looking eastward for hundreds of years in anticipation of the Fair God's return.

As elusive as Quetzalcoatl himself was Tula, where the Fair God was said to have dwelt twenty years—years that were called "the wonder age" of the Toltecs.

> In the days of ancient Tula
> There in grandeur rose his temple;
> Reared aloft its mighty ramparts,
> Reaching upward to the heavens.

But where were those mighty ramparts?

Tula was the reputed capital of the Toltecs, and legend had much to say about both. Fernando de Alva Ixtlilxóchitl (*c.* 1568–*c.* 1648), a native prince and a learned man who "kept his ear pressed close to the lips of tradition," had written that the Toltecs founded Tula in days remote. These Toltecs, said Ixtlilxóchitl, knew how to write and to reckon, to rule with justice, and to build magnificent temples. Toltec soldiers, he said, wore copper helmets. Their empire had endured some five hundred years, he believed, before it succumbed at last to famine and strife. All of this dovetailed with other traditions which credited Quetzalcoatl with bringing the art of picture writing from the Land of the Sun, introducing major reforms in government, and teaching the Toltecs to become master builders, as their name implies. And always the legends named as the Toltec capital Tula or Tulla or Tollan.

Centuries passed. In the materialistic philosophy of the nineteenth century, Tula and Quetzalcoatl were lumped together as preconquest myths. Few scholars saw fit to defend such tenuous tales at the risk of their reputations. It would be folly to seek Tula, some declared, for it did not exist—had never existed; likewise Quetzalcoatl. The Toltecs too came to be regarded by many as a fabricated people out of the sun myths. Moreover, at that time American archaeological endeavors and funds were directed largely to Old World sites while their own back yards lay fallow.

All this time it was common knowledge that some fifty miles north of Mexico City lay the modest and sleepy village of Tula in the State of Hidalgo. But this modern Tula had little to recom-

mend it as the erstwhile capital of an empire—only a few unpromising mounds overgrown with vegetation. Nevertheless, in
the 1880's Désiré Charnay, a Frenchman who was examining
Mexican ruins at the behest of the French Ministry of Public
Instruction with the financial assistance of the American tobacco
manufacturer Pierre Lorillard, decided to have a look. Perhaps
Charnay was influenced in part by the fact that twenty years
earlier a poor shepherd-boy, while scratching the moist ground
at Tula, had uncovered a vase containing five hundred ounces
of gold (which is his innocence he quickly parted with for a few
coppers). But even more Charnay listened to legend.

His search at Tula was rewarded by a strange assortment of
finds. Among the strangest was a fragment of stone sculptured in
the form of feet and legs. The sandaled feet, as shown in Figure 7,
are four feet long. Nearby lay a fallen column, its parted segments
revealing that once they were held together by tenons. Charnay
found also the vestiges of a pyramid; and a distance away, where
time had eroded the soil, a bit of ancient brick wall was bared.
Digging further there, he uncovered a Toltec house. On one wall
of it was a bas-relief depicting two bearded men (Figure 9).

Charnay reported his finds in detail, with illustrations; but
no headlong assault on Tula ensued. In fact, the archaeological
world little noted nor long remembered, and as recently as 1940
the argument was raging still as to whether Tula had ever existed
and, if so, where.

In 1940 the Mexican archaeologist Jiminez Moreno be-
thought himself of the lore of the Aztec sages as recorded by
Father Sahagún. In the sixteenth century Father Sahagún had
written that Quetzalcoatl lived in "Tula next to Xicococ." Near
this same little Tula in Hidalgo is a hill called Xicococ. Moreover, in the sixteenth century the Spaniards had erected a massive church at Tula, a tip-off that on this site they had probably
destroyed a pagan temple.

In 1940 Moreno decided that excavations should be undertaken at Tula. Beneath the soil the spade touched stone. Bit by
bit the ancient city, long ago burned and destroyed (perhaps
about 1116 A.D.), has emerged from its earthy shroud. Now partially restored, it stands revealed as a proper capital of the mighty
Toltecs.

Here lies the little that yet remains of a Pyramid of the Sun

FIGURE 7. Fragment of a column found at Tula.

FIGURE 8. Broken column showing tenon, Tula.

FIGURE 9.   Bas-relief depicting two bearded men; from the wall of a house in Tula.

FIGURE 10.   Fragment of a mural painting depicting a lotus, found by Charnay in a Toltec house.

once apparently quite imposing. Here too are other temples and structures and a great ball court on which the natives played a game that we shall encounter again in Mayan country. As for Quetzalcoatl, the Toltecs did not forget their teacher. One of the most impressive structures at Tula is the Temple of Tlahuizcal-pantecuhtli, "Lord of the House of Dawn, Venus, the morning star, variant of Quetzalcoatl."[7] Although the roof that covered the patio in front of his temple no longer exists, some of its amazing pillars still stand. These pillars are atlantes or telamones (the male form of caryatids)—sculptured columns of gigantic stone warriors. The heads of the warriors alone achieve the height of a man (Figure 11). The fragment that Charnay had discovered almost sixty years before was recognized now as a part of one of these atlantes. Around the walls, belled jaguars parade in endless succession (Figure 12).

Tula and the Toltecs, at least, have thus stepped out of mythology into history, their legendary reputations confirmed by recent excavations. And off in the limbo of discredited historians, Sahagún and Ixtlilxóchitl must have enjoyed a chuckle together.

True, beneath those unpromising mounds at Tula lay proof that Toltec artisans had labored there hundreds of years, just as

FIGURE 11. Toltec warrior, Tula. (Feuchtwanger, *Kunst im alten Mexiko,* Atlantis Verlag, Zürich.)

FIGURE 12. Relief on the temple of Quetzalcoatl, Tula.

the legends stated, and that the Toltecs had long preceded the
Aztecs. The Aztecs, however, represent what Brogger might have
termed "the end phase." To an Aztec repeating his native lore in
the sixteenth century, another people who preceded his own by
hundreds of years—a people, in fact, who preceded the people
who preceded his own—might have seemed ancient indeed and
the fountainhead of all wisdom. For the Aztecs themselves did
not come down from the north till the latter part of the twelfth
century. Arriving as poor and bellicose nomads, in the Valley of

Mexico they saw and partially assimilated the higher culture that lay about them. In 1325 they founded Tenochtitlán, the present Mexico City, Montezuma's lake-ringed city of gleaming white temples that dazzled Cortés in 1519.

In scaling thus swiftly up the ladder toward civilization, the Aztecs were only repeating the rapid ascent of the Chichimecs, their immediate predecessors and teachers. When the Chichimecs entered the Valley of Mexico a century earlier, they were barbarians who dressed in animal skins and dwelt in caves. After coming in contact with the last vestiges of Toltec culture, the Chichimecs were soon weaving and making pottery. Led by a few surviving Toltecs, Chichimecs even started erecting pyramids and were presently painting codices.

How many times this civilizing process was repeated in the long history of the Valley of Mexico—or in the history of savage America—is the crucial question.

The fountainhead of this flood of civilization may possibly have been the Toltecs; in fact, the name Toltec, meaning "master builder," could have been a generic term applied to both earlier and later pyramid-building peoples, or the proud name itself might have been usurped. More likely, however, the Toltecs in turn, like the Aztecs and Chichimecs, borrowed from a yet older people. Tracing the stream of Middle American civilization backward through time and terrain to its headwaters is a task which is still going on, for the stream meanders deviously into and out of far places.

We turn now to follow that stream and the trail of Quetzalcoatl which runs alongside it. Where the stream meanders, pyramids stand and legends of bearded white gods still linger. For the Quetzalcoatl of Tula was not the first of his name. Our search has only begun.

5

PYRAMIDS AND ZIGGURATS

BEFORE THE REDISCOVERY of Tula in 1940, archaeologists who stubbornly held that there must once have been such a place were hard pressed by disparagers to produce it. One possible site stood out, recommending itself by the size as well as the obvious antiquity of its ruins—but the Aztecs called it Teotihuacán, not Tula. Still, tradition insisted that the great Montezuma himself had visited Teotihuacán, literally "Place of the Gods," to offer sacrifices. So, as time passed and no ancient Tula emerged, this site came to be regarded by some as the elusive capital of the Toltecs.

Today the tourist who visits bustling Mexico City may drive thirty miles northeast to the village of San Juan Teotihuacán (the "San Juan" being obviously a postconquest appendage) and view these silent ruins. As he stands on a height overlooking a broad plain, an eerie sight spreads before him: a huge and venerable pyramid seems to rise from out of another time, another world. Dominating the landscape, it stretches more than seven hundred feet along the base—roughly two city blocks—and rises to 216 feet, which is almost the height of a twenty-story building. If the visitor crosses the plain and stands small and mortal at the base of the pyramid, he can comprehend in part its deep religious significance; for, looking up, he cannot glimpse the summit—only the innumerable stately stairs that seem to lead straight into heaven.

The tourist who comes without prior knowledge, as a few still do, finds himself abruptly disabused of any vestigial notion that the New World harbored only savages whose noblest architectural efforts wrought the tepee. He may even see at once the hand of ancient Egypt. But one who has come in the expectation of finding a true Egyptian pyramid suspects uneasily that somebody oversold him. He notes, for example, that the pyramid does not rise smoothly to a point but has instead a flattened look, as if lopped off by a mammoth sword or depressed by a giant hand (Figure 13).

The plain fact is, American "pyramids" have been misnamed. They resemble more closely than anything else the ziggurats of Mesopotamia. Both are sometimes referred to as "temple towers" or "stepped pyramids," but by definition a single word would suffice: ziggurat.

Not only the Pyramid of the Sun at Teotihuacán is flat on top. All early American pyramids are flattened, truncated, for each once formed the gigantic base of a temple or *teocalli*. Babylonian ziggurats too were truncated and were topped with temples. For, whereas Egyptian pyramids were built by the backbreaking toil of thousands of slaves to serve as the tomb of a single pharaoh, American and Babylonian ziggurats—by whatever forced labor they may have been built—served a communal purpose: they were places of worship.

This is demonstrated today by the outside staircase that catches the eye at Teotihuacán. One who has trudged up the 222 steep, narrow steps to the top will never forget this feature. Babylonian ziggurats too had outside staircases leading steeply up the face. Egyptian pyramids had none.

Once the temples that topped Mesopotamian ziggurats housed the likenesses of Babylonian gods. And once, it is said, the temple that graced the top of Teotihuacán's great pyramid

FIGURE 13.   Pyramid of the Sun, Teotihuacán, Mexico.

housed a colossal statue of the sun god, his breastplate of burnished gold and silver facing the east to catch the first rays of his prototype. This statue, still standing when the Spaniards arrived, was demolished by Bishop Zummáraga, official "protector of the Indians," whose indefatigable hand fell, as William H. Prescott put it, "more heavily than that of Time itself" on Indian monuments.[1]

Most important architecturally, all ancient American pyramids rose in a series of stories or terraces, each rectangular terrace smaller than the one on which it was superimposed. The Pyramid of the Sun at Teotihuacán has four such terraces. The Temple of Tlahuizcalpantecuhtli (or Quetzalcoatl) at Tula has five. Ziggurats too were terraced pyramids. And here a strange feature emerges, for the earliest pyramids of Egypt also were terraced or stepped. The Step Pyramid of Sakkara, built for Zoser (Djoser) in about 2750 B.C., has the outward appearance of a Mexican pyramid (Figure 14). The Step Pyramid of Medum, built for Snefru some fifty years later, although it now retains only three of its seven steps, looks more like a ziggurat than like the Great Pyramid of Khufu (Cheops), which followed shortly.

What does one make of all this? At the moment only a mental note, for nothing is more treacherous than the quicksands of similarity—or more alluring. We shall venture upon those quicksands, but not without further provocation.

Although the Pyramid of the Sun dominates the plain at Teotihuacán today as in ages past, once this plain was a vast ceremonial center with pyramids great and small, avenues, temples, and a stadium that seated thousands, all oriented astronomically, planned by skillful priest-architects and built by vast legions of laborers under a powerful centralized authority. Many of these buildings, invisible now, still lie beneath open fields, for complete excavation would cost millions of dollars. At one time the entire area, approximately three and a half miles long and almost two miles wide, was paved with red stucco. Here stood a smaller Pyramid of the Moon. And here today, relieved of later construction that buried it, stands the Temple of Quetzalcoatl.

Smaller by far than the massive Pyramid of the Sun is the Temple of Quetzalcoatl, only part of which has survived. This portion, however, is lavish with ornamentation. Jutting from the

FIGURE 14 (*above*). Egyptian step pyramid of Sakkara.
FIGURE 15 (*below*). Temple of Quetzalcoatl, Teotihuacán. (Feuchtwanger, *Kunst im alten Mexiko*, Atlantis Verlag, Zürich.)

façade at regular intervals are the great carved heads of feathered serpents, the symbol of Quetzalcoatl. Some of the eyes still glitter blackly with polished obsidian insets—the few that curio hunters have not yet plucked out. Alternating with the feathered serpent is the symbol of Tlaloc, the rain god, identifiable by the eye rings. On the wall behind them, carved in low relief, is an undulating design suggestive of waves. The spaces between are filled with carvings of sea shells (Figure 15), all of which, according to Vaillant, are Caribbean varieties, although Teotihuacán lies nearly two hundred miles inland across the mountains. It is almost as if the builders who bestowed such infinite care on this temple were trying to convey the message that Quetzalcoatl had come to these parts out of the Caribbean.

As for dates, those indispensable guideposts as we grope our way back through the misty past, Teotihuacán has demonstrated the difficulty of obtaining reliable radiocarbon dates—as if the shades of departed worshipers were jealously guarding their secrets from the prying present. But this much is known: its earliest structures reach back into pre-Christian times, back to about 150 B.C. The entire site was later extensively altered, redecorated, even completely rebuilt, possibly because of a change in religion and possibly too out of sheer religious fervor. The early American elite were ardent rebuilders—much like the Babylonians and quite unlike the Egyptians, who never again touched a completed pyramid, no matter how great the need.

The ceremonial center of Teotihuacán is believed to have flourished for many centuries, and its people seem to have had contact with other cities in Mexico, notably Cholula, and even as far as Guatemala. Then presently the whole vast, tediously constructed site was abandoned. Why? At the end of its third phase, possibly around 850 A.D., Teotihuacán was burned and sacked, and the greater part of the city was destroyed. The Teotihuacanos departed, and presently the Toltecs moved in.

Who can unravel the mystery of Teotihuacán, which only a few short decades ago was attributed to the Toltecs? C. A. Burland looks at it this way:

"Well, now that we know Tollan [Tula] to have been situated at Tula, what are we going to do about Teotihuacán? This greatest of all ruined sites in Mexico is an embarrassingly heavy

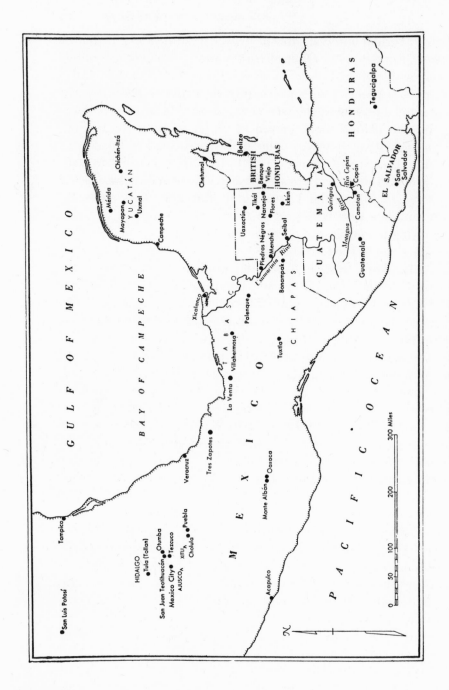

Archaeological sites of Middle America

baby to be left on archaeologists' hands. But that is just what has happened. We do not know how this great city began, nor why it was abandoned half-ruined by its nameless builders. . . . We cannot tell, so, for the sake of clear thinking, we just call these people the Teotihuacanos. They built other great centres, as you know, at Cholula and Azcopotzalco. These all included temples and courtyards, and many-roomed houses with frescoed walls."[2]

So we take up the search once more, attempting to follow the trail of Quetzalcoatl, and again the legend serves as our guidebook.

When the Fair God left or was driven from Tula, the legend tells, he first buried his treasure. (Belief in this treasure is so enduring that natives are seeking it still.) Then he wandered about in Mexico for a time. After that he moved on to Cholula (about sixty miles southeast of Mexico City), where he lived, governed, and taught the arts of civilization for the next twenty years.

In Cholula, according to legend, the people erected numerous temples in his honor. The truth of this statement was impressed upon Cortés, who declared that he counted four hundred "towers" at Cholula. They later imposed a stupendous task on the conquering Spaniards, who vowed that each pagan temple would be smashed and replaced by a Christian church. Today Cholula, an ex-metropolis that has shrunk to a mere 11,000, is known as the City of Churches. The visitor stands on the summit and looks out over a sprawling landscape dotted with domes—one for each day of the year, it is said, and the figure 365 seems scarcely to be an exaggeration. Long before the prophet Mohammed was born, Cholula was the Mecca of Middle America, the Holy City of Anahuac, the City of Quetzalcoatl to which pilgrims journeyed from near and far.

Of all its churches, Cholula is famous for one: its *tlahchiual-tepetl* or Artificial Hill. Atop this high hill today stands a large Catholic church dedicated to Nuestra Señora de los Remedios. Inside the great grassy hill itself, however, and forming the base of the Catholic church, is a pagan pyramid (Figure 16). Once long ago, before the Spaniards destroyed it, the pyramid supported instead of the church a temple dedicated to Quetzalcoatl. The

FIGURE 16.   Great pyramid of Cholula, topped by a Catholic church.

pyramid covered forty-five acres, a larger area than the Great Pyramid of Khufu, and rose to a height of 210 feet, making it one of the largest structures in the world in terms of cubic content. But size is not the measure of its importance.

For many years Mexican archaeologists have been exploring inside the pyramid, digging labyrinthine tunnels which total a mile in length. They have learned that the pyramid is constructed of sun-dried bricks and covers an even more ancient ceremonial precinct composed of a maze of temples, where they have come across frescoes similar to those found at Teotihuacán, including one fresco painted in red, black, and yellow depicting grasshoppers. Like other Mexican pyramids, that at Cholula is truncated, terraced, and so erected that its four sides face the four cardinal points of the compass.

"The big temple of Cholula," wrote the late George Vaillant, one of the foremost Mexicologists, "is incredible. It seems like the counterpart of Babel, to which the friars compared it."[3]

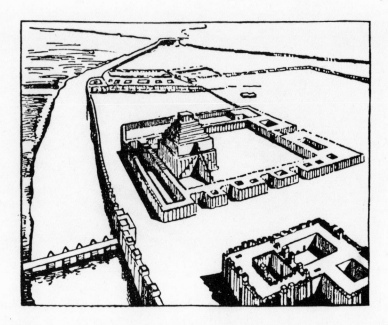

FIGURE 17.   The Babylonian ziggurat of Etemenanki, the Tower of Babel. In left foreground, a bridge across the Euphrates. (A reconstruction.)

Now, the Tower of Babel was a ziggurat. Babel was, in fact, *the* ziggurat, famous throughout the ancient world, "the epitome of human arrogance" and the envy of all. Rising in seven terraces, it towered above the Euphrates and glittered grandly across the Mesopotamian plain. There were many impressive structures at Babel (the city known to us through the Greeks as Babylon), but the Tower of Babel dimmed them; it was stupendous.

Other ziggurats, smaller and less ostentatious, rose in every large city in Babylonia—and quite a few rose elsewhere. Ziggurats came in assorted sizes. There was even one only four feet tall at Gebal, a Phoenician port city on the Mediterranean.

The ziggurat type of structure may have originated farther south in the Fertile Crescent, perhaps near the Persian Gulf. Temporally it goes back to the days of ancient Sumer in the lower Euphrates valley, where dwelt the non-Semitic Sumerians whose civilization rivaled and coexisted with that of most ancient Egypt. Sumer's was possibly the oldest culture on earth, a wondrously

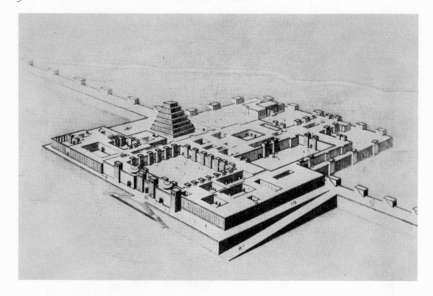

FIGURE 18.   Reconstruction of the Assyrian palace at Dur Sharrukin, near Nineveh. At left, court; right, royal quarters; rear, the temple tower.

fertile culture whose generative power is not known to have been exceeded in the history of the world. Semites moved in and shared the land and the culture, and others have been partaking of that culture ever since. One who looks sees the handprint of Sumer down through the ages, visible yet today. And Sumer too had its ziggurats, including a splendid one at Ur in Chaldea.

Like Ur, the Tower of Babel goes all the way back to the period described in Genesis. Small wonder that many a student, gazing on Middle American pyramids, may have wondered privately at the resemblance to Old World ziggurats but has gone his way without comment. What could one say? Is the resemblance purely coincidental? Or is this perhaps the form of construction which lent itself best to tools of the time? Or *could* these American pyramids conceivably have been erected in imitation of ziggurats?

Consider first the time element. The Tower of Babel dates from the dimmest reaches of human memory. But time was not telescoped then as now. Man in his leisurely progress upward from bestiality was only a few millennia removed from his aeons as hunter and fisher, and just so far in the past lay the date of his foremost invention, agriculture, accelerator of human progress. Ancient buildings, like ancient civilizations reared by the small *avant garde* in the great river valleys, endured so marvelously long when measured by present standards that the modern mind can scarcely conceive their span. The Tower of Babel, like its Mesoamerican counterparts, was remodeled, repaired, and rebuilt. It was Nabopolassar who said: "Marduk commanded me to build the Tower of Babel, which has become weakened by time and fallen into disrepair." And well it might have, for Nabopolassar reigned from 625 to 605 B.C. Thus, suddenly, the Tower of Babel has moved from out of primordial mists into our line of vision, into the years of the greatness of Tyre.

The first positive indication of a possible connection between Old and New World ziggurats is to be found here at Cholula. The striking physical resemblance between the pyramid of Cholula and the Tower of Babel is augmented by an equally striking similarity between the Biblical account of Babel and the preconquest Mexican legend which entwined this largest American pyramid.

According to the account in Genesis, *after the deluge* and even before the days of Abraham surviving mankind journeyed from the east to a plain in the land of Shinar [Sumer]. There they said one to another, "Go to, let us make brick. . . . Let us build up a city and a tower, whose top *may reach unto heaven.*" But the Lord came down to see the city and the tower which the children of men had built, and the Lord said, "Behold, the people is one, and they have all one language; and this they begin to do; and now nothing will be restrained from them, which they have imagined to do." And He forthwith *confounded their language* so that they could no longer understand one another's speech. . . . [4]

In Middle America the echoing preconquest legend runs thus: *After the deluge* which destroyed the primeval world, seven giants survived. One of them, Xelhua, then built the great pyramid of Cholula *in order to reach heaven.* But the gods destroyed the pyramid with fire and *confounded the language* of the builders.

If one could say how the story of the confounding of tongues reached early America—and how it came to be associated with the construction of a ziggurat attributed to a time "shortly after the flood"—one could write a new and amazing chapter of American history.

And perhaps one can.

6

THE MYSTERY
OF MONTE ALBÁN

ONE OF THE STRANGEST histories of America ever penned was that set down in the sixteenth century by the Indian savant Ixtlilxóchitl in his *Relaciones* after he had investigated all available preconquest records and legends, aided by his ability to understand the native tongue and decipher the hieroglyphs.

Ixtlilxóchitl's ambitious history of Middle America began with the creation of the world by the supreme god Tloque Nahuaque. This first era lasted 1716 years, until floods swept over the earth. In the second period the world was populated by giants, most of whom vanished when earthquakes ended this era. (From time to time through the centuries the bones of extinct mammoths, some of them larger than present-day elephants, have turned up in Mexico. The hypothesis has been advanced that primitive men, seeing these mammoth bones, attributed them to an extinct race of giants. Traditions of prehistoric giants are, however, almost universal. The earliest inhabitants of Canaan were, according to Hebrew tradition, giants.)

During the third era, according to Ixtlilxóchitl, human tribes —the Olmecs and Xicalancas—lived on the earth. These people, he wrote, founded Cholula and later migrated eastward to the present State of Tabasco in southeastern Mexico. (Tabasco lies on the Bay of Campeche along the southern lip of the Gulf of Mexico.) Also during this third era a fabulous person named Quetzalcoatl appeared, bringing civilization. Disappointed in the people's response to his teachings, Quetzalcoatl returned to the east. The fourth era is the present.

Other legends of Quetzalcoatl agree that after his twenty years in Cholula the bearded teacher returned to the east. His goal was believed to have been Tlapalla; but Tlapalla has not been discovered in recent times. Whether it never existed or whether it lies today beneath burgeoning tropical vegetation or across the sea beneath the dust of ages remains for the curious-hearted of future decades to ascertain. In the legend according to Sahagún, at the seashore Quetzalcoatl commanded that a raft of snakes be constructed for him, and in this he put to sea, his destination Tlapalla.

Some of the legends hold that when Quetzalcoatl reached the east coast he sent back the following prophecy: that in time to come surely his brethren, bearded and white like himself, would come to these shores by way of the sea where the sun rises, and that these men would rule the land. The Mexicans never forgot his promise.

Like Quetzalcoatl, we depart from Cholula walking into the sunrise. But soon the path forks: we could continue generally east or could veer instead southeast and follow the route of the flour-ishing trade between the Valley of Mexico and the highlands of Guatemala. "In Cholula," wrote the sixteenth-century Spanish chronicler Torquemada, "these people [of Quetzalcoatl] remained and multiplied, and sent colonies to Upper and Lower Mizteca and the Zapotecan countries." Following the route of merchants and colonists, three hundred miles southeast of Cholula we come to the crossroads of trade, where once the Mixtecs and Zapotecs dwelt.

Down in a valley lies Oaxaca, capital of the state of the same name. Oaxaca is a charming old city unchanged since colonial times; and yet it is a comparatively recent settlement, having been founded only six years before Columbus reached the West Indies. Above the city and seven miles distant looms a small mountain, Monte Albán.

In ages past—long, long before old Oaxaca was founded—armies of laborers arduously leveled the summit of this mountain to create a gigantic platform. On this man-made plain overlooking the valley the indefatigable worshipers then erected their ceremonial center. Almost two millennia later its crumbling ruins still stand—temple-pyramids, tombs, terraces, even ball courts—deserted now, lifeless, reverberating with the poignant silence of a ghost town (Figure 19).

"Is there," asked the German journalist Egon Erwin Kisch in a sweeping query, "any other spot on earth so completely enwrapped in darkness, so mute in the face of all our questions?" And Kisch's questions were many. "What tribe, what race once dwelt at the foot of Monte Albán? Who were the builders, who the architects of these pagan temples? . . . What were the tools of the stonemasons made of? . . . How to explain why several of the urn-figures seem to depict an Egyptian sphinx, another the bird-headed god Ra, and why the reliefs in the 'Gallery of Dancers' are partly in Assyrian style, partly a portrayal of Negroid types? How? Why? Whence?"[1]

After three decades of excavations, Monte Albán continues mute in the face of these queries. For every question it reluctantly answers, it poses a dozen new ones.

The task of excavating Monte Albán was undertaken by the Mexican archaeologist Alfonso Caso in 1931. As one might expect at the crossroads of trade, he found traces of many cultures, for the inhabitants of Monte Albán appear to have served as cultural intermediaries between the Toltecs in central Mexico and the Old Empire of the Mayas along the east coast, and to have had contacts also with peoples even as far removed, perhaps, as Peru.

Before the advent of Cortés, Monte Albán had been occupied by three different peoples, Dr. Caso learned. Most recent of these were the Mixtecs, who moved down from the north, overran the Valley of Oaxaca, and wrested the site on the hill from its previ-

FIGURE 19. Monte Albán, Oaxaca, after excavations. (Feucht-

wanger, *Kunst im alten Mexiko,* Atlantis Verlag, Zürich.)

FIGURE 20.   Monte Albán. Drawing by Gisela Kuske.

ous owners. The Mixtecs claimed descent from the Toltecs and
were skilled in the arts of those capable craftsmen. In 1932 Dr.
Caso discovered an undisturbed tomb of a Mixtec official, Monte
Albán's famous Tomb No. 7, which yielded a golden treasure,
for the state was rich in that precious metal. Here he found ex-
quisite jewelry of gold, copper, jade, pearls, and turquoise; polished gems; golden tiaras and a golden mask; earrings "woven
from tears and thorns"; a twenty-strand necklace; brooches, bracelets, and rings.

Before the puzzling Mixtecs moved in, a little-known people
called Zapotecs dwelt at Monte Albán. Much of the magnificent
ceremonial center is credited to their labors. There was ample

time for building: Zapotecs are believed to have worshiped here more than a thousand years. During their early period the Zapotecs built an astronomical observatory and possessed a hieroglyphic writing. This period has been placed between 200 B.C. and 350 A.D., and more recently a specimen from it was radiocarbon-dated as of 272 B.C. ± 145 years—only fifty years after the death of Alexander the Great and a few years before the first of the Punic Wars between Carthage and Rome.

Early settlers though they were, the Zapotecs were not the founders of Monte Albán. How large their cultural debt to their predecessors may have been it is difficult at this late date to say. The cat god of the previous residents lingered on at Monte Albán, where the Zapotecs adopted it, and they seem to have adopted more.

So little is known of the earliest comers to Monte Albán that their very identity was until recently in dispute. Ceramics from this initial period are similar to Olmec ceramics, but once they were thought to have been carried to Monte Albán by traders. Now these ceramics are believed to have been produced on the site. Moreover, the general cultural pattern of early Monte Albán bears a marked resemblance to that of the Olmecs, most enigmatic and most exciting of all preconquest Americans.

Ixtlilxóchitl in his history of the world described the Olmecs as the people who succeeded the race of giants and, more significantly, as *the people who flourished during the era when Quetzalcoatl appeared,* bringing the gift of civilization. If, then, the founders of Monte Albán were Olmecs, and if Quetzalcoatl arrived when the Olmecs were flourishing, we may have in Monte Albán the first tangible clue to the dates of the original Quetzalcoatl, assuming him to have been a man or living men and not a fleshless fabrication.

The date of the Olmecs' arrival at Monte Albán is controversial, as are most dates in Mexico's scrambled prehistory, but radiocarbon tests indicate that it occurred no later than 500 B.C. An average of several tests yielded the date 666 B.C. ± 160 years.

These early residents of Monte Albán stand near the top of the list of remarkable Americans. Long before ancient Rome had achieved her grandeur and even before the golden age of Athens, the people of Monte Albán were writing in hieroglyphics, main-

FIGURE 21.   Olmec "dancers" at Monte Albán. Figures carved in relief on building blocks, some accompanied by hieroglyphs.

taining a calendar, and computing by the bar-and-dot system, of which more presently. They were also carving life-sized figures on large rocks which were then employed in the construction of buildings (Figure 21).

These rocks tell a fabulous story, for carved in enduring stone are "dancers" who must once have dwelt and probably danced on this man-made plateau. The "dancers" have flat noses, round faces, and thick lips. In short, their appearance suggests that the dancers of Monte Albán were Negroes (Figure 22).

Do these Negroid representations in association with a higher and very early culture indicate that the bringers of civilization were Negroes? Not necessarily. For here alongside the dancers another physical type is portrayed. One of the faces carved in

FIGURE 22.   Closeup of an Olmec "dancer."   (Feuchtwanger, *Kunst im alten Mexiko,* Atlantis Verlag, Zürich.)

FIGURE 23.   A bearded Olmec of Monte Albán, possibly an artisan at work.

stone at Monte Albán (Figure 23) is an Old Testament type with a convex nose and a spatulate beard, another feature alien to beardless American Indians.

There are yet the unanswered questions of Egon Erwin Kisch. How to account for such a conglomeration: an Egyptian sphinx, the Egyptian god Ra, an Assyrian style, and Negroid types—and in addition, as we have just seen, a bearded face of Semitic aspect? Where else on the face of the earth were these once blended?

Where else? In the ancient Orient, a term employed in scholarly convention to indicate the ancient Near East or the "Mediterranean East." More specifically, in the Syro-Palestinian region, including Phoenicia, which linked together the great river valleys of Egypt and Mesopotamia and freely partook of the cultures nurtured by both.

Rather than draw important conclusions from a single site, however, we shall move along, still in pursuit of bearded Fair Gods, still seeking to sift from the legend the kernel of truth from which it grew. So our path, like Quetzalcoatl's, lies again to the east and the strange and provocative things which the swamps and jungles have yielded to the spade of the archaeologist. Monte Albán is only a preview of what has lain hidden for hundreds of years in the jungles of eastern Mexico hard by the "sea where the sun rises."

⚜ ⚜ ⚜

7

⚜ ⚜ ⚜

THE REDISCOVERY
OF THE MAYAS

IN NOVEMBER, 1839, when the ancient Mayas were almost unheard of and their great ceremonial centers had long since been swallowed by the jungle, an American lawyer and antiquarian named John Lloyd Stephens was pushing through the tropical wilds of Honduras "with the hope rather than the expectation," as he expressed it, "of finding wonders." During the preceding two centuries, ever since 1650, very little had been added to the fragmentary story of the Mayas as set down by the early Franciscan fathers and converted natives. But Stephens' curiosity was piqued: there was more to be known, more to be seen, and Stephens proposed to find it.

Slogging along behind him now was his friend and fellow adventurer Frederick Catherwood, an English artist. Ahead of them, slashing a path through the tangled woods with a machete, was the native guide José, the only man—so they had been told—who "knew anything about" the ruins the two outsiders were seeking.

Scratched, sodden, despairing of success, Stephens and Catherwood emerged from the wet green gloom of the woods and stood dejectedly on the bank of the Río Copán, tributary of the Motagua, which empties into the Caribbean. Glancing across the river, they saw directly opposite them a stone wall perhaps a hundred feet high. Despite its mantle of overgrowth they saw at once that the wall was man-made. With resurgent energy the party forded the rapid river, hacked their way through the undergrowth, and ascended the wall by large stone steps. Presently they found themselves on a terrace enveloped by a dense forest.

The guide José pushed forward, clearing a path with his machete, then stopped to slash away matted vines that enwrapped a toppled fragment of stone half buried in the earth. In the forest's faint light they could dimly discern its elaborate sculpturing. José moved along, machete swinging, and they came to a massive structure which, as nearly as they could make out for the trees, was a pyramid. Some of its wide stone steps had been heaved apart by saplings. Working their way deeper into the woods, the threesome came upon a square stone column about fourteen feet in height, sculptured in bold relief. "The front," as Stephens described it, "was the figure of a man curiously and richly dressed, and the face, evidently a portrait, solemn, stern, and well fitted to excite terror. The back was of a different design, unlike anything we had ever seen before, and the sides were covered with hieroglyphics."[1]

Stumbling along, the interlopers came in time upon fourteen more monuments, some pushed aslant by enormous roots, some locked in the branches of trees, some bound to the earth by gigantic vines, and "some in worksmanship equal to the finest monuments of the Egyptians"—all in the forest's appropriate gloom and silence. Only the monkeys disturbed the quiet of the buried city as they swung through the trees overhead with the sound of wind, forty or fifty at a time in swift procession, some with little ones wound in their arms. Amid these strange monuments they seemed to Stephens "like wandering spirits of the departed race guarding the ruins of their former habitations."

In this frame of mind Stephens returned at length to the wall, his first glimpse of ruined Copán, and sat there pondering the mystery that lay all about.

"Who," he asked, "were the people that built this city? In the ruined cities of Egypt, even in the long-lost Petra, the stranger knows the story of the people whose vestiges are around him. America, say historians, was peopled by savages; but savages never reared these structures, savages never carved these stones. We asked the Indians who made them, and their dull answer was 'Quien sabe?' 'Who knows?'

"There were no associations connected with this place; none of those stirring recollections which hallow Rome, Athens, and 'the world's great mistress on the Egyptian plain'; but architecture, sculpture, and painting, all the arts which embellish life, had flourished in this overgrown forest; . . . glory had lived and passed away, and none knew that such things had been, or could tell of their past existence. Books, the records of knowledge, are silent on this theme. The city was desolate. . . . It lay before us like a shattered bark in the midst of the ocean, her masts gone, her name effaced, her crew perished, and none to tell whence she came. . . . All was mystery, dark, impenetrable mystery, and every circumstance increased it. In Egypt the colossal skeletons of gigantic temples stand in the unwatered sands in all the nakedness of desolation; but here an immense forest shrouds the ruins, hiding them from sight, heightening the impression and moral effect, and giving an intensity and almost wildness to the interest."[2]

Next morning, back at the hacienda outside the miserable village of Copán with its half-dozen corn-thatched huts, a new complication presented itself. A native came forward, identified himself as "the owner of the idols," and stated that no one could step on the land without his permission. As proof of this claim he presented his title papers.

Later that day an idea was born to Stephens. Resolving that the ruins "belonged by right to us," he conceived a grandiose scheme to buy the entire site, remove the monuments, and set them up elsewhere as the nucleus of a great national museum of

FIGURE 24 (*opposite*).   Mayan altar at Copán, Honduras. The death's-head altar is seven feet square and four feet high, its flat top grooved, perhaps for use as a sacrificial table. Behind the altar stands a god carved in stone. Drawing by Catherwood.

American antiquities (a plan which was to prove infeasible because of problems in transportation). With this scheme in mind, however, he approached the owner and asked the price of the ruins. "I think he was not more surprised than if I had asked to buy his poor old wife, our rheumatic patient, to practice medicine upon. He seemed to doubt which of us was out of his senses. The property was so utterly worthless that my wanting to buy it seemed very suspicious."

There were other considerations also, including proof of character, which Stephens supplied in the form of a letter from General Cascara and credentials from the mighty United States government. Even these, however, failed to convince the villain in this comic opera. Whereupon Stephens opened his trunk and put on his diplomatic coat with its profusion of large gilt-eagle buttons. "I had on a Panama hat, soaked with rain and spotted with mud," Stephens added, "a checked shirt, white pantaloons, yellow up to the knees with mud." But the eagle buttons did it. The property owner bowed and yielded, and the ancient ruins of Copán, Honduras, changed hands.

"I paid," says Stephens, "fifty dollars for Copán. There was never any difficulty about price. I offered that sum, for which Don José Maria thought me only a fool."[3]

Stephens' companion, Frederick Catherwood, set to work to make drawings of the sculptured stelae. The dense shade baffled his efforts, and it became necessary to fell the trees around each object selected for reproduction. Indians were hired, but they had no axe. "But we had been buffeted into patience," wrote Stephens, "and as we watched the Indians while they hacked with their machetes, we even wondered that they succeeded so well." When a space was cleared, Catherwood set up his frame. Standing ankle-deep in mud, his hands gloved for protection against mosquitoes, with monkeys grimacing at him from nearby trees, Catherwood worked from daylight to dark producing the careful and infinitely detailed drawings which were later to startle the world (Figure 24).

Stephens meanwhile slogged deeper into his jungle city, discovering more and yet more ruins. When work was resumed there a century later, it was found that the ceremonial center comprised a main group and sixteen subgroups, one of them seven miles

FIGURE 25. Overview of Copán, Honduras, Stephens' $50 purchase. Reconstruction drawing by Tatiana Proskouriakoff.

away. The Acropolis—a complex of pyramids, temples, and terraces—covers twelve acres. The Main Structure—the Acropolis plus five adjoining plazas—sprawls over seventy-five acres.

One of its most interesting features was revealed by the tooth of time and the river. After the site was abandoned in the early ninth century, the Río Copán changed its course, swept closer, and gnawed at Copán's Acropolis, exposing a vertical cross section which rose to a maximum height of 118 feet and was almost a thousand feet long at the base. This "largest archaeological cross-section in the world" showed clearly that Copán, like similar early American sites, had been built and rebuilt and built yet again, layer upon layer, with the floor levels of many earlier constructions now visible simultaneously. Twentieth-century engineers have restored the river to its original course to prevent further erosion.

Leaving Copán, Stephens wandered through much of Middle America discovering ancient wonders. In 1841 he published his *Incidents of Travel in Central America, Chiapas, and Yucatán* with illustrations by Catherwood. Before that date the existence of ancient jungle cities was almost unknown outside of Middle America. From Stephens' buoyant account most American readers —bored with tepees and tomahawks—learned for the first time that America's past was as rich and ripe and fertile as the jungle itself. The impact of the book was instantaneous and far-reaching.

Stephens today is known as "the father of Mayan archaeology," though he was never a professional archaeologist, and as "the rediscoverer of the Mayas." Modern exploration in the land of the Mayas begins with John Lloyd Stephens.

Like a giant thumb the Peninsula of Yucatán thrusts northward into the Gulf of Mexico. This thumb, its base, and adjacent webbing were the land of the Mayas, America's ancient savants, who flourished from shortly after the time of Christ till the coming of the Spanish conquistadors. Approximately 125,000 square miles in area, the Maya "empire," a group of city-states, was roughly equivalent in size to New England plus New York and New Jersey. In addition to the Peninsula of Yucatán with its present Mexican states of Campeche and Yucatán and the territory of Quintana Roo, the Mayan domain included also the eastern

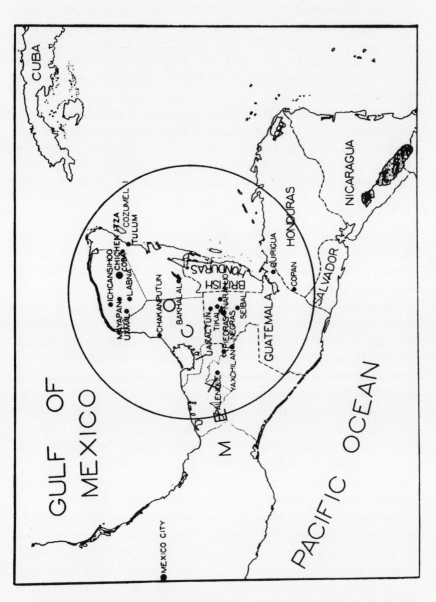

The domain of the Mayas

part of the state of Chiapas, much of Guatemala (particularly the panhandle), British Honduras, and the western fringe of Honduras.

At the southern extremity lies Stephens' Copán in Honduras. At the northern extremity lies Chichén Itzá in northern Yucatán. These two cities represent also extremes in time: the so-called Old Empire and the New. For the Mayas achieved not one but two eras of greatness, with Chichén Itzá the center of the later Mayan culture.

In 1855 Edward Herbert Thompson, "the Schliemann of Yucatán," set out to locate fabled Chichén Itzá, confident of its existence because he believed that the old written records reported facts. His faith was vindicated one moonlit night when, riding along at the end of an arduous, racking journey, he saw a magnificent temple rising above the dark sea of treetops.

Today Pan American Clippers fly visitors to the modern capital of Yucatán, Mérida, and a subsequent drive of 77 miles brings them to the old New Empire capital, Chichén Itzá. There Mayan children, unaware of their ancestors' greatness, tumble in play amid the ruins of temples and pyramids.

Chichén Itzá is more than impressive. To look upon something as tangible as solid stone and find it incredible is uncanny. Yet here it is the Temple of the Warriors, suggestive of ancient Greek temples (Figure 26); and everywhere the familiar Greek fret. Here too is the Castillo, Temple of Kukulcan, reminiscent of earlier Babylonian ziggurats (Figure 27). Some archaeologists believe that this pyramid is a summation of the Maya calendar, its ninety steps in each of the four stairways plus the top platform representing the three hundred sixty-five days of the year; its nine terraces, each divided by a stairway, representing the eighteen months; and these multiplied by the four sides representing the fifty-two years in a Calendar Round. Here too at Chichén Itzá is a crumbling observatory, its thick walls oriented in accordance with the instructions of Mayan astronomers: one line of sight, for example, bisects the setting sun on the day of the vernal equinox (Figure 28).

Jutting from corners and sprawling on columns all over Chichén Itzá are portraits of bearded men and feathered serpents, symbol of Quetzalcoatl. "The people of Yucatán," wrote the six-

FIGURE 26. Temple of the Warriors, Chichén Itzá. This structure takes its name from the pilasters, which are carved in relief with warriors in the style of Tula. Reconstruction by Kenneth Conant.

FIGURE 27. Temple of Kukulcan, Chichén Itzá. This perfect pyramid, 24 meters high (78¾ feet), is also called The Castillo. (Feuchtwanger, *Kunst im alten Mexiko*, Atlantis Verlag, Zürich.)

FIGURE 28. Astronomical observatory, Chichén Itzá. The Caracol (snail), as it is sometimes called, was partially restored by the Carnegie Institution of Washington. Incense burners dot the balustrade of the upper platform.

teenth-century Spanish chronicler Torquemada, "reverenced this Quetzalcoatl, calling him Kukulcan and saying that he came to them from the west, that is from New Spain [Mexico], for Yucatán is eastward therefrom. From him it is said that the kings of Yucatán are descended who call themselves Cocomes, that is to say, 'judges or hearers.' "4 Other sixteenth-century writers referred to this Quetzalcoatl-Kukulcan as a Mexican captain who entered and captured Chichén Itzá, established a new religion, and in 987 A.D. founded the walled city of Mayapán.

Although Yucatán seems far removed from the Mexican plateau, recent excavations at Tula have clearly established the interrelation. Chichén Itzá, except for some basic Mayan architecture, has been called "a grandiose duplicate of Tula."5 Architecture, sculpture, and other art work which closely resemble or even duplicate those brought to light at Toltec Tula are found in Mayan Chichén Itzá (Figure 29), and it is accepted as fact that the Toltecs conquered Chichén Itzá in the tenth century. As for Quetzalcoatl, today most Mexicanists conclude that the conqueror of Chichén Itzá merely bore the name of the Toltec culture god but was quite another person who lived centuries later.

At Chichén Itzá some visitors pass by the crumbling ruins to stare down seventy feet into the somber water of the Sacred Cenote, the enormous Well of Sacrifice into which the Mayas, amid the heady reek of incense, cast precious gifts of jade, copper, and gold—and in times of crisis also humans, including the most beautiful virgins—in the hope of appeasing the gods.

Another magnetic attraction is the old Mayan ball court, where athletes almost a thousand years ago indulged in a game vaguely similar to modern basketball, maneuvering the solid rubber ball not with the hands but with agile hips and knees. Passing the ball through the high stone ring was a feat so rare that the player who achieved it had the right to claim the jewels and cloaks of all the spectators. As a result, one basket quickly emptied the stadium. The same game, to judge by identical courts and stone rings found in the Valley of Mexico, was a favorite sport of the Toltecs. Chichén Itzá had no less than seven ball courts.

Those who will may see in these ball courts the character-

FIGURE 29.   Bearded Atlas on a Mayan capital supports a ceiling at Chichén Itzá. A similar capital was found at Tula.

building "playing fields of Eton," but fifty years ago Professor William E. Gates termed the ball courts and other splendors of Chichén Itzá "the false activity of decay," reared at a time when the national energy had "turned in and begun to feed upon itself." In such a period of decay, he stated, "the national impulse has changed from achievement to gratification, more and more sources are drawn upon to minister to its enjoyment, and that enjoyment becomes an art; forms of every kind are subtly refined in its service, and linguistic forms with them. And this is then the very period when all these material, formal elements are pointed to with pride as the evidence of culture and progress. The thought-life of the nation has lost itself in the conflict and confusion, in the distractions of the forms into which it has molded the matters its creative force has entered."[6]

It is generally conceded that the Mayan New Empire, epitomized in Chichén Itzá, was culturally inferior to the Old. As Gates has put it, though somewhat overstating his case:

"The stately and incomparable compositions and architecture of Palenque, Copán and Quiriguá have yielded to the ball courts and local strifes of Chichén Itzá. . . . The later the date, the lower in every case the culture. . . . Of course we see the rise of the Aztec nation, a small cycle, but like the Gothic upon the Roman, it comes at the end of the general American break-up—an incursion of barbarians settling on and preserving for us fragments of the culture that preceded them, just as happened over and over again all over the world. And the same with the Incas in Peru. And yet even the Mexican culture demands our high respect, comparing favorably with European of the same period."[7]

The words of Professor Gates have indicated our next stop. Our path leads away from the ball courts and subtler refinements of Chichén Itzá, backward through time to "stately and incomparable" Palenque, where stirring finds have been made in the last decade.

8

IN THE PALENQUE
TOMB

SOUTH THE LENGTH of the Yucatán peninsula from the expiring greatness of postclassic Chichén Itzá lie the older ruins of classic Palenque, an important Old Empire religious center.

In 1949 the archaeologist Alberto Ruz was investigating Palenque's Temple of Inscriptions, a temple atop a pyramid. Others had examined the temple before him, but Ruz discovered that its inner walls continued on below floor level. Looking further, he found in the floor a flagstone with circular perforations. These, he deduced, were fingerholds, and he promptly tested his theory. The slab lifted out, and Ruz looked down into a staircase completely filled with rubble in the manner of Egyptian pyramid builders.

That year Alberto Ruz and his assistants laboriously cleared twenty-three steps, wondering the while whether all they would find at the bottom might be the end of the stairway; for it was

generally accepted that Mesoamerican pyramids were not constructed as tombs but merely as pedestals for temples.

The following year, 1950, another twenty-three steps were
cleared. They ended at a passageway. In 1951 Ruz investigated
two apertures in this passageway which resembled windows.
Clearing them, he found them to be air passages which extended
through the pyramid about twenty-five feet to its west side. By
this time Ruz and his associates had devoted three years to the
project and had little but rubble to show for their labors—until
they came to another stairway which led off the same landing,
this time downward in the opposite direction.

Twenty-two steps later, about sixty-five feet below the floor

FIGURE 30. Cross section of the Ruz tomb, Temple of Inscriptions,
Palenque.

of the Temple of Inscriptions, this second flight was blocked by a stone wall. Leaning against the wall was a masonry box which contained three earthenware plates, three shells, a pair of jade earcaps and stoppers, seven other pieces of jade, and one fine pearl: scarcely sufficient treasure to have warranted the building and blocking of two flights of stairs. So Ruz dug on.

When the wall had been cleared, a huge triangular flagstone was revealed, standing on edge. At its base was a rude grave containing six skeletons, five male and one female, apparently adolescents. Many of the bones crumbled or broke when removed. Now the investigators noticed a crack along the base of the triangular slab and, shining a flashlight through it, descried a shadowy room (Figure 30). They tried turning the vertical slab on its base. It moved, and four more steps came into view which led down into the room itself.

Breathlessly Ruz swung his torch and lighted the ghostly room. It seemed to be carved from ice, for seeping water had calcified with time. Long stalactites trailed from the high ceiling and slender stalagmites rose from the floor like a curtain of petrified vines, partially obscuring the stucco bas-reliefs that decorated the walls (Figure 31). These bas-reliefs depicted a procession of nine priests, elegantly attired, bearing puppetmaces (Figure 32).

Dominating the long, narrow room and occupying almost the width of the floor was a large sarcophagus approximately seven feet wide and ten feet long, resting on sculptured stone legs (Figure 33). The monolithic sarcophagus resembled an altar, its outer surface elaborately sculptured with a representation of a man whose large nose and Mongoloid cast of features mark him a typical Maya (Figure 34). Astronomical glyphs circle the slab, and fifty-four hieroglyphs are carved on the sides.

In November, 1952, the top of the sarcophagus, a huge slab of stone almost ten inches thick, was lifted, revealing another stone slab which fitted precisely into the sarcophagus. This too was removed, exposing the skeleton of a man, doubtless a distinguished priest or lord (Figure 35). Every finger bore a ring, and his arms were adorned with bracelets. The crumbling skeleton still wore a breastplate of beads, and over his face could be discerned the fragments of a mosaic mask constructed of jade—jade, esteemed by the Mayas as gold was precious to Old World

FIGURE 31.   Stalactites and stucco bas-reliefs, Palenque.

FIGURE 32.   A bearded priest of Palenque.

FIGURE 33.   Palenque sarcophagus viewed from steps.

FIGURE 34.   Relief on the Palenque sarcophagus.

FIGURE 35.   Sarcophagus and ancient Maya, Ruz tomb, Palenque.

peoples. (Eighty-four years earlier, when Heinrich Schliemann was excavating prehistoric Mycenae, he brushed the dust of ages off dissolving skeletons attired in golden breastplates and golden masks, for these were believed to protect deceased kings from malign forces after death. Golden masks have been found, too, on corpses interred in the tombs of Phoenicia.)

The shape of the great stone coffin at Palenque also warrants attention. The Mayan stonemason, chiseling arduously with whatever tools he may have had, invested considerable time and effort to fashion a foot, a flared and flattened base (Figure 35). Why did he bother? Interestingly, the same question has been asked concerning similar stone sarcophagi found in Phoenician tombs, sarcophagi with rounded heads and flattened bases—and occasionally with the stone sides indented slightly at ankle height, as here, then flared at the foot. Archaeologists and art historians quickly supplied the answer as to Phoenician sarcophagi. Obviously, they said, these sarcophagi were modeled after Egyptian mummy-cases. The Egyptians constructed their mummy-cases of wood, and the light, movable cases were sometimes stood upright; the wider base then increased the stability. The heavy stone sarcophagi of Phoenicia, however, were always found lying flat, as was the sarcophagus of Palenque. The ancient Phoenicians, archaeologists agree, merely continued to copy a detail of their model long after its *raison d'être* had ceased to exist. Did the Mayan stonemason likewise have a model in mind when he provided the heavy stone envelope of Palenque with a wide base?

A tiny object laid inside the Palenque sarcophagus near the corpse is sometimes dismissed with a word: a carved jade "idol." Identified by archaeologists as Kinich Ahau, the sun god, this small figurine stirs large conjectures. For in the populous and interrelated pantheon of the Mayas, Kinich Ahau, Lord of the Eye of the Sun, is intimately associated with Itzamna, Lord of Day and of Night, and the blended god is sometimes called Kinich Ahau Itzamna. Significantly, Kinich Ahau Itzamna was worshiped by the Mayas as the first of all priests, patron of medicine, learning, writing, and books.

Once more this smacks of mythology and the infant years of religion. Yet here is a god of learning depicted in jade, a face which may or may not resemble that of a deified human (Figure 36). A bearded face, moreover, unlike the Mayas who dwelt here but strongly suggestive of faces one finds even today in the Holy Land and the Levant, a face that would not have seemed out of place at the helm of an ancient Phoenician ship.

Who served as the subject for this strange likeness? When had a Mayan sculptor gazed upon such a face? There are indications that this is perhaps a stylized likeness which may have

FIGURE 36.   Jade figurine of an Old Empire Maya god found in the Palenque sarcophagus.

evolved through centuries, not unlike the depiction of Christ on a modern crucifix. But how long ago, if ever, the prototype of the figurine walked through the streets of Palenque remains a riddle, or by how long a span of time he antedated, if human, the bejeweled corpse which lay so long in its clammy tomb that the lid of its stone sarcophagus sprouted stalagmites.

9

MEN WITH
PETTICOATS

IT MAY BE MORE than sheerest coincidence that an ancient
legend tells of a stranger who came to this same Palenque in
the long, long ago and acquired in time the status of culture god.

This Votan, it is written, came to America "by divine command" and brought along some of his people for the purpose of
founding a settlement. The natives looked at the newcomers,
who were strangely attired in long robes, and quickly dubbed
them "men with petticoats." But the same natives who had
scoffed at the colonists' robes "soon exchanged ideas and customs
with them, submitted to their rule, and gave them their daughters
in marriage."[1]

The source of much information concerning Votan is a book
which Votan himself reputedly wrote on the origin of his people.
A copy of this book, written in the Tzental or Quiché language,
was once in the possession of Nuñez de la Vega, Bishop of Chiapas;
but the good bishop burned it in 1691. Both the bishop and one
Ordoñez Aguilar, however, had previously written extracts from

it, in keeping with that maddening Spanish custom of trying to preserve with one hand what they destroyed with the other.

From this Bishop of Chiapas and Ordoñez de Aguilar we learn that Votan set out from the land of Chivim (unidentified), passed by the "dwelling of the thirteen snakes" (which some nineteenth-century scholars took for the thirteen islands of the Canaries group off West Africa), arrived at the land of Votan (thought by some to be Cuba or the adjacent West Indian island of Hispaniola), passed through the island-strewn Laguna de Terminos, went south up the Usumacinta River, and on one of its tributaries founded Palenque.

These interpretations were merely large guesses, but this can be said in their favor. Though the Antilles may seem far distant from Mexico, only the Yucatán Channel with a breadth of about 125 miles separates westernmost Cuba from the low cliffs of northeastern Yucatán. Bernal Díaz, that trustworthy early Spanish reporter, relates that when he and a group of adventurers first went ashore on the east coast of Yucatán they encountered a young Indian woman who spoke to them in the language of Cuba, which the Spaniards had learned. They asked her how she came to be in these parts, and she explained that she was one of ten Jamaica Indians who two years earlier had paddled out from their island a distance in a large canoe to fish but had been caught by the current and carried to this new land.

By whatever route an early voyager may have reached the arid peninsula of Yucatán, from Cuba or riding the Gulf Stream westward farther south, if he then attempted to follow the Yucatán shoreline he would presently dip south (down the inner side of the thumb, as it were) and would come in time to a vast bay, the Laguna de Terminos. Here, where the Peninsula of Yucatán joins the mainland, the country becomes fertile. Near the western end of this great bay a navigable river, the Usumacinta, leads invitingly into the luxuriant land to the south. Some fifty miles farther south in the Usumacinta Valley, in the state of Chiapas, lie the ruins of ancient Palenque, one of the early Mayan cities.

Four times Votan returned, it is written, to his former home. On his first return voyage he came to a great city where a magnificent temple was under construction. Returning to Palenque, Votan found that more of his countrymen had arrived there.

Long after his death (if one may dare to assume that he

lived), Votan was associated in the minds of these people with jade and with snakes. Why snakes? In fact, why was a writhing serpent also the symbol of other American culture-gods? The names of the Fair Gods Quetzalcoatl in the Aztec language, Kukulcan in the Mayan, and Gucumatz in the Quiché all have an identical meaning: "the feathered serpent, the snake covered with feathers, the green-feathered snake."

To be sure, in ancient Egypt the uraeus or sacred asp, appearing above the forehead, was the symbol of sovereignty. In Phoenicia it crawled on the scepter of the king of Gebal—and perhaps on the scepters of others whose remains have not yet been recovered. But another and broader explanation might be this: The lowly snake, as Bancroft once noted, is always and everywhere the symbol of healing. Two intertwined snakes as the emblem of healing, wisdom, and fertility were early employed in Babylonia, and from there the symbol spread east and west. A Phoenician stela now in the Louvre bears two caducei; and, according to Berger in his *Les Ex-voto du Temple de Tanit,* the caduceus was no uncommon object on Carthaginian stelae. The Greek god of medicine, Asclepius, was represented by a single snake, and this single snake continued in use as the symbol of medicine in the western world until the sixteenth century, when it was replaced by the caduceus, two snakes twined round a winged staff, which is still today the symbol of the physician.

One of the more dependable patterns of history is the clutching for medical aid when primitive natives recognize the stranger in their midst as a person of higher culture. Thus, within historic times, the Indians appealed to the Spaniard Cabeza de Vaca to cure their ills when he wandered alone across the Southwest in the sixteenth century. Thus, three centuries later, the American lawyer-diplomat John Lloyd Stephens and his artist friend Frederick Catherwood found themselves in constant demand as physicians and were soon dispensing healing and medicines by the hour while they fretted to get on with the digging and drawing at their fifty-dollar Copán. And thus, in our generation, the crew of the raft *Kon-Tiki* were pressed into service as lay physicians by South Sea Islanders. These men had the misfortune to live too late, or perhaps they also might have been deified in the form of a writhing serpent.

All of which seems to suggest that the very early American

strangers may likewise have been recognized as persons of higher culture, just as the legends hold, to whom the natives appealed for medical treatment. Quetzalcoatl in addition to being a culture-god was also god of the air, the healing air, and some of the ancient Mexican legends specifically state that he brought a knowledge of medicine. Itzamna, the Mayan god of medicine and knowledge, is often depicted as an ugly old bearded man with a protruding tooth and a nose that out-noses Cyrano's; and then again, particularly on the monuments in the old cities toward the south, we see Itzamna represented as a serpent with scales and rattle, whereas the serpent representation of Kukulcan is covered with feathers. Even the natives who transmitted the legends of Itzamna and Kukulcan to the Spanish chroniclers shortly after the conquest sometimes confused the two serpent gods, for both were also gods of medicine.

And now Votan, a culture hero and serpent.

Varied claims have been made on behalf of Votan. Within the last century several families named Votan have been found in this area who claimed descent from the hero-god. J. G. Müller, who devoted many years to the study of Indian myths, pointed out one which suggests that Votan was the grandson of Quetzalcoatl.[2] Obviously this Quetzalcoatl was not the Mexican captain and conqueror but instead a much earlier Quetzacoatl, or perhaps a blending of Quetzalcoatl and Itzamna. For an ancient manuscript dates Votan's arrival as a thousand years *before Christ*.

A few nineteenth-century scholars, accepting this date, suggested that Votan and his "men with petticoats" were Phoenicians. Now, Votan is said to have departed from the land of Chivim—or so the name was written in the Tzental or Quiché language—but no Chivim is known. The Phoenicians said of themselves that they came from the land of Canaan; and the original name of their land, so several Greek writers reported, was $\chi\nu\hat{a}$. This would be transliterated into English as Chna; the Greek alphabet had no character which transliterates into our letter "v." The name has also been written in English as Kena'an or Kan'an, the vowel variance stemming from the fact that the Phoenician alphabet, like the Egyptian, lacked symbols for vowels. None of these is, of course, Chivim, but transliteration has accomplished many strange things. Among ancient place names one other is also vaguely similar to Chivim: the Chittim of the Old Testament, which is Cyprus, early settled by Phoenicians and described by Homer in the *Iliad* as a land thoroughly Phoenician.

Pablo Cabrera went farther, averring that the Phoenician inscriptions on two marble columns found long ago at Tangier, Morocco, west of Gibraltar, trace the route of Votan.[3] His opinion was not widely shared, and indeed recording a route for all to follow seems totally out of Phoenician character—except in those centuries between the decline of Crete and the rise of Hellenic Greece when theoretically there was none to challenge or follow, even as far as the marble columns beyond Gibraltar. These six centuries or so of Phoenician supremacy embrace the date in question.

As for the tower which Votan is said to have seen under construction on his first return from Palenque, Ordoñez de Aguilar in his manuscript entitled *Historia de Cielo,* reputedly a copy of extracts from Votan's own book, states that this tower had been intended to reach to the heavens, but linguistic confusion had doomed the project. The other copyist of portions of Votan's book, Bishop Nuñez de la Vega, was even more specific in his identification. In his *Constituciones Diocesianos de Chiapas* he writes: "It is also said that he [Votan] . . . saw the great wall, namely, the Tower of Babel."

On first thought these statements seem utterly mad, at odds with every known fact. The Tower of Babel was built in the time of Genesis. Moreover, Votan, allegedly en route from America to Phoenicia, could not have glanced up from the helm of his ship to see this most famous of ziggurats because Babylon lies not on the Mediterranean but on the Euphrates. And yet—

If we are to give the legend of Votan any semblance of fair consideration, we must admit that this date of 1000 B.C.—which stems from a different manuscript rather than from Votan's own account—is its most questionable element, and that the "great city" as well as the "magnificent temple under construction" are far less likely to be in error. The great city might conceivably have been that greatest in the Middle East, Babylon, visited possibly for purposes of trade, for Babylon was a favorite market of Phoenician merchants. And the magnificent temple might indeed have been that most magnificent Tower of Babel. Anyone who looked upon it, looming high above the plain and dwarfing all around it, would not soon forget the sight. Such was the Tower of Babel as *rebuilt* by Nabopolassar and his successor Nebuchadnezzar in the seventh and sixth centuries B.C.—a date, by the way, which corresponds better with the possibility of four successful round-trip transatlantic voyages.

It would be as foolhardy to erect an elaborate hypothesis on the nebulous foundation of a single legend as on the treacherous quicksands of similarity. And yet, on this subject of similarity, only a person whose curiosity was blunted could gaze on the ruins of Palenque, Copán, Piedras Negras, and other Old Empire Mayan cities and fail to wonder how the architectural marvel of the Tigris-Euphrates Valley could be duplicated halfway around the world, with the trail of the temple-pyramids leading, not down from the northern narrows southward through Canada, but rather, it seems, from the shores of the Caribbean.

Bishop Nuñez de la Vega, discussing extracts from Votan's book, notes that "in the little history" the heathen recorded the names of all the provinces and cities in which he had tarried. One of these was Huehueta (Huehuetlán), where Votan claimed to have placed a treasure in a damp, dark, subterranean house. The treasure was said to consist of lidded clay jars, green stones, "other superstitious images," and of a room where portraits of "the ancient heathens who were in the calendar" were engraved in stone. Votan appointed a woman as chieftain of the treasure, with keepers to guard her, and apparently the treasure remained thus safe and protected through countless centuries.

In 1691, to history's eternal loss, Bishop Nuñez inspected this province. The chieftainess herself and her guardians, he peremptorily announces, surrendered all these ancient heathen treasures, which were then publicly burned in the market place. The only copy of Votan's book was burned in the same market place, along with other manuscripts, in this year of holocaust.[4]

The parallels between this account and the recent finds of

Alberto Ruz at Votan's Palenque are striking. In particular, one wonders whether the nine priests elegantly attired and bearing puppetmaces (Figures 31 and 32) might just possibly have been "the ancient heathens who were in the calendar."

More than a whim directed the hand that laid a small jade figurine inside a sarcophagus—stalactite-adorned when Alberto Ruz came upon it in 1952—in a room hewn deeply beneath a pyramid in Mayan Palenque. Could this be an image of Votan?

Behind the bearded and hook-nosed face the head is strangely misshapen. This might seem at first glance a matter of slight significance, for head deformation was a practice the Mayas indulged in immoderately, as so many old Mayan murals and stelae illustrate. The late Sylvanus Griswold Morley described the practice thus:

"Depressed foreheads," wrote Morley, "were considered a mark of beauty among the ancient Maya, and this deformation was achieved by binding the heads of the babies between a pair of flat boards, one at the back of the head, the other against the forehead. These boards were left in place for several days, and after they were removed, the head remained flattened for life. Maya representations of the human head in profile show that this practice must have been almost universal, at least among the upper class."[5]

One questions only Morley's assumption that the purpose was purely aesthetic. Was this "mark of beauty" rather a mark of prestige? We know that certain Maya mothers strove also to make their small children cross-eyed by attaching a ball of wax to a forelock and leaving it to dangle between the eyebrows, and we know from his portraits that Itzamna, that beak-nosed god of knowledge, was cross-eyed. We know too that certain adult male Mayas, in order to make the bridge of the nose seem higher, wore artificial nose pieces. Then there was head deformation, which, Bernal Díaz reported from observation, "seems to have been confined to the priests and nobles"—perhaps as an indication of rank and noble descent? If so, what was there about a misshapen head that made it prestigious?

In a society not only class-conscious but also bound by tradition one looks to the past: one looks for illustrious forebears with

FIGURE 37.   Stucco bas-relief at the palace, Palenque, showing Mayan
head deformation. Drawing by Catherwood.

heads misshapen. And here in the tomb of Palenque lies one
accorded the title of god, a god with a crescent-shaped nose and a
pointed beard—in fact, a god who could have passed for a native

in ancient Phoenicia; for there too head deformation was prac-
ticed, as indeed it was practiced in many places throughout the
Fertile Crescent. Yahweh himself found it needful to enjoin the
Hebrews: "Ye shall not round the corners of your heads."[6]

The arm of coincidence is notoriously long. But too many
coincidences centered about a given locale become just that: too
many. There comes a point, perhaps not yet reached in our investigation, where "coincidences" seem no longer coincidental,
no longer lacking in causal connection. The little-known legend
of Votan deserves to be re-examined in the light of recent archaeological finds. There may be a causal connection between these
elements—the flat-headed, bearded figurine; the legend of Votan's men with petticoats who exchanged ideas, customs; and
marriage vows with the natives; the distant land which, ancient
Greek writers stated, the Phoenicians had found and wished to
settle; and the lines which Fray Lizana set down in his *Historia
de Yucatán*. Recording traditions that were current among Yucatán Mayas at the time of the Spanish conquest, Fray Lizana observed that in their ancient language the Mayas had denoted the
east "in another way than today." Anciently, he said, they called
the east *Cenial* (the small descent) and the west *Nohenial* (the
great descent). "And the reason they say this is because from the
part of the east there came down to this land few people, and
from that of the west, many, and with this word they understand
few or many, the east and the west; and the few people from one
part and the many from the other."[7]

If a few shiploads of people from across the Atlantic long
ago landed in Yucatán and there intermarried with the flood of
natives who had earlier migrated down to Yucatán from the north
and west, this might have been precisely the way in which their
much later descendants would have described the two immigrations.

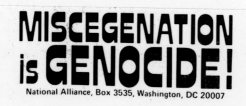

MISCEGENATION is GENOCIDE!

National Alliance, Box 3535, Washington, DC 20007

IO

THE LORE OF
THE JUNGLE SCHOLAR

IN NORTH AMERICA the colonists who came as a flood from
1620 onward brought along their old way of life: their religion, their customs, their mores. These people pushed the Indians
away, kept them at musket length always ahead in the westward
thrust, and in approximately two centuries erected a European
civilization across a continent. In Middle and South America the
influx, though it began a century earlier, never achieved the
volume or velocity of a flood. There a high percentage of the immigrants intermarried with natives; purebred natives lived all
about them, and some still do. These Europeans too brought
along their own way of life, tried to stamp out the old, the pagan,
and impose the new. But the moribund old, seemingly in its death
throes these four centuries, has never expired. Instead, the two
ways of life have achieved a curious blend—a hybrid.

If colonists also arrived here from out of the ancient world—
Phoenicians or Greeks or Romans—not in a flood or a stream but
only in a trickle, one might expect the point of balance to lie

heavily with the native, the numerically overwhelming old. One might expect incongruous contrasts: elements of a more advanced culture superimposed but spottily, puzzling traces of Old World erudition alongside typically Indian customs. This is precisely what one appears to find.

But vague similarities lure the observer aground on the reef of overhasty conclusions. We need to examine further, to attempt to ascertain the degree of any such cultural similarity, to explore insofar as we can the mind of the jungle scholar and what it may have evolved out of its own convolutions.

This overambitious program would be the labor of several lifetimes. But in the next few pages I shall attempt to set forth very briefly the Mayas' major intellectual concepts, some of the questions which they give rise to, and several tentative answers—partial, inconclusive, controversial, and therefore provocative.

The Mayas are often called the savants of early America. Not only their temple-pyramids astounded the Europeans. The Mayas had also a calendar sometimes described as more accurate than the Christian calendar in use at the time of Columbus. They possessed, too, a mathematical system, a rather impressive knowledge of astronomy, and a form of hieroglyphic writing—each a notable intellectual achievement. As John Lloyd Stephens might have expressed it, savages never evolved the concept of zero, savages never devised this remarkable calendar.

But who did? This question embarrasses all. It embarrasses the independent inventionists who, as Earnest A. Hooton once put it, "have set up for Aboriginal America a sort of *ex post facto* Monroe Doctrine and are inclined to regard suggestions of alien influence as acts of aggression." Now, a culture evolves from the first stick-digging of the first local agriculturalist to an elaborate civilization like that of the Mayas only through untold centuries of slow intellectual growth. But, early though agriculture appeared in Middle America, evidence of Mayan intellectual development is as yet inadequate to carry the cause for the staunch supporters of a home-grown American culture. Gladwin has repeatedly pointed out that the independent inventionists are caught in "the trap of time."

This question of the roots of Mayan knowledge, however,

also acutely embarrasses the diffusionists, those who hold that alien brains arrived to supplement local brawn. Similarities with Old World cultures are numerous, but very little of the lore appears to have been carried over intact. The most glaring example perhaps is the writing, for Mayan hieroglyphs bear only the most superficial resemblance to any the Old World has to offer.

This would seem at first glance to close the subject. But the history of writing takes many strange turns, and one of the strangest is that labeled "stimulus-diffusion." A. L. Kroeber's theory of stimulus-diffusion or idea-diffusion holds that the knowledge of the *existence* of writing can stimulate—has more than once stimulated—the development of a new and different expression. Professor Kroeber's theory is now rather widely applied to explain the origin of various Old World scripts which were apparently designed for monumental purposes—that is, for writing on stone, as the Mayas also used theirs. The Hittite hieroglyphic writing, often placed in this category, will exemplify the process.

Back in the Old World of the thirteenth century B.C., the scripts of various peoples were still in a fluid state and many had not yet been devised. It was during this time that two behemoths of antiquity, the Hittites and the Egyptians, the latter resurgent under their Ramses the Great, met head-on in battle. The peace treaty, drawn in about 1280 B.C., was recorded at the Hittite capital, Boghazköy, in three scripts: Egyptian, Babylonian, and Sumerian. The Hittites, it would seem, had not yet invented their own writing. When at length they got around to devising it, their hieroglyphs bore little or no resemblance to Egyptian, Babylonian, Sumerian, or any other known form of writing.

Such stimulus-diffusion has certainly occurred within historic times, as evidenced by the Cherokee Indian alphabet invented in 1821 by a half-breed Cherokee named Sequoyah and the Bamun script of the Cameroons created by the sultan of the Bamuns in the twentieth century. These examples are recent and incontestable. But where the event occurred long ago, positive proof is missing. As David Diringer observed, "Obviously this process is one which will ordinarily leave a minimum of historical evidence; the specific items of cultural content, upon which historians ordinarily rely in proving connection, are likely to be few or wholly absent."[1]

To suggest that this may have occurred in Middle America is no mere clutching at a straw. In earlier times the knowledge of writing was jealously guarded, first by Egyptian priests, who had three different forms of writing but spurned the simplified script and clung to their intricate hieroglyphs for the very reason that they were and would remain unintelligible to the masses. The Maya priests too were jealous guardians of their learning, and only the nobility and the priesthood were initiated into the mysteries of reading and writing or admitted to the inner circle of knowledge. The Phoenician alphabet, precursor of our own, was a simplified instrument that in time became the tool of the merchant princes; and now, three millennia later, a variation of this same alphabet places literacy within the grasp of infants. Would it have been the purpose of Phoenician colonists in a remote and primitive site to place this powerful instrument at the command of hordes of natives or, instead, to devise an impressive and baffling substitute?

In short, the fact that the Mayas from ancient times possessed a form of hieroglyphic writing is grist for nobody's mill. It is neither proof of idea-diffusion and hence knowledge of Old World writing, nor is its lack of resemblance adequate proof that no such contact was ever made.

Speaking of Mayan inscriptions of the Old Empire, Diringer wrote: "At the time of their first appearance, the Maya script and astronomical and mathematical knowledge are fully developed, and this presupposes a previous evolution of long development—of which nothing is known—unless there was some cultural importation, which is hardly thinkable."[2]

Or is it?

Whatever stand one takes on early Mesoamerican cultures, certain aspects appear to be "hardly thinkable." Take, for instance, the Mayan mathematical knowledge which Diringer mentioned.

Mayan mathematics, like that of other American aborigines, was vigesimal (by twenties, the sum of fingers plus toes) as distinguished from decimal (fingers only). In fact, the word "digit," which derives from the Latin *digitus,* meaning finger or toe, throws altogether too much light on the *modus operandi* of early mathematicians.

The Mayas indicated numerals in two different ways. The simple notation for numbers from one to nineteen was in bars and dots, each bar (perhaps once a twig) representing five, and each dot above it (perhaps once a pebble) signifying one. Thus nineteen was written as shown here.

The Mayas also, however, used glyphs or "head-variant" numerals, elaborate carvings of human heads (some of which warrant a closer look), to represent each number from one to nineteen and—surprisingly—zero.

(19)

Many historians of mathematics hold that the concept of

FIGURE 38.   Stucco glyphs, Palenque.

zero—so noticeably absent from Roman numerals—occurred first among the ancient Mayas; but others believe that the honor of this momentous discovery belongs to the Babylonians, who very early signified nullity by a blank and later introduced a special character corresponding to our zero. What happened to the Babylonian concept of zero after that is not yet known. Zero appears to have been forgotten until, somehow, it reappeared centuries later among the Mayas and later still in India.

Like the Babylonians, the Mayas also used place value, a form of positional mathematics involving multiplication. To label it so formidably is to disguise a process familiar to every schoolchild, for in writing the number 11,338, for example, we have multiplied the digit on the extreme right by 1, the digit to the left of it by 10, the next left by 100, the next by 1,000, and the digit on the extreme left by 10,000. Anyone who questions the importance of this simple concept should try to compute his income tax in Roman numerals!

The Mayas indicated place value vertically rather than horizontally, and they multiplied by twenty instead of by ten. Thus to write the numeral 20 an ancient Maya drew the symbol for zero, a shell, and placed one dot above it.

To cite a more complicated example, a Maya would have written the number 11,338 as shown in the column on the left, with the top dot in the position of 8,000's, the second tier 400's, the third tier twenties, and the fourth or bottom tier the simple number.

$$\cdot \quad \times\ 8{,}000 = 8{,}000$$
$$\cdots$$
$$\underline{\quad\quad} \times\quad 400 = 3{,}200$$
$$\cdot$$
$$\underline{\quad\quad} \times\quad 20 =\quad 120$$
$$\cdots$$
$$\underline{\underline{\quad\quad}} \times\quad 1 =\quad \underline{\ 18}$$
$$\quad\quad\quad\quad\quad 11{,}338$$

The Mayas often are called the New World's outstanding mathematicians. Among Europeans that distinction has been accorded the ancient Greeks, from whom the great structure of European mathematics is said to derive. The prime contribution of the Greeks, however, was in geometry. The basis of their mathematics was borrowed, it has been said, from earlier peoples—from Egyptians and from Phoenicians. The Phoenicians, so

Strabo reported, "are described as active investigators in astronomy as well as in the science of numbers, having been conducted thereto by arithmetical skill and by the practice of nocturnal navigation, both of which are indispensable to trade and to maritime intercourse." Mathematicians though they were, the Phoenicians themselves were among the most avid borrowers, and their mathematics in turn is believed to have derived in small part from Egypt and in large part from Assyria and Babylonia.

The point of all this is that Babylonian and Assyrian mathematics are known to have shared another important feature with Mayan in addition to place value and the concept of zero: the ability to express large numbers—infinitely large.

This is a comparatively recent concept. The Australian aborigines, typifying primitive man today, can count to two, some of the brainier ones to four, but their word five is "many." Even the ancient Greeks are said to have regarded the number 10,000 as "a large, uncountable aggregation." Says C. W. Ceram: "Not until the nineteenth century did the concept of a million become common in the West. By contrast, a cuneiform text found on the mound of Kuyunjik [Mesopotamia] records a mathematical series the end product of which in our number system would be expressed as 195,955,200,000,000. This means, in other words, a number that did not again enter the realm of calculation until the days of Descartes and Leibniz."[3]

The Babylonians, incidentally, achieved their results despite a cumbersome system derived from a fusion of the Sumerian sexagesimal and the Semitic decimal systems. This fusion necessitated the use of reckoning tables or "antique slide-rules."

Not only certain mathematical concepts were common to the Mayas and the scholars of the ancient Orient. Certain astronomical concepts too appeared in the Fertile Crescent and again among the Mayas.

Astronomy was not a late-blooming flower on the Maya stalk. Observatories are found in the earliest structures, and peepholes were let into ancient stone walls to provide a line of sight. The Mayan priests, however, stood like watchdogs guarding from the profane their cherished astronomical lore. Each time that the priests accurately predicted a solar or lunar eclipse, the masses believed that their priests had indeed communed with the gods. When at last the priesthood succumbed to war, disease, and Spanish fanaticism, their lore died with them.

A classic example of modern decadence was reported by Gregory Mason, a field archaeologist. One night when Mason was on an expedition in Maya country a member of his party, a surveyor, was taking a star sight. Out of the darkness stormed a twentieth-century Maya, the chief of the Tuluum Indians, and threatened irately to have the surveyor shot. "We don't want you white men moving our stars around!"[4]

Before the fall of ancient Rome the ancestors of this Tuluum chief were charting accurately the synodical revolutions of Venus. That aberrant white beacon appears for a while as the morning star, again as the evening star, and during conjunction appears not at all. For this reason Venus was once, long ago, believed to be two stars, Lucifer and Hesperus, which signaled the coming and going of day. But Assyrians recognized the two as identical— and Mayan astronomers likewise.

Living in jungles, without recourse to modern instruments, Mayan astronomers managed to overcome these handicaps by utilizing the temples that topped their pyramids. The temples thus served a dual purpose: they were observatories as well as religious shrines. Off in the Fertile Crescent, ziggurats too were topped with temples, and ziggurat temples also served a dual function as observatories and shrines.

In these high temples the lines of sight were sufficiently long to permit observations with such simple devices as crossed sticks lined up with fixed objects on the horizon. Demonstrating that the power of abstract thought is not negated by primitive instruments, the Mayas managed to achieve notable results—for example, in lunar determinations.

Now, modern astronomers have calculated the length of a lunation as 29.53059 days. Mayan arithmetic had no fractions, and this one is particularly unwieldy. Yet Mayan astronomers were able to compile a table of 405 consecutive lunations with a discrepancy of less than a day. This table and other astronomical tables have come down to us in the Codex Dresdensis, one of only three pre-Columbian Mayan manuscripts which survived the fanatical zeal of Bishop Diego de Landa and his cohorts. Among the ancients those who were notable for the accuracy of their lunar determinations were the Babylonians, who are said to have calculated the lunar revolutions within four seconds.

The calendar, that amazing Mayan time machine, was a lunar calendar, as was the early Jewish calendar. No inferences should be drawn from this, for in many ways the Mayan calendar was unique. Its accuracy can be illustrated with a few comparisons, each of which shows the length of a year:

Modern calculation . . . . 365.2422 days
Mayan calculation . . . . 365.2420 days
Present corrected Gregorian calendar   . 365.2425 days
Julian calendar (replaced 1582) . . . 365.2500 days[5]

With a calendar of such precision and with dates recorded in stone on every occasion, one might think that the dating of Mayan history would be child's play. Nothing is simple, however, nothing is lucid in the muddle of Middle American origins, least of all the matter of dates. The Mayan initial-series time count can now be read. But to be meaningful the dates must still be properly placed alongside the Christian calendar. Similarly, a hypothetical archaeologist from Mars, visiting the atom-wrecked earth in the twenty-first century, might find the inscription "A.D. 1789" decipherable but still without meaning.

As our own calendar begins with the birth of Christ, the ancient Greek with the first known Olympic Festival in 776 B.C., and the Jewish calendar with the suppositional date of the Creation in 3761 B.C., so the Mayan calendar too is anchored deep in the past. The zero date of the Mayas, representing some unknown or mythical event or perhaps the Creation, is 4 Ahau 8 Cumhu, which antedates the first known use of the Mayan calendar by more than 3,000 years. The Mayan zero date, like the Jewish initial date, goes back to the fourth millennium B.C., but the exact year is still in dispute. Herbert J. Spinden puts it at 3373 B.C., Goodman at 3113 B.C.; and latterly an expert on radiocarbon dating has suggested that neither correlation reaches quite deep enough into the past.

Another important question is this: When was the Mayan calendar originally devised?

"The hieroglyphs of Mayan months," Spinden declared, "carry the tell-tale marks of the year when they were first drawn on paper." By a series of calculations too intricate to detail here, Spinden computed that the Mayan calendar was first devised during the thirty-three years between August 6, 613 B.C., and December 22, 580 B.C.[6]

It should come as no great surprise that others, basing their calculations on the same data, have arrived at different answers. Thus S. G. Morley wrote: "There is internal evidence in the Maya chronological system that it was first devised either at the end of Baktun 7—7.0.0.0.0 of the Maya Era (353 B.C.)—or shortly after—7.6.0.0.0 (235 B.C.)." Elsewhere he adds: "Some time during the fourth or third centuries before Christ, the priests devised a system of numeration by position, involving the conception and use of the mathematical quantity of zero, a notable intellectual accomplishment." And again: "Something fundamentally important took place in northern Peten [the Department of Petén, the panhandle of Guatemala] sometime during the three or four centuries immediately preceding and following the beginning of the Christian era. Was this cultural impetus due to some outside influence, or was it of autochthonous origin? Perhaps we shall never surely know."[7]

Morley's question remains valid, but the correlation on which he based his dates has of late been questioned. When dated objects were subjected to radiocarbon testing, the results suggested that the Goodman-Martinez-Thompson correlation on which Morley leaned was guilty of underestimating the age. The Spinden correlation, on the other hand, fared well.

Here we have a period of thirty-three years, tentatively 613 B.C. to 580 B.C., during which the calendar is believed to have been devised and during which (if we may redate Morley's analysis, with ample justification) the priests devised a system of numeration by position and employed the concept of zero. In short, this was a period of sudden, unaccountable cultural impetus.

For whatever light it might throw on this shadowy subject, we could do worse than to glance across the Atlantic to see what was going on in the Old World between 613 and 580 B.C. that may have incited an emigration.

Beneath the towering Rock of Gibraltar, ships were patrolling the gate to the Outer Ocean with the intention that none but their own should pass beyond. In 613 B.C. the sentinels of the sea were still—after six hundred years—the Phoenicians.

Back in their homeland at the eastern end of the Mediterranean, however, the proud Phoenicians had long been humbled, yet humbled at first in a painless and prideful way. Since about 876 B.C. little Phoenicia had worn the yoke of mighty Assyria, had donned it without resisting when the armies of Ashurnasirpal were still in the distance. Realists rather than cowards, Phoenicians were fond of peace and prosperity. "Qualified subjection" under the rule of their own city-kings had seemed to this nation of merchants the likeliest way of assuring their uninterrupted well-being. Their bargaining power lay in tribute; so tribute they paid and willingly over the years, renting their peace with the profits of peaceful trade.

For a century and a half the yoke of Assyria seldom rubbed. The Assyrians themselves scorned commerce, but tribute flowed when caravans toiled and ships sped over the ocean. Assyrian patrols protected Phoenician caravans as they snaked ubiquitously over the sprawling empire, and Phoenician ships roamed the seas at will with Assyria's blessing if not her protection.

Presently Assyria, however, employing the tactics later indulged in by Rome, attempted to draw the bonds tighter. Whereupon, in about 728 B.C., Tyre and Sidon rebelled. Island Tyre, blockaded from shore by Assyrian forces, held out for five years and brought the titan to terms. This earned the Tyrians a respite of twenty years.

In 701 B.C. the Assyrian armies—"whose arrows are sharp and all their bows bent," as the prophet Isaiah described them—were marching again. Sidon surrendered, but once more Tyre resisted. Assyrian archers protected by wicker shields rained death on the city, and the aging king of Tyre took ship and fled to Cyprus. In neighboring Israel, Isaiah rejoiced that the mighty had fallen: "Who hath taken this counsel against Tyre, the crowning city, whose merchants are princes, whose traffickers are the honourable of the earth? The Lord of hosts hath purposed it, to stain the pride of all glory, and to bring into contempt all the honourable of the earth. . . . Arise, pass over to Cyprus; there also shalt thou have no rest."[8] No rest awaited the Tyrian king in Cyprus: only death. And off in Nineveh, Sennacherib boasted: "As one gathers eggs that have been abandoned in fright have I gathered the whole earth."

But now the Assyrian yoke was galling the nation of merchants, who overlooked no slightest chance of throwing it off. Next time it was Sidon that revolted. In 677 B.C. a vindictive Esarhaddon came thundering down with charioteers, cavalry, foot soldiers; with bowmen, lancers, and slingers; with battering rams and "tanks." When he had finished with Sidon, he disdainfully "cast its walls into the waters." The king of Sidon, "who from the face of my soldiers into the midst of the sea had fled, like a fish from the midst of the sea I caught him, and cut off his head."

Till at length, since nations are as mortal as men, Assyria weakened. And presently, some time around 640 B.C., all Phoenicia slipped from the empire's moribund grasp.

By 613 B.C., to come again to that signal date in Middle American history, Phoenicia was at the height of her sea power and had enjoyed several decades of independence. Her trade was booming, her coffers were brimming, her ships probing ever farther. Tyre, as if in defiance of Isaiah's premature epitaph, was firmly established as the ascendant city of a Phoenicia now savoring her freedom and enormous prosperity.

This too, however, was to pass away. Giants were stirring: Egypt and Babylonia had awakened at last from slumber. In 608 B.C. Pharaoh Necho of Egypt looked to the north with covetous eyes and thought to garner those lands which expiring Assyria could no longer hold. Phoenicia yielded to Necho without a battle. But the peace of Egypt which Phoenicia once had enjoyed for golden centuries was not to be repeated. The ancient East was in upheaval, and only three years later it quaked again as armies rumbled.

In 605 B.C. Nabopolassar, who as king of a resurgent Babylonia considered himself the legitimate heir to the Assyrian Empire,

commissioned his son Nebuchadnezzar to take possession. Con-
fronted by Nebuchadnezzar's army of conquest, every Phoenician
city again submitted without a struggle.

After a time the Phoenicians, already reeling from too many
swift turns of fortune, heard the voice of Egypt whispering in their
ear, urging them to throw off Babylon's yoke before it was hope-
lessly settled upon them. And presently Tyre revolted.

Back came Nebuchadnezzar, this time bringing allies. He
bore down upon Phoenicia with an army reputedly numbering
10,000 chariots, 120,000 cavalry, and 100,000 foot soldiers. Sidon
(rebuilt since 677) he crushed. Then he moved on to mainland
Tyre and proceeded with the awful dismemberment described by
Ezekiel.[9] He broke down her walls and destroyed all her pleasant
houses; and her stones and her timbers and her dust he cast into the
water. A certain number of the defenders, the historian George
Rawlinson avers, "may have taken ship and escaped by sea, but the
greater part, of the males at any rate, fell in a massacre where no
quarter was given."[10]

Tyre—the "merchant of the people for many isles . . . Tyrus,
of perfect beauty"—was, like many Phoenician cities, a double
city, part of it built on a narrow plain at the foot of towering, isolated, snow-crowned Mount Hermon, the rest on an offshore
island, a convenient location for sea traders. Now the Island
Tyrians out on their crowded rock, defiant behind tremendous
stone walls that towered a hundred fifty feet in the sky, awaited a
similar fate rather than submit to the empire-building Nebuchadnezzar.

The Babylonian was in no mood to brook defiance from this
handful of upstarts. His helmeted thousands camped on the shore
and waited. For thirteen years they waited. Every head was made
bald, Ezekiel tells, and every shoulder was galled. Meanwhile, out
on their island not a mile long the rebel Tyrians ate what food
they could come by, drank of their brackish water, looked across
at the mainland black with the enemy host, and waited. Thirteen
years they waited.

What were their thoughts as they waited? What but of peace?
What was there during these thirteen years to sustain their hope
of reviving trade? Egypt, often Phoenicia's rod and its staff, was
now but a broken reed: it pierced the hand that leaned upon it.

Ashore the army of Nebuchadnezzar camped, ready to wait, it seemed, till eternity. No Assyrian coming down like a wolf on the fold had had less of charity in his heart. Off to the north the Medes had united. They too were to look with hungry eyes on Phoenicia. Off to the west the Greeks, long a maritime threat, were gathering in the lines of trade, the markets Phoenicia had reserved for herself when she and Carthage had divided the known world's commerce between them.

In a later day Diodorus Siculus was to write of a land which lay far to the west and was known to none but Phoenicians and Carthaginians "because of its distance from the entire inhabited world." The Tyrians, Diodorus continued, "at the time when they were masters of the sea, purposed to dispatch a colony to it."[11]

Now, if this distant refuge had seemed attractive to Tyrians in their heyday, probably within the memory of living men, how much more alluring must it have seemed when the bristling armies of Nebuchadnezzar were camped on the opposite shore? Escape by sea was a time-honored course for Phoenicians. History records no major exodus, and probably none was ever attempted. But it seems unlikely also that every Tyrian shipmaster waited in his island prison for thirteen years.

This is not to say that any who escaped sailed promptly to Middle America. But if ever Phoenicians attempted to establish a colony on New World soil, this might have seemed to them a propitious moment.

These, then, were the years that archaeologist Herbert J. Spinden denominated as crucial, as developmental, in Middle American culture: 613 to 580 B.C.

The date which Spinden ascribed to the devisal of the Mayan calendar had one peculiar aspect: it antedated the Mayas. This fact seems to have made little impression, and the Mayas continued to be regarded as the fountainhead of Middle American culture. Then, a few decades ago, several objects came to light whose discovery was no less than jarring. For carved in stone on these objects were dates—earlier dates than any inscribed on the Mayas' own monuments.

Archaeologists at first assumed that these early dates were in error, that ignorant imitators had misunderstood and misused the Mayan calendrical system, giving an impression of too great antiquity. This point of view, however, has been losing ground in the last decade, and now the results of recent Carbon-14 tests are hastening it to a quiet burial. For adumbrating the Mayas were the Olmecs, who not only used the "Mayan" calendrical system but seem to have invented it. The Olmecs seem also, on the basis of recent radiocarbon tests, to have developed the Mayan system of numeration.

One is reminded of a similar revelation in Old World cultures. Two centuries ago what we now look upon as parvenu Rome was regarded as second in antiquity only to glorious Greece. Now even Hellenic Greece has yielded to older cultures. As Leonard Woolley so admirably expressed it: "We have outgrown the phase when all the arts were traced to Greece and Greece was thought to have sprung, like Pallas, full-grown from the brain of the Olympian Zeus; we have learnt how that flower of genius drew its sap from Lydians and Hittites, from Phoenicia and Crete, from Babylon and Egypt. But the roots go farther back: behind all these lies Sumer."[12]

Just so, behind the Mayas lay the earlier Olmecs, whom we shall consider next—and what, if anything, lay behind the Olmecs.

THE FACE OF
THE OLMEC

LIVING AZTECS kissed the ground at the feet of Cortés in 1519. Living Mayas were impaled upon Spanish lance points ten years later. But the Olmecs, buried long and deep, were even then faceless and voiceless: a name without substance. And so they remained, into our own lifetime.

Now at last the miracle of archaeology has resurrected the fabled Olmecs and given them faces: portraits graven in stone or clay some two millennia or more ago. These images stand today in scattered museums, defying not only time but also comprehension; for the faceless Olmecs have become a people of several faces—faces that seem to depict three different races. Voiceless still, their stone lips mute, these visages hint at a curious story which has not as yet been pieced together. At this moment we have, to paraphrase Pirandello, characters in search of a plot.

Meanwhile the epilogue is already written, telling how, within recent times, a name without substance acquired a face—or too many different faces.

In 1858 a native in the State of Veracruz was hacking at a patch of virgin jungle when he felt his machete bounce off an object harder than wood. The Mexican parted the undergrowth and saw, protruding slightly from the soil, what appeared to be the rounded bottom of a gigantic kettle. No kettle would be buried so deep without purpose, the peon reasoned, and a kettle so huge might hold a vast treasure. He hurried to the proprietor of the hacienda and reported his find, and a crew of men were put to work digging for buried treasure. As their spades bit deeper into the heavy clay, however, what slowly emerged was not a kettle at all but an enormous carving of a human head, time-blackened until the basalt resembled iron. The workers and the proprietor trudged disgustedly back to the hacienda and admitted failure.

Years passed. The jungle reclaimed the giant head, and only the local tradition lingered on.

In 1902 a native working in a tobacco field about fifteen miles away, near San Andrés Tuxtla, was attracted by a glint of sunlight near his feet. Leaning over, he saw a pale green stone about eight inches long. He picked it up, pressed off encrusted dirt with his thumb, and found himself holding a curious carving with the face of a man, the bill of a duck, and a shapeless plump body covered with strange incised markings. The peon carried it off, and in time the jadeite statuette found its way to the United States National Museum, where archaeologists deciphered the band of bars and dots that run vertically up the small figure's stomach.

The date, these archaeologists decided, was 98 B.C.—earlier than the earliest dated Mayan object. Presently other archaeologists correlated the bars and dots and came forth with different dates, 162 A.D. by the G-M-T correlation. But by whatever system of computation, the dates being relative, this Tuxtla statuette remained the earliest *dated* object recovered up to that time in the Western Hemisphere.

What should have brought jubilation, however, became instead a cause for concern. Had someone been using Maya-style dates before the Mayas, or was an earlier event commemorated "as we might erect a monument to George Washington in 1939 and put on it the date of 1776"? The date was expressed in the Mayan manner; yet the spot where the statuette was found lay 150 miles outside the Maya area, and the carving of the figure had a different air. Had the portable statuette been carried here from afar? Archaeologists stirred uneasily.

Another generation passed. In 1938 Dr. Matthew W. Stirling of the Smithsonian Institution was visiting in Veracruz. He knew of the Tuxtla statuette, and having also heard rumors of a colossal stone head partially uncovered in a Veracruz jungle eighty years earlier, he resolved to have a look at it. A bruising eight-hour horseback ride carried him down to the village of Hueyapa, where the head was reputedly buried, but at Hueyapa he learned that it lay instead near Tres Zapotes. There, a mile from the village, he found the object he sought—almost unrecognizable, buried again to its forehead. As his trained archaeologist's eye roved over the surrounding terrain, he realized of a sudden that the kettle-like dome protruding here was no isolated phenomenon: it lay in a plaza formed by four mounds. "Investigating the neighborhood further," Stirling reported, "I found that somewhat to the east of this plaza was another group of very large mounds, one of which was almost 450 feet feet in length. Beyond these, on an elevated piece of land, was a third group, the central feature of which was another plaza surrounded by four large mounds."

Perceiving that the excavation would be a major undertaking, Stirling returned to Washington, where he obtained the cooperation of the National Geographic Society and the Smithsonian Institution. Early the following year, 1939, a joint expedition set forth.

This time Stirling elected to travel by water, for Tres Zapotes lies close to the Gulf of Mexico. Engaging a venerable launch, the archaeologists cruised down the Gulf as far as the town of Alvarado, then chugged up the Papaloapan River. In so doing they inadvertently followed the route that the Spanish adventurer Pedro de Alvarado had sailed on a trading mission in 1518, at which time Alvarado had found the land hereabout so inviting that he had returned to Cuba to request permission to colonize. Now the archaeologists too noted the undisturbed beauty of land and river and commented on the masses of water hyacinths that often choked the maze of winding channels, on the luxuriant vegetation that grew denser and more tropical as they approached the higher land toward the foot of the mountains, and on the peace that was shattered from time to time by the squawking of parrots overhead.

At the base of the Tuxtla mountains and in their shelter, on fertile alluvial soil lay the village of Tres Zapotes. Nearby the archaeologists located the "kettle," set up camp, and hired a crew of natives.

Promptly the crew set to work digging away the heavy clay from the smooth black dome of what presumably was a head and perhaps a body also. On the second day it stood revealed in all its immensity (Figure 39). "Carved from a single massive block of basalt," Stirling reported, "the head was a head only, and it rested on a prepared foundation of unworked slabs of stone. . . . Cleared of the surrounding earth, it presented an awe-inspiring spectacle. Despite its great size the workmanship is delicate and sure, the proportions perfect. Unique in character among aboriginal American sculptures, it is remarkable for its realistic treatment. The features are bold and amazingly negroid in character.

"Fully exposed to view for the first time in modern times, it still remains as great a mystery as ever, for it fits into no known aboriginal American cultural picture. Approximately 6 feet high and 18 feet in circumference, it weighs over 10 tons.

"How was this great block of stone transported more than ten miles from its source near the base of Mount Tuxtla? This problem, which would tax the ingenuity of an engineer with the benefit of modern machinery, included crossing the 30-foot-deep gorge of the arroyo. The ancient engineers, however, performed the feat of successfully quarrying a flawless block of basalt and transporting it in perfect condition without the aid of the wheel or domestic animals."[1]

In Stirling's account one fact, above all, amazes. Stirling himself appropriately used the word in describing the giant head: "The features are bold and *amazingly* negroid in character." Thus Stirling conveys in a single word, never enlarged upon, the astonishment that he and his colleagues must have felt as they stared at the round face, the wide nose, the thick, drooping lips, each unmistakable in its immensity and so skillfully carved that the Negroid aspect could not possibly be ascribed to the artist's inepti-

FIGURE 39.   Colossal head found at Tres Zapotes, Veracruz.

tude. For if no Negro slave was ever transported into the New World before the advent of Columbus, how is one to account for these features?

Obviously the head antedated Columbus (and has since been shown to antedate him by about two thousand years). To be sure, some anthropologists believe that one of the very early migrations into the New World—perhaps 15,000 B.C. or before—was Negroid, but it was apparent that no such age could be claimed for this head. Primitive men of the glacial and immediately postglacial period, moreover, were not given to carving human faces in the round in perfect proportions. And if black men long ago wandered eastward the breadth and northward the length of Asia, crossed to the New World via the glacial land-bridge, and then wandered southward nearly the full length of North America, the features would almost surely have carried the marks of racial intermixing during the long trek. It is inconceivable that racial intermixing would not also have occurred during the fifteen thousand years or so in the Western Hemisphere, dimming the characteristics further. *How then to account for the presence of a Negro in Middle America in the millennium before Christ?*

More than twenty years have elapsed since this colossal head was discovered, and the question remains unanswered. Meanwhile, to get ahead of our story, other such heads have been found in similar ancient sites near the Gulf of Mexico, indicating that the person portrayed in stone at Tres Zapotes was no biological sport. Other archaeologists, warily circling around Stirling's frank use of the word Negroid, have termed these faces "swollen" and then "infantile"—until at length archaeologists settled on a nickname for all these gigantic heads, calling them "Baby-faces."

True, the only proof that the heads are of Negroes lies in the eye of the beholder, and other eyes may see in them other features. We recall, however, the bejeweled dancers of Monte Albán and their Negroid features. There is little doubt that the dancers of Monte Albán were adults—and of the same race as the "Baby-faces." The question, then, of whence they came still stands.

In quite a different context the English archaeologist R. J. C. Atkinson recently wrote: "I do not myself believe that the archaeologist who offers his wares to the public has any right to take refuge in a smug nescience, by an appeal to the strict canons of archaeological evidence, when faced with perfectly legitimate questions of this kind." He added this stipulation, however: "If, then, the archaeologist is willing to leave the dry land of fact and set out upon the uncharted sea of conjecture, in an attempt to find answers for questions of this sort, he must first make it quite clear what he is doing."[2]

With this word of warning we sail forth upon that uncharted sea in an attempt to account for the presence of a Negroid head in Middle America in the millennium before Christ. In propounding the following theory, which is my own, I must emphasize that Matthew W. Stirling can in no way be held responsible for it.

If one grants that the massive head was Negroid, that it represents an actual portrait of a living Negroid seen in Middle America, that such a person or his immedate forebears did not arrive on foot, there remains only one possibility: the artist's model must have come by ship. To deny any one of these three allegations is to fly in the face of logic. To grant them is to explode the myth of total isolation.

If, then, the artist's model came by ship, where did the ship sail from? At the date usually assigned to these colossal heads, approximately 500 B.C., the eastern and central Pacific islands are believed to have been uninhabited; furthermore, the Polynesians as we know them today are a hybrid people not strongly Negroid in appearance. Ruling out the Pacific, therefore, what remains except the Atlantic? In fact, the location of the heads suggests an Atlantic crossing.

Jumping over to western Africa, one seeks in vain for early Negroes who possessed the ships and the nautical experience to undertake such a voyage, or who sailed often and far out to sea where they might have been driven, willy-nilly, westward. Moving yet farther afield, then, into the ancient civilizations that flourished half a millennium or more before Christ, what do we find? We find Greece, definitely a sea power but with limited egress to the Outer Ocean (though Pytheas slipped through in about 330 B.C. and doubtless others, and by the second century B.C. the bars were down). We find also the great states of the ancient Orient—Assyria, Babylonia, Syria, Egypt—not one among them a sea power. And we find Phoenicia and its offspring Carthage, sea powers par excellence and guardians of the gate to the Outer Ocean.

These two qualifications do not of themselves, however, place these Semitic seafarers in Middle America. That Phoenician and Carthaginian ships—and their mariners too—were capable of a transatlantic crossing will be shown in a later chapter, and also why the landfall would probably have been made in the same general area of the Western Hemisphere where the colossal heads have been found. None of which yet hints at cause or associates Negroes with Phoenicians. The fact is, both the Phoenicians and the Carthaginians were known throughout the ancient world as slave traders, both are known to have trafficked along the West African coast, and both stood well out to sea on occasion, where a chance storm and the prevailing winds and currents might have driven them westward across the Atlantic toward the Antilles.

It would seem, therefore, that the Negroes who fetched up in Middle America were transported there in Phoenician or Carthaginian ships; and they possibly arrived there inadvertently, as did Columbus himself.

This I must clearly label hypothesis, but the fact remains that the Negroid portraits, whether we call them dancers or "Baby-faces," are found in pre-Christian Olmec sites along with evidence of an unexplained higher culture and unexplained portraits of keen-visaged men with Semitic noses and with beards that were quite un-Mongoloid.

Meanwhile at Tres Zapotes, to return to that point of departure, the members of the National Geographic–Smithsonian expedition under Stirling looked at the colossal head, the first of its kind ever discovered, saw that it wore a helmet somewhat resembling those worn by American doughboys in World War I, and decided to nickname their new-found friend "The Dough-boy." In 1939 the purpose of the expedition was to dig; the time to assess their finds had not yet arrived. In those years, one must remember, the Mayas were still the favored people; the Olmecs were only just beginning to emerge from millennial mists; and who could say what manner of people once dwelt in this Veracruz jungle?

Presently, as the digging at Tres Zapotes progressed, there occurred one of those happy accidents that serve to remind archaeologists to "leave no stone unturned." Twelve natives were maneuvering wooden poles, trying to turn a fallen stela the face of which was blank. The natives "labored mightily," as Stirling described it, and at last the heavy slab flipped over—revealing that the other side too was blank. Stirling had walked two miles from the camp to examine this stela and, being in the vicinity, he decided that they might as well tackle an inconspicuous stone that protruded only a few inches above the ground on the edge of a nearby cornfield.

As the digging went deep, the day became broiling hot and

the stone proved larger than expected. In time it became apparent that the front of this stela had been worked; but weather and age had chewed on the low-relief carving, and Stirling could discern no pattern. To complete the day's failures, the back of the stone appeared to be blank. Doggedly Stirling instructed the crew to clear all mud from the back with their hands. Presently a native on his knees in the excavation called out, "Chief! Here are numbers!"

"I don't know," Stirling wrote later, "how my illiterate workman guessed it, but there, running transversely across the back of our stone, was a beautifully carved row of bars and dots in the form of a Maya calendrical date . . . the thing we had all secretly hoped might show up in the course of our work, but which not one of us had had the temerity to expect."

Stirling copied the characters and hurried back to camp, where his wife sat down at once to make the calculation. She announced the date on the stela as November 4, 291 B.C., by the Spinden correlation—the oldest recorded date yet found in the New World, earlier by 193 years than the Tuxla statuette. "Biggest thrill of the expedition," Stirling called it.

Such a find represents more than the fruit of skill and endeavor. As the farmer's harvest is great or small at the whim of the weather, so the archaeologist reaps what chance has preserved. The series of coincidences which led to the recovery of Stela C, as the dated stone at Tres Zapotes is called, was already building back in pre-Christian times. Stirling reconstructs the chain of events thus:

Misfortune long ago overtook the people who erected Stela C. They departed or vanished. The stone itself fell or was toppled over and lay on its back for centuries, its carved face exposed to the weather but its dated back protected. Then came another migration. The new inhabitants of the site, finding the stone too large to handle and being undeterred by respect for the gods of their predecessors, broke the stone into several pieces for easier handling. The middle fragment, because it was wider than long, the newcomers stood on end before a stone altar, "where once more, serving different gods, the stela looked out on strange ceremonies. Time passed," Stirling concluded, "the city was again abandoned, and gradually Nature buried the monument with its altar so that it all but disappeared from sight, until just now our spades have brought it to light. . . . If three inches more had been broken off either the top or bottom of the monument, the date never could have been determined."[3]

Once again, in the wake of the news disagreement erupted as to the date the stela bears. It was jarring enough that the Tuxtla statuette bearing Maya numbers should antedate the Mayas themselves, but here was a date almost two hundred years older. The series of five numbers carved on this Stela C is a typically "Mayan" date, for whereas we would require only three time periods, as in 11/28/1962, the Mayas recorded five, denoting respectively from top to bottom the number of *baktuns* (periods of 144,000 days each), *katuns* (7,200 days), *tuns* (360 days), *uinals* (20 days), and *kins* or single days which had expired since a certain established date.

Soon the theory was advanced that perhaps this date had been computed in a different system. The Spinden correlation itself had already been challenged, and now its moorings were shaken. The Goodman-Martínez-Thompson correlation, giving considerably later dates, came to be widely regarded as sounder.

But Herbert J. Spinden was to see his calendrical calculations defended a decade later by a silent witness. A series of radiocarbon tests were made on three wooden lintels found at another site, Tikal, each bearing the Maya date 9.15.10.0.0, which is June 30, 741 A.D., by the GMT correlation and October 30, 481 A.D., by Spinden's. Results, including two different samples from Tikal tested at the University of Chicago laboratories, showed:

Lamont Laboratories, Columbia U.. .	481 A.D.	± 120 years
University of Chicago Laboratories . .	469 A.D.	± 120 years
University of Chicago Laboratories . .	433 A.D.	± 170 years

The finding of the exact date 481 A.D. is less conclusive evidence in favor of the Spinden correlation than it might seem, for the age of the lintel beams at the time the date was carved on them must also be considered. But the Spinden correlation is exonerated at last of the charge of overestimating the age.[4]

Stirring further the muddied waters that swirled around Stela C was the Mayan practice of occasionally recording dates which were not contemporary, equivalent to the example cited of carving

1776 on a recent statue of George Washington. Matthew W. Stirling believed that the date on his time-weathered Stela C was contemporary; others did not. And stone does not yield to radiocarbon dating.

Stirling believed that he had stumbled onto a site not only very old but also different and exciting. Other mysterious objects in addition to Stela C and the massive head were coming to light here at Tres Zapotes, including what Stirling judged to be "one of the finest examples of stone carving ever found in Mexico"—a large stone box elaborately carved with scrolls and with "gods engaged in cosmic combat." This too was baffling, for the features of the gods are "strongly Mayan in feeling, but the nature of the remainder of the carving is unique." Near the box lay a sacrificial stone which suggested to Stirling that these unidentified people had engaged in human sacrifice in the manner of the Toltecs. Who, Stirling wondered, were these people who seem to have had ties with both the Mayas and the Toltecs? Were they perhaps the shadowy Olmecs emerging at last from legend?

The following year, 1940, he therefore returned in the hope of discovering more. And once again his magic spade uncovered strange and wonderful things.

In the Western Hemisphere, we have long been told, there was never a wheel—never before the time of Columbus. Believers in the absolute isolation of the American Indian remind us that the ancient Egyptians sped to battle in wheeled chariots, as did the Assyrians and Babylonians, the Greeks and the Romans. Why, then, was only the Western Hemisphere ignorant of the wheel?

In Tres Zapotes, Veracruz, the Stirling expedition in 1940 discovered—of all things—wheels. Eight wheels, tiny in size as well as in number, but large in their implications. The wheels are, in fact, small clay disks on which, apparently, pottery toys were propelled. For alongside the eight clay disks lay a pottery dog and a pottery jaguar, each with two tubes attached to its feet. If today wooden axles were inserted into these tubes and the eight wheels at hand were attached, the toys would still roll.[5]

This was a rather startling discovery in 1940, and that fact alone may be suggestive. It intimates that scientists, faced with a piece of information which refuses to fit into their intricately as-

FIGURE 40.   Wheeled toy discovered by Charnay.

sembled jigsaw puzzle, have tended to lay the piece aside for the
moment rather than to start reassembling the picture. For wheeled
toys similar to those discovered at Tres Zapotes had been found
and reported more than fifty years before.

Désiré Charnay, the nineteenth-century French explorer
whom we first met at Tula, in the course of his roaming and digging in Mexico climbed Popocatepetl, the great mountain visible
from Mexico City, and then crossed to nearby Monte del Fraile.
There, at an altitude of 13,000 feet, with a view of the stately
pyramid of Cholula far below, he discovered a cemetery which he
believed to be Toltec. Excavating tombs, he came upon playthings
analogous to those discovered by Stirling at Tres Zapotes, archaic
in appearance, made of terra cotta. These toys, Charnay conjec-
tured, bereaved mothers had placed in the tomb beside the bodies
of their children. Here were toys in the shape of elongated dogs or
coyotes and tiny wheeled chariots, some broken, some with their
four wheels still intact. The wheels fit into four terra-cotta stumps;
but again, in the damp tombs where even the pots were filled with

FIGURE 41. Wheeled toy
found at Remojadas,
Veracruz.

water, the axles were missing. Whereupon Charnay fashioned axles
from wood, and behold: "My chariots rolled!"

His announcement was dubiously received. Perhaps the objects, it was proposed, were modern fabrications? To which Charnay replied with Gallic heat, *"Je laisse tomber l'objection, qui
serait une insulte à ma bonne foi."*[6]

In the last two decades, archaeologists have discovered still
other wheeled toys in Mexico—principally in the States of Veracruz
and Oaxaca—and in the Isthmus of Panama. The dog shown in
Figure 41 was found in Remojadas, Veracruz, a site occupied
contemporaneously with Tres Zapotes.

If these wheels appear strange to twentieth-century eyes, they
might have appeared less strange to the ancient Phoenician who
modeled in terra cotta the small wheeled chariot, eight inches
high, depicted in Figure 42. Many such miniature clay chariots
have been found in Phoenician tombs; in fact, when found in
cemeteries of the Old World they have been termed "the peculiar
property of Phoenicia." Perrot and Chipiez warn against regarding the chariots as toys. "They embody an allusion to the state
and circumstance which, after surrounding the occupant during
life, was supposed to follow him in his supreme migration."[7]

But to return to the matter of wheels. The wheels discovered
in Tres Zapotes and Remojadas and those found half a century

FIGURE 42. Miniature chariot, Phoenician. Louvre.

earlier by Charnay pose a single question: If the principle of the vehicular wheel was known, why have no large wheels been discovered in Middle America?

The answer may lie in part in the climate, for large wooden wheels, like the wooden axles, would long since have rotted away. But this in turn would indicate that a wide span of time had elapsed since the last wheel rolled. If the principle of the vehicular wheel was once known in Mexico, why was it lost?

Possibly, strange as it sounds, the wheel was merely abandoned, for it is widely known that pre-Columbian Americans had no horses, no mules, no donkeys or burros, no oxen or any bovines.

"The almost universal use of wheeled vehicles today," Atkinson has noted, "makes us forget that sledges are not merely for use in snow, but are also by far the best way of carrying heavy or bulky goods over dry ground, where wheeled vehicles or pack animals are not available. Indeed there are still farms in Wales and Ireland today where the horse-drawn sledge is still the main and sometimes the only vehicle."[8]

No chariots, I might add, bore warriors of the ancient Orient into battle before strangers swept down out of Anatolia, bringing horses. The chariot, in other words, followed the horse. Yet putting the cart before the horse is somehow expected of Mesoamericans, and their failure to have done so has long been specifically pointed to as proof of their uninterrupted isolation.

One further question concerning wheels. How does it happen that wheels were found at both Toltec and Olmec sites? Like the Aztec-Chichimec-Toltec chain of culture, this might be another example of idea-diffusion, for Indians recording their native legends reported that Olmecs and Xicalancas were present at the coronation of Chalchiuhtlanetzin as King of the Toltecs and swore allegiance to the new king. If we accept this as fact the chain is complete, extending from the halls of Montezuma in 1519 eastward to the jungles rimming the Gulf and backward through time some two thousand years.

FIGURE 43. Clay head found at Tres Zapotes.

FIGURE 44.   Prone figure found at Tres Zapotes.

Before our glance was deflected towards wheels and a dated stela, we were scanning faces: the multiple countenance of the Olmec. The giant head with flat nose and thick lips was not the only type honored by representation at Tres Zapotes. Archaeologists digging in a mound near there in 1940 uncovered a pottery head, a suave early-day Mephistopheles with mustache and pointed beard. "Because of its life-like appearance," Stirling noted, "it is probably a study of a prominent person."[9]

One might go further and venture the guess that this prominent person was either a ruler or a priest. On what basis? Because Middle American rulers and priests were often (until the advent of bearded Spaniards) given to wearing beards—at least when they

FIGURE 45.   Front view of face, same figure.

sat for their portraits. Montezuma was able to grow a sparse one. Others, to judge by their plastic representations, resorted to artificial beards in the the manner of Egyptian pharaohs. As far back as higher civilizations flourished on Middle American soil—

through the Aztecs, Mayas, Toltecs, Zapotecs, back to the Olmecs
—so far back and no farther the leaders and gods were sometimes
depicted as bearded, though Indians today are not and can scarcely
achieve such adornment.

Why was a beard a badge of high office, possibly even more
prestigious than a skull that was pushed out of shape? Was the
source of the beard as a mark of esteem the Fair God himself,
the bearded white "bringer of civilization," whether one man or
the composite image of his people? The bearded face of the prominent person of Tres Zapotes may or may not be that of a white
man, but its carefully modeled features bear little resemblance to
those of an Indian.

Another highly interesting bearded face is that of the lordly
gentleman receiving homage in the background of Figure 44, too
important to be overlooked while concentrating on the almost
terrifying visage in the foreground. The massive, mature Negroid
head is shown again, front view, in Figure 45. Both men, one surmises from the realism of the portraiture, must have been residents of early Tres Zapotes.

Here, then, at Olmec Tres Zapotes—a few miles in from the
Gulf of Mexico—were wheels, the earliest dated object yet found
in the Western Hemisphere, bearded faces, and Negroid heads: a
combination far too provocative to be pushed aside like unwel-
come pieces of a jigsaw puzzle.

Tres Zapotes was not the only abode of the Olmecs. When
Stirling was writing his first report, another such site had less
than a year left in which to lie undisturbed in its earthen shroud.

12

OF SHOES AND SHIPS

AS THE NEEDLE turns to the north, so Stirling's thoughts, while he sat in his office pondering the possible lines of attack for his next expedition, kept turning again to the giant head. He recalled a photograph he had once seen which showed the top of another such head pushing out of the ground, one large, unblinking eye exposed. That photograph had been snapped fifteen years before at La Venta, Tabasco, by members of a Tulane University exploring expedition headed by Frans Blom and Oliver La Farge, whose one-day visit to La Venta in 1925 had allowed no time for excavating and little enough for locating and photographing jungle-cloaked monuments. Stirling, seeing in retrospect that rounded stone helmet so much like the headgear worn by his own Tres Zapotes Doughboy, perceived that here was another site that bore the mark of Olmec habitation. Accordingly, when he and his group sailed away on their next expedition their goal was La Venta.

Their course lay south on the Gulf of Mexico to Coatzacoalcos, Veracruz, on the southermost dip of the Gulf. In the Nahuatl language Coatzacoalcos means "Serpent Sanctuary." It was here, where the Coatzacoalcos River enters the sea, that Quetzalcoatl reputedly bade farewell to Cholulan friends who had accompanied him on his eastward journey; and then, according to legend, the Fair God disappeared over the ocean.

The archaeological expedition, sailing thence eastward a short distance, arrived at Tonalá. There in 1518 the ships of the Spanish explorer Juan de Grijalva put into the mouth of the Tonalá River and, while their ships lay to, the ubiquitous Bernal Díaz and friends had scouted the town and later slept in "a temple atop a high mound."

Stirling's launch chugged up the wide, shallow Tonalá River and entered the Blasillo, which Stirling described as a deep and sluggish small tropical stream of coffee-colored water, its current so slight that the placid river mirrors the high jungle growth that flanks its sides.[1] After an hour on the beautiful Blasillo followed by an hour of alternately slogging and wading through the swamps of the deep jungle, the archaeologists came upon higher ground, dry and sandy, where patches of corn and bananas flourished in small clearings. Another half-hour of fast walking brought the group to their destination.

The buried city of La Venta lies on a swamp-girded island close to the western border of the State of Tabasco and only about twelve miles inland from the Gulf of Mexico. Scientists believe that long ago, before innumerable river inundations deposited silt around it, the island stood higher.

Stirling procured as guide a native who lived nearby and professed to know the location of several stones, though he said that the present inhabitants "had never paid much attention to them" and the jungle had closed over many.

There the following morning the crew commenced the long task of excavating a site now believed to have been the religious and possibly also the political capital of the Olmecs, whose rulers dominated the hinterland, collected tribute, commanded armies of laborers for construction purposes, and perhaps created the first true civilization in Middle America.

As the days went by, the crew uncovered stone after stone, but the giant head failed to reappear, and none of the natives knew its location. Till one day fifty yards into the jungle they came upon a smooth hemispherical stone, vine-sheathed and almost unrecognizable with both eyes buried. Excavating around it, the workmen in due time exposed a colossal head about eight feet high—two feet higher that that at Tres Zapotes—carved in the same realistic style with the same broad nose and thick lips.

While the crew were digging around this head, a small boy stood watching curiously. After a while he turned and remarked to Stirling that he had seen some large stones near the *milpa* his father was working. Stirling followed the peon's son half a mile into the forest, where the lad stopped and pointed to three rounded boulders lying about thirty yards apart in a straight line. Stirling put a crew to work trenching around them, and in time three more colossal heads emerged, all facing east.

The facial features and style were similar to those of the first head, but these three heads were no mere copies. Two of the three had been laboriously provided with teeth, a comparatively rare feature in early American art. One of the heads, eight and a half feet high and twenty-two feet in circumference, wears circular ear plugs with a cross carved on each. This head, like much at La Venta, had been mutilated by hostile hands, probably those of a conquering people; but the lines of cheek and jaw remain eloquent: the weary lines of maturity, strongly Negroid in aspect.

These giant heads, like that at Trez Zapotes, wear a distinctive headgear somewhat resembling a football helmet. Something about the headgear suggests a warrior, an association which may have been implicit in the mind of Stirling and his colleagues when they called that first great head The Doughboy. The purpose of the heads remains a mystery. The first four discovered stood morose and forbidding like giant stone sentries, recalling to mind the menacing figures of Bes, the pygmy god, that Phoenician sea captains mounted on the prows of their ships to frighten the almost savage tribes with whom they traded. But the last great head disinterred at La Venta is smiling.

Other colossal Negroid heads have since been discovered elsewhere in the jungles of southeastern Mexico.

Again, if these were African natives captured by slave traders, where are the portraits of the alleged merchant-captain and his astronomer-navigator? The trenchant answer remains the same. Here at La Venta as at Tres Zapotes and Monte Albán, where a

FIGURE 46. "Baby-face" found at La Venta, Tabasco. Designated as Monument No. 1 at La Venta, this head, carved from basalt, stands almost nine feet high. This and many other monuments have been moved from La Venta to open parkland at Villahermosa, Tabasco, a project undertaken by the Mexican poet, Carlos Pellicer.

Negroid type is depicted, there too are the likenesses of bearded men who bear little resemblance to American Indians.

When the members of Stirling's joint expedition had arrived at La Venta several months before and had stood and thirstily drunk in their first view of these ancient ruins, their eyes were drawn at once to a huge pyramidal mound. Rising to a hundred feet in the center of the site, it stood on an enormous base approximately three hundred feet square. Beyond it to the north the archaeologists noted a curious curblike construction which enclosed a rectangular area roughly as large as a quarter of a city block.

Later, when the crew began to shovel away the drifted sands of two millennia, it became apparent that the "curbing" was actually the crowns of columns. Slowly there emerged a solid stone wall constructed of hundreds of cylindrical columns set so closely together that each column touched the next. To enclose their ceremonial center the Olmecs had carried or dragged more than six hundred basalt columns—each column ten feet tall and weighing two tons—from the nearest quarry some sixty *miles* distant. It remained to discover what sacred treasure within had seemed to warrant such stout protection.

In the middle of the enclosure a wide stone jutted out of the ground three feet and leaned steeply forward. Members of the expedition, peering beneath, saw delicate carving on the protected underside. Did this carved stone hold a clue to the history of La Venta?

Before the digging could begin, the monolith had to be propped with logs (mahogany logs because they lay close to hand) to prevent it from toppling and crushing a workman. By evening a depth of five feet had been reached, and the carved design was rooted yet deeper in the earth. All through the following day the digging continued, while the immense stela, bolstered by still more mahogany logs, leaned precariously over the crew working deep in the pit. Not until dusk of the second day did the stela stand fully exposed—fourteen feet high, seven feet wide, and almost three feet in thickness. Now the men gathered round and carefully brushed off the dirt that clung to its face.

The scene they exposed shows two human figures seven feet

tall facing each other, apparently in conversation. One is a commanding presence, remarkably handsome, with an aristocratic high-bridged nose and a long, flowing beard. His features reveal no trace of Mongoloid, Negroid, or Australoid; nor does he resemble an American Indian. Instead his nose and beard call to mind that familiar character Uncle Sam; so Uncle Sam he was dubbed by members of the expedition. The face of his companion had been broken off. Above these two figures were others, possibly deities, floating in air.

"The figures," Stirling pointed out, "are executed with a sure and delicate touch, and in many ways have a different flavor from the others on the site. . . . Both wear tall and elaborate headdresses. Like all the other headdresses shown at La Venta, these are particularly interesting because they do not make use of the plumes of birds. . . . Both figures wear shoes with odd pointed, upturned toes."[2]

These upturned toes give one pause. They seem, somehow, curiously inappropriate. One thinks of Mexican Indians today as frequently barefoot. The typical Indians of early American novels were moccasin-shod. But the preconquest Aztecs often wore sandals, and the Mayas, even in the earlier centuries of the Christian era, were shod in sandals not unlike those of various Old World peoples. Now here at La Venta were men who wore shoes —shoes with odd pointed, upturned toes—and wore them, moreover, at a site of surpassing antiquity. Peculiarly disturbing.

Have we possibly here, recorded in stone, not only a hint of contact but also a tangible clue to the identity of the earliest Olmecs? If so, who else in the New World or in the Old was wearing similar shoes so long ago?

But how long ago? The first question, then, is when did the Olmecs inhabit La Venta?

The answer to this query startled the archaeologists themselves, even the members of a National Geographic-Smithsonian-University of California expedition that later continued Stirling's excavations at La Venta and did splendid work there in 1955. As recently as 1956 they placed La Venta temporally well inside the Christian era. "About A.D. 410," wrote members of this expedition, "as the barbarian Visigoths swarmed over Europe and sacked

ancient Rome, a tribe of American Indians were building elaborate tombs and monuments of basalt rocks and green serpentine in
a swampy rain forest of southern Mexico."[3]

The members of the expedition took the precaution, however, of obtaining nine samples of wood charcoal from the La
Venta ceremonial court—from whence Uncle Sam had been disinterred—and submitted them to radiocarbon time tests. When
the results were announced in 1957, the La Venta phase of Olmec
culture made a sudden leap backward in time.

Five samples taken from what seemed to be the original construction at La Venta yielded the average date of 814 B.C. with a
margin for error of 134 years.

Like other Mesoamericans, the builders of La Venta had not
been content with their original construction. In fact, the 1955
excavations revealed that the La Venta ceremonial court, called
Complex A, had undergone not just one but three major altera-
tions. "We wish to emphasize," stated archaeologists Philip
Drucker, Robert F. Heizer, and Robert J. Squier, "that these are
site construction phases only, *not* cultural stages; we found no
clear evidence of cultural change during the time that complex
A was in use."

A charcoal sample from the second phase of construction
dated it at 804 B.C. plus or minus 300 years.

Still another sample submitted to Carbon-14 testing was
taken from the base of the great pyramid. "The date," in the
opinion of the same archaeologists, "almost certainly refers to
one of the later stages of construction of the pyramid." This later
date, radiocarbon tests indicated, was 574 B.C. plus or minus 300
years. Summarizing the results of these time tests, the three archaeologists stated: "We would place the end of the La Venta
phase IV within the period 450-325 B.C., probably near the early
part of that period. Complex A thus appears, from the radiocarbon determinations, to have been constructed and used during
approximately the four centuries 800 to 400 B.C."[4]

These, then, are the temporal guideposts in our search for
shoes with upturned toes. Inasmuch as the excavating archaeologists found "no clear evidence of cultural change" during the
four centuries that the ceremonial court was in use, the initial
date would seem to be more to our point than the terminal. The

original construction at La Venta, we recall, yielded the averaged radiocarbon date of 814 B.C. plus or minus 134 years.

Who, besides Uncle Sam of La Venta and his faceless companion, was wearing shoes with pointed, upturned toes between 948 B.C. (which includes the margin for error) and, say, 600 B.C.?

In such a search one must lay aside preconceived notions and "leave no stone unturned." In fact, one soon develops a feeling of kinship with the frustrated archaeologist who digs out unadorned stelae. Having now examined pre-Christian feet on far-flung art works *ad nauseam,* I can report results which in the end proved not only rewarding but also, I believe, exciting. I have turned up three candidates and submit them here for consideration.

First, the Hittites, because upturned toes were their hallmark (Figure 47).

Only in the last eighty years have scholars suspected that the insignificant Hittites who wander about in the Bible were identical with the powerful Kheta of Egyptian records and the people called Khatti by the Assyrians. Early in the second millennium B.C. these seminomads poured into Asia Minor and began to spread over Syria, their movements facilitated by "their peculiar animal," the horse. These Hittites are believed to have sacked Babylon, overthrowing the Hammurabi dynasty. In 1500 B.C. the dominant power in Asia was Egypt; but as the might of Egypt waned, the strength of the Hittites waxed. By 1400 B.C. the Hittite Empire was the colossus of western Asia, with its capital at Boghazköy in Asia Minor.

A military power, the Hittites advanced gradually southward, drawing others, including little Phoenicia, into their orbit. It was Egypt's Ramses the Great who thought to check the Hittite advance, and the titans met in a great battle fought at Kadesh. The peace treaty, drawn in about 1280 B.C., gave to the Hittites "Syria and all western Asia from the Euphrates to the sea"[5]— including, of course, Phoenicia. It was this treaty, as noted earlier, that was recorded at Boghazköy in three scripts, none of which left a telltale mark on the hieroglyphic writing that the Hittites themselves presently created.

The records of Boghazköy, the northern Hittite capital, are silent after about 1200 B.C., when the head of the empire seems

FIGURE 47.   Two Hittites slay a lion. Carchemish, *c.* 9th century B.C.

to have been lopped off; but the body survived in fragments some five centuries and for a time even flourished in its dismembered condition. The push toward the south and east accelerated, and Hittite city-states dotted Syria as far south as Palestine. Till presently, off in the east, another colossus arose and picked up his wicker shield. Assyrian armies came surging across the scattered domain of the Hittites. But the Hittite people lived on, in their own city-states and others, for it had been their custom after sacking a city for some to return and dwell there as friends. Clinging to the shreds of their vanished glory, the Hittites mingled and intermarried with the peoples about them.

I have lingered somewhat over the Hittites for more reasons

than the upturned toes on the Olmec stela at La Venta. The vigorous art of the Hittites had other characteristics in common with Middle American art.

The Hittites, particularly in their southern period after 1000 B.C., were assiduous carvers of monuments: figures in relief on stone stelae, sometimes against a plain background but occasionally surrounded by hieroglyphs; also large statues carved in the round and sometimes small figurines—all of which are likewise found among peoples of higher culture in Middle America. But more than this. Both Hittites and Mesoamericans were given to carving two figures facing each other in conversation, the greater one sometimes larger than life and clearly indicating by superior height that he was more exalted than his smaller companion (Figures 48 and 49). Both peoples also occasionally carved figures standing on the backs of others. And for a distinctive touch they sometimes, though rarely, depicted a band of rope-molding running around several sides of a monument.

As for attire, both Hittite and early Mesoamerican figures are represented as garbed in robes or in thigh-length tunics. Often these figures are wearing earrings. Hittite men frequently wore their hair in a pigtail (Figure 47); Maya men are sometimes shown with a queue which dangles behind. Tall headgear seems to have been the fashion in both these worlds: Middle American headgear dazzles the viewer with its barbaric splendor, but barbaric splendor was an accouterment too of Old World culture (Figure 50). And finally, Hittite soldiers wore crested helmets, as did, according to native tradition, the gods of Mexico.

One could go on. But at the moment we are trying to trace a single feature: shoes with pointed and upturned toes like those of the bearded patriarch of La Venta. Who besides Olmecs were wearing such shoes so long ago? Hittites certainly. A remarkable people, the Hittites, whose sculptures bear an uncanny resemblance to Middle American. But as potential cultural ministers they lacked one essential qualification. They lacked, in fact, a fleet. The Hittites are not known to have been a seafaring people.

Though upturned shoes were characteristically Hittite, other ancients donned them too. The subtle Etruscans, sometimes known as Etrurians, who early dwelt in central Italy also were fond of pointed and upturned toes. It has been said of the Etruscans,

FIGURE 48.   Hittite god 11½ feet tall (left) and king-priest (right).

"Their shoes curve, their beards curve, their eyes are beaded slits curving in profile" (Figure 51).

Since slitted eyes are the stock indication of a secretive nature, the Etruscan artist depicted his compatriots more prophetically than he knew. Etruscan history cannot yet be written, and Etruscan secrets are buried still in unexcavated tombs. Today a device called a potentiometer is locating hidden Etruscan tombs. Small holes are then drilled in the unopened tombs, a camera and flashlight mounted on an arm are pushed through the holes, and the rotating camera enters the past. Its roving eye quickly records for

FIGURE 49. A Maya with artificial beard receiving homage, as depicted on a stela at Tepatlaxco, Veracruz.

FIGURE 50.   Accoutered Hittite deity sculptured on a building-block in Malatia.

the archaeologist which tombs warrant priority and which can wait yet another while.

Like the Phoenicians, the Etruscans were middlemen of antiquity. Migrating westward from Asia Minor (in the opinion of their first historian, Herodotus, and of their latest, Raymond Bloch), they carried with them into Italy the Bronze Age civilization of the eastern Mediterranean and elements too of the Greek, thus contributing in still undetermined degree to the stockpile of western European culture, our own. The Etruscans (they called themselves "Rasena") walked not only in the upturned shoes of the Hittites but also in Hittite footsteps, learning early the techniques of smelting iron which the Hittites had developed. Precisely what the Etruscans' association with the Hittites was—or who in fact the eclectic Etruscans were or where they had come from—all these are unanswered questions.

Unlike the land-bound Hittites, the Etruscans took to the sea. By 700 B.C. their maritime might was a factor in the battle for Mediterranean power—though perhaps not a dangerous factor,

one suspects, for the wary Phoenicians smiled upon them as friends. And so it continued for several centuries, while Greece expanded, Carthage expanded, and the upstart Romans encroached on a city long ruled by Etruscan kings: we call it Rome. Till at length the Romans carried the day. The Etruscans did not vanish; they were merely absorbed. Like the Carthaginians, their story thereafter was told by their bitter enemies.

How far did Etruscan ships venture? In those earlier days of adolescent energy and rapacious ambition before the Etruscans lapsed, like an aging businessman, into a sybaritic enjoyment of wealth and success, did their ships ever quit their Italian peninsula and their Mediterranean islands—Sardinia, Elba—and run the Phoenician blockade at Gibraltar? It could be done. Pytheas managed, and the Roman shipmaster too who thought to follow a Phoenician ship to the Tin Islands. Did Etruscan ships also leave these towering cliffs in their wake?

Present opinion holds that Etruscan ships did not. This may be only an echo of the time-honored thinking (but not the ancient) which regarded the Mediterranean "lake" as closed at both ends. It was not the opinion of Alexander von Humboldt, who believed instead that the Canary Islands were "known to the Phoenicians, Carthaginians, Greeks and Romans, and perhaps even to the Etruscans."[6] The Canary Islands are far indeed from the New World, but they are the gateway to the Great Western Searoad, as Columbus in due time heard or discovered.

Of these five seafaring ancients listed by Humboldt—Phoenicians, Carthaginians, Greeks, Romans, Etruscans—the Etruscans would seem the least likely to have found their way to American shores. And yet, one can scarcely say. One can scarcely say *much* about the Etruscans—except that their actual story is still to be told.

Finally, one other category of ancients is depicted in shoes with upturned toes: western Asiatics who were strongly under the sway of the Hittites.

In about 859 B.C., when a new way of life had only just touched or was soon to touch a swamp-girded island near the

FIGURE 51 (*opposite*).   An Etruscan: from a tomb painting.

Gulf of Mexico, a scene that was possibly of surpassing importance to our investigation was being enacted beside the Mediterranean. The Assyrian Shalmaneser III, having succeeded to the throne the preceding year, had crossed the Euphrates and, to test the might of his growing empire, imposed an annual tribute on those fringe states no longer subject to Hittite rule. We can see him yet, sitting grandly beneath a parasol in his camp by the sea and watching the bales and bundles come pouring in as the tribute-bearers, each in his native costume, bent under their loads. By happy chance another was watching too: the artist of Shalmaneser, whose unknown hand has preserved in stone the minute details of dress of those who bore tribute to Shalmaneser.

Here are nobles in long, sweeping robes and upturned shoes —the Hattini. And men in short robes and plain-toed shoes— Aramaeans. And men with long robes, pointed beards, and up-turned toes—Phoenicians.

We move in closer to scrutinize these Phoenicians. Young King Matten of Tyre had placed his tribute in the care of two of his merchant princes, who rowed ashore in long, narrow boats with soaring prows and soaring sterns carved in the shape of a camel's head. Bearers unloaded the boats in the shallows and carried ashore the bales of blue wool dyed to the color of lapis lazuli and the ingots of gold, silver, copper, and lead. The Phoenician ambassadors, as they stepped before Shalmaneser, were "clad in long clinging double robes, turbans wound round with ribbons, pointed beards, and upturned toes." The Phoenicians' servants followed, "bearing trays with sweet-meats, boxes over their shoulders, and big kettles on their heads like caps."[7]

It would be more surprising, as a matter of fact, if those avid cultural borrowers the Phoenicians had *not* adopted the Hittite mode of attire. Their ties with the Hittites over the centuries were many and varied. Genesis 10:15 records that "Canaan begat Sidon his firstborn, and Heth," the Hittites. This is sometimes interpreted as saying that, already in the time of Genesis, the Phoenicians had settled in Canaan and Hittites had advanced that far south.

At any rate, time and circumstance were to draw these two wandering peoples closer together. This was more than a matter of trade relations, although both were nations of traders, handling

FIGURE 52. Stela from Amrit in northern Phoenicia. Hittite, Babylonian, and Egyptian influences are combined in this broken stela. The lion is walking across mountains, depicted in the same manner as in the Ninevite reliefs.

the heavy flow of traffic between three continents, the Hittites by land, the Phoenicians by land and by sea. Both served also as cultural intermediaries, and each has been called "a veritable link between Babylon and Egypt."

To commerce and infiltration, by way of contact, was added conquest. Militarily the Phoenician city-states were no match for the northern titan. When the Hittites warred with Ramses the Great, the Hittite king could "summon" contingents of Phoenicians to his aid. The three-language peace treaty formalized the Hittite hold on Phoenicia. Forty miles south of Tyre and ten miles south of Phoenician Akko (Acre) rose the line of fortresses which formed a bristling frontier between the Hittites and the Egyptians. Presently Hittite cities encircled Phoenicia, and Hittites dwelt long among the Phoenicians.

Small wonder, therefore, that the vestiges of Phoenician art often bear distinctive marks of the Hittite. Skillful imitators, clever with their hands, the Phoenicians too were prolific sculptors, producing, as did the Hittites, figures in relief on stone stelae, large statues carved in the round, small figurines by the thousands, figures facing each other in conversation, and figures wearing tall, elaborate headdresses, long robes, or thigh-length tunics—and sometimes shoes with upturned toes.

Who else in the New World or the Old between 948 and 600 B.C. was wearing the same strange style of shoes as the two men sculptured at Olmec La Venta? I have turned up only those mentioned. Among them, the Hittites were land-bound; if they reached this site twelve miles inland from the Gulf of Mexico, they came in the ships of others. The Etruscans, at least in the present state of our knowledge, would seem to have had scant reason or opportunity for any such voyage. Opportunity during these early years, however, could have rattled the Phoenicians' purple sails with alarming frequency on their homeward voyages from various African ports of call, as we shall presently see when we investigate the longer Phoenician voyages.

The thornier question remains unanswered. Are the shoes at La Venta a strong indication of contact; or are they merely a happenstance, an independent invention that chanced to be made at about the same time?

Looking around for an answer here at La Venta, what do we see? First, Uncle Sam with his upturned toes, his generous beard, his chiseled un-Mongoloid features. There are also Mongoloid faces at La Venta, for the Olmec had many faces—too many faces, representing more widely differing types than one might expect in a single Indian tribe.

There are, in addition, monstrous "Baby-faces," three of them lined up staring ever eastward, wearing rounded helmetlike head-dresses. These helmets might also have been invented quite independently, but the Assyrian artist of Shalmaneser who depicted the ambassadors from Sidon and Tyre with their curling toes depicted too their servants—wearing rounded helmetlike head-dresses: "big kettles on their heads like caps." It is interesting that the same analogy occurred to the peon in a Mexican jungle whose machete bounced off a rounded object which he mistook for a kettle. And however one accounts for the similarity of the head-gear, the presence of the "Baby-faces" themselves must still be explained.

Thus the oddly assorted Olmec cast—Mongoloids, whites, and Negroids: characters in search of a plot. A fiction writer could spin a fair yarn around them: a bearded Phoenician shipmaster in about 850 B.C., attired in the Hittite robe and shoes befitting a merchant prince, trafficking well down the West African coast; a raiding party going ashore, the seamen wearing rounded helmets; a cargo of captured blacks; a northbound route that regularly carried the single-sail vessel well out to sea to escape the battering head winds; a storm. . . .

Others might follow, but somebody had to come first; and distant lands have been stumbled upon in less likely ways.

THE DARK RELIGION

THE BASIS of primitive society is religion. Religion is the constant preoccupation of primitive man and the inspiration of his artistic expression. It was thus too with all early civilizations, including the Olmec, Mayan, Egyptian, Assyrian, Babylonian, and Phoenician. Therefore it was peculiarly fitting that the first object pointed out by the native guide to the first archaeologists who dug at La Venta should have been an altar—an immense stone altar that had fallen forward at a sharp angle and was almost buried by the sediment of centuries. There the following morning the crew began the long task of disinterring what eventually proved to have been the religious capital of the Olmecs.

Carved from a single block of basalt, Altar 1, as it is designated, is impressive, even startling in conception and execution. Under a niche in the front of the altar a life-sized figure sits cross-legged in an easy, natural pose; he wears an elaborate headdress and a wide, beaded collar. Life-sized figures in the round are rare in early American art, and this one is free of stiffness and conventionalization. Its style is almost incredibly advanced for what is believed to have been the earliest site of a people who antedated even the Old Empire of the Mayas by centuries.

This seated figure holds the end of a rope which runs around the base of the altar, forming a molding or border, and is fastened to the wrist of a figure carved in relief on one end of the altar. Now, the artistic device of a rope border was long in favor in Syria and Asia Minor. In fact, when found in the ancient world it is generally accepted without question as an indication of Hittite influence. The Hyksos are believed to have carried it into Egypt in the seventeenth century B.C.; the seals of Khian, greatest Hyksos ruler of Egypt, bear a twisted-rope pattern. The Hittites were still employing the same pattern at Carchemish some five centuries later. In the meantime the Phoenicians too had adopted it. A rope border, carved in stone, encircles the sarcophagus of Ahirom, king of Gebal (Figure 53). This Phoenician sarcophagus can be dated by two alabaster vases found with it, each bearing the cartouche of Ramses II (c. 1304-1237 B.C.). Ahirom's sarcophagus is notable also because it bears the earliest known inscription in the Phoenician alphabet. Centuries later, Phoenicians were still bordering some of their seals with this same twisted-rope pattern.

FIGURE 53. Sarcophagus of Ahirom, king of Gebal, showing rope molding.

And now, here at La Venta in southern Mexico, were Olmecs employing the same design, whether by coincidence or otherwise, and using it as it was used in Phoenicia—as a border. How to account for the duplication in Middle America of an artistic device that is distinctly North Syrian—as North Syrian, in fact, as the pointed shoes with turned-up toes which were found at this same La Venta?

Probably the most unusual feature of Altar 1 is the seated figure who peers out from beneath the altar. It is disquieting, therefore, and possibly worthy of mention, that a figure also peers out from beneath a curious ceramic piece, now in the Louvre, which was found in Cyprus and which is believed to have been consecrated to the Phoenician goddess Astarte.

From Altar 1 the crew at La Venta moved on to another great stone, and presently a second altar emerged—and with it another

FIGURE 54. Ceramic sculpture found on Cyprus, now in the Louvre. The doorway is flanked by two lotus-headed shafts. Two other terra cotta models from the same general area, both with figures peering out, may also be found in the Louvre.

puzzle. Altar 2 depicts the upper portion of a man, again real-istically carved in the round, leaning forward out of a niche and holding an infant in his arms. Other infants carved in relief on the same altar are depicted with deep clefts in their heads. These infants appear to be struggling to escape from the adults who are holding them.

Stirling found Altar 2 profoundly disturbing, for "it is prob-able," he said, "that the real meaning of the composition has a rather grim portent, suggesting infant sacrifice."

Infant sacrifice must be clearly differentiated from infanti-cide. The latter practice, growing out of economic want, was not uncommon among primitive peoples whose food supply was in-adequate. Even in most of the Greek city-states, in Rome, and among the Norsemen before they accepted Christianity, it was the father's right to determine whether his newborn child should be accepted and nurtured or instead be abandoned—simply left to perish from exposure. But in infant sacrifice a father offered this most precious gift to the gods. Thus Abraham was told: "Take now thy son, thine only son Isaac, whom thou lovest, and get thee into the land of Moriah; and offer him there for a burnt offering upon one of the mountains, which I will tell thee of."[1]

The practice of infant sacrifice seems to have been forsaken early by the Semites, but it was revived in Phoenicia during its darkest period of wild religious fanaticism. First-born children and newly-born infants were sacrificed to Phoenician gods not only in Tyre and Sidon but also in Phoenician colonies, where the practice endured some centuries longer. Carthage continued it till the end of her days, while the rest of the civilized world observed with a shudder.

Before we start delving into religious practices, however, we must realize that archaeology can answer with certainty only par-ticular kinds of questions. As that philosophical archaeologist R. J. C. Atkinson put it, "One has only to think how difficult would be the task of future archaeologists if they had to recon-struct the ritual, dogma and doctrine of the Christian Churches from the ruins of the church buildings alone, *without the aid of any written record or inscription*. We have thus the paradoxical situation that archaeology, the only method of investigating man's past in the absence of written records, becomes increasingly less effective as a means of inquiry the more nearly it approaches those aspects of human life which are the more specifically human."[2]

This impediment notwithstanding, what faces us here is a challenge. We have at La Venta not only a rope molding, Negroid heads, bearded faces, and upturned toes. We have also a strong suggestion of infant sacrifice, which was practiced in Phoenicia during this same period. And of burnt offerings too, for in excavating the area directly before Altar 1 the crew uncovered a clay floor "of mixed burned material."

Was there a causal connection?

In order to explore this possibility we must first learn more of the religion and rites of Phoenicians during the years that La Venta was founded and its religious pattern established.

Fifty years after the death of that friend of David and Solomon, King Hiram of Tyre, the high priest Eth-baal (Itto-baal) assassinated the then Tyrian king and seized the throne. Eth-baal (899–867 B.C.) was a high priest of the goddess Astarte (Ashtoreth) and a religious zealot of the first water. To what extent he should be taxed with the degradation of the Phoenician religion is unclear, but certain it is that Eth-baal from his seat on the throne proselyted the neighboring peoples and spread the pernicious practices.

He married his daughter Jezebel to the king of Israel and sent her forth from Tyre with a sacerdotal entourage consisting of four hundred priests of Baal, the sun god, and four hundred priests of Astarte, the moon goddess. All eight hundred feasted daily at Jezebel's royal table. This forceful young woman induced her husband, King Ahab of Israel (874–852 B.C.), to build a sanctuary to Baal-Melkarth on a hill in Samaria. Ahab was busy completing a palace which was modeled after the palace at Babylon, but he granted Jezebel her sanctuary. An altar was installed, and Phoenician deities carved on pillars of wood soon graced the interior. Baal alone, carved on a pillar of stone, stood grandly before the temple. Astarte, as moon goddess and goddess of fertility, was worshiped in the form of an emblem instead of a statue. Less than a century after the time of David and Solomon, then, the gradual defection of the Israelites began, and in time their whole people fell away from the worship of Jehovah, as the second book of Kings records:

"And they left all the commandments of the Lord their God, and made them molten images, even two calves . . . and served Baal. And they caused their sons and their daughters to pass through the fire, and used divination and enchantments."[3]

Jezebel's daughter continued the work of proselyting the neighbors. She married the king of Judah and introduced the same orgies, the same licentious practices. In time the people of Judah were led back to Jehovah, but so deeply infused was the Phoenician religion that when staunch Hezekiah died in 692 B.C. the conservatives of Judah forced his successor, his twelve-year-old son Manasseh, to permit a return to "the good old days." The high places were restored, incense wafted again through the sanctuaries, and once more the children were passed through the fire.

This, then, was the religious atmosphere of Phoenicia throughout the ninth century before Christ and for many generations thereafter, as described by Döllinger in his *Heidenthum und Judenthum*:

"In earlier times Baal had been worshipped without an image in Tyre and its colonies; but for a long time now his worship had grown into an idolatry of the most wanton character, directed by a numerous priesthood, who had their headquarters at Tyre. . . . Besides the incense consumed in his honour, bulls also were sacrificed to Baal, and probably horses too. . . . *But the principal sacrifice was children*. This horrible custom was grounded in part on the notion that children were the dearest possession of their parents, and, in part, that as pure and innocent beings, they were the offerings of atonement most certain to pacify the anger of the deity. . . . The sacrifices were consumed by fire. . . . and the sound of complaint was drowned in the din of flutes and kettle-drums. Mothers, according to Plutarch, stood by without tears or sobs; if they wept or sobbed they lost the honour of the act, and their children were sacrificed notwithstanding. Such sacrifices took place either annually on an appointed day, or before great enterprises, or on the occasion of public calamities, to appease the wrath of the god."

Still more spectacular and revolting was the manner in

which Phoenician children were sacrificed to the goddess Astarte. At the spring festival, so Döllinger recounted graphically, "they were put into a leathern bag and thrown the whole height of the temple to the bottom, with the shocking assertion that they were calves and not children. In the fore-court stood two giant phalli. To the exciting din of drums, flutes, and inspired songs, the Galli [eunuchs of the temples] cut themselves on the arms; and the effect of this act, and of the music accompanying it, was so strong upon mere spectators, that all their bodily and mental powers were thrown into a tumult of excitement; and they too, seized by the desire to lacerate themselves, inflicted wounds upon their bodies by means of potsherds lying ready for the purpose. Thereupon they ran bleeding through the city."[4]

This last bloody scene calls to mind a sight that repeatedly greeted the Spanish explorer Fernández de Córdoba in 1517 as he worked his way down the southwestern coast of Yucatán, where every island dotting the coast bore its pyramidal mound with steep stone stairs and atop it a squat temple-tower gleaming whitely, the smoke of incense floating above. Going ashore in Campeche, Córdoba again saw many temples. "From each there swarmed angrily forth half a score of priests, armed with braziers, and clad in white mantles down which fell their hair, long, black, and disheveled—so matted and clotted with blood, from their own ears lacerated in penance, that one strand could not be separated from another."[5]

Out of a religious feeling that is universal at a certain level of social advancement flow expressions which also are universal. Doubtless some of the resemblances between religious practices in Phoenicia and Middle America are no more than the natural efflorescence of this universal religious feeling. In this category one might place, for example, the worship of a sun god and moon goddess, each with a multiple personality; a populous pantheon; possibly also the building of high places to the gods, and a numerous and influential priesthood. There comes a point, however, where these treacherous similarities seem more than coincidental, more than the natural religious effusion of such widely different peoples. Recognizing this hypothetical point is a task which requires an Olympian detachment that few can achieve.

The Spanish conquistadors, marching across Mexico behind the banner of the cross, thought that they had come upon positive proof of previous contact when they found American Indians worshiping the same symbol. The cross, as other Spaniards later learned, was the symbol of Quetzalcoatl. Some students then placed in Middle America the legendary lost island visited by Saint Brendan, the seagoing Irish monk, and accepted him as the Fair God. Others saw in Quetzalcoatl an earlier missionary: Saint Thomas, the doubting apostle.

"Few causes," wrote Godfrey Higgins in his *Celtic Druids,* "have been more powerful in producing mistakes in ancient history than the idea, hastily taken up by Christians in all ages, that every monument of antiquity marked with a cross, or with any of those symbols which they conceived to be monograms of Christ, were of Christian origin."[6]

For the cross is not solely a Christian symbol. It was earlier employed on at least four continents, and here at La Venta it was chiseled in stone five centuries or more before the birth of Christ. Long before that the ancient Egyptians mounted crosses along the Nile to measure its life-giving overflow. If the flood reached the crossbar, crops would flourish; short of it, famine would follow. From this humble utilitarian beginning the cross evolved into the symbol of life and generation, and as such the Egyptians worshiped it. Then presently those avid borrowers the Phoenicians and other Semites too were employing the symbol.

Midway between Tyre and Jerusalem, in Beth Shan, a temple dating from the second millennium B.C. has been excavated during the twentieth century. Here, carved in high relief on the upper surface of a basalt altar, is the sign of the cross. The Semitic faithful had placed upon it their offerings of jewelry and pottery. This altar, however, was not the focus of worship. There was also a great stepped altar; and another altar, cylindrical in form, on which incense was burned; and yet another altar for the meat offering, which was proffered and then roasted. The sign of the cross seems to have been carried to Beth Shan from Egypt, for here too was Ptah, the god of Memphis. But, like the sign of the cross, Ptah was only one feature in a highly syncretistic worship. The Phoenician goddess Astarte was variously represented. There were reliefs of a lion in action: the Babylonian pest (or plague) god Nergal. A bearded local deity in ornamented collar was the essence of cosmopolitanism, wearing the Babylonian conical helmet, holding the Egyptian *waz* scepter in his hand, and receiving an offering of two lotus flowers. Finally, to descend abruptly from the sublime, the drainage of the temple was excellent, featuring a pipe with male and female joints—strange companions of the cross that with it have survived the ages.

The sign of the cross was found not only at Olmec La Venta but also at Toltec Teotihuacán, at Mayan Palenque, and elsewhere. It is the symbol of Quetzalcoatl and his alter ego Kukulcan, god of the four winds, and also the symbol of Tlaloc, the rain god. The Mexican word for cross is *tonacaquahuitl*, meaning "tree of life," which conveys the same idea of fertility as the Egyptian cross, symbol of life and generation.

Diffusion? Or repeated independent invention of a basically simple design in association with the universal concept of fertility? Who can say?

Near the main mound at La Venta, where the jungle had closed in densely, the archaeologists came upon a third large buried stone. Surrounding trees had first to be felled and their matted roots painstakingly disengaged. When at last the soil was cleared away, the stone stood forth as yet another altar, again unique, again surprising.

La Venta's third altar was formed in the image of a human head, a broad-nosed colossal "Baby-face" looking eastward, flattened on top for use as an altar. Closer scrutiny revealed a second ancient function: the altar had served as an oracle. In grayest antiquity a priest of the Olmecs had whispered into this giant ear, and his sonorous words had emerged from the great stone lips. Much mutilated, rather by the hand of man than nature, the altar still retained intact its speaking tube, a hole which enters at the left ear, runs like a Eustachian tube through the head, and emerges through the center of the mouth.

This altar had, in Stirling's opinion, a look of considerable age. "If any extensive gap of time exists between the various monuments on this site," he said, "it appears to me that this stone must have been one of the oldest at La Venta."[7]

Oracles were common to many nations in the early stages of civilization. And, like so many religious practices, their use persisted throughout millennia, for through divination one could ascertain the will of the gods—or, conversely, through oracles the priests could hope to impose their will on gullible people. The oracle of Delphi is probably the most widely known, but, earlier and later, western Asiatics too were devoted to the use of oracles in various forms. One who frequently consulted an oracle was the Biblical David. A thousand years later, so Tacitus tells, the Roman emperor Vespasian, wishing to consult the famous oracle of Mount Carmel on the southern border of Phoenicia, found there neither temple nor statues but only an altar standing, like that of La Venta, in open air.[8]

Among American Indians, divination was widely practiced but in forms which were, if not simpler, at any rate more elementary than the oracle of La Venta. The Incas of Peru, for example, starved a black llama, cut out its heart, and examined it to see if it augured good or ill. The famous Apurimac oracle of Peru was a tree trunk set up in a house and attired in feminine apparel. In 1534 A.D. a Spanish prisoner who was present when Manco Inca consulted this oracle heard the tree trunk reply to the question in a feminine voice. But to find in the Western Hemisphere two thousand years earlier an oracle such as that of La Venta, to visualize Olmec priests manipulating thus the lives of the faithful, strikes somehow a discordant note in the sylvan symphony.

If Phoenicians brought oracles, infanticide, and the cross to La Venta, why then, one might ask, did they leave behind in their homeland other more practical elements of their culture?

Some of the practical features had not yet come into use in Phoenicia itself. Coins, for example, did not appear there until shortly before 500 B.C., during Phoenicia's Persian period, and coinage came even later to Carthage. But the Olmec culture had certainly its practical and intellectual features, whatever their origin—astonishing features in view of the early date. These are best described by the archaeologists who, in 1955, after a long lapse due to the war, continued Stirling's task and carried the excavations at La Venta layer by layer deeper.

"These people [the Olmecs]," wrote archaeologists Drucker and Heizer, "had developed a knowledge of mathematics and apparently of hieroglyphics, and were using an excellent pre-Mayan calendar. Their citizens included some first-rate architects, engineers, artists, and jewelers. Incredibly, they managed to move single stones weighing as much as 30 tons to La Venta from quarries 60 miles away."[9]

The fact is, almost any one of the seemingly alien creations, skills, or religious practices at La Venta could have been independently invented on the site by natives. It is rather the startling *combination* of similarities, accumulating like grains of drifted sand, building and ever building, which begins to disturb the observer who attempts to rationalize each alone into insignificance. What is a sand dune but an accumulation of innumerable particles, each grain infinitesimal, each in itself insignificant?

Looking at the La Venta finds in the aggregate, what do we see? By way of devotional remains: a cat god, a cross, a pyramid, a profusion of altars, an oracle, and indications of those rites of a dark religion—burnt offerings and infant sacrifice. By way of intellectual or practical achievements: a knowledge of mathematics, of writing, of architecture and engineering. By way of distinctive artistic devices: a twisted-rope border, plus another curious parallel with art of the ancient East—deities depicted as floating horizontally overhead (Figure 55). Also, at the same site, representation of three distinct physical types, including faces of Negroid aspect and a man with a generous beard. This un-Mongoloid-looking hero wears shoes of a style which Phoenicians are known to have worn in the ninth century B.C. And for good measure: La Venta also has figurines whose heads are distinctly deformed.

All this at a single Olmec center erected on an island twelve miles in from the Gulf of Mexico in the ninth century *before* our era—four centuries before Pericles lifted Athens to her glorious apogee and even before the she-wolf had suckled Romulus and Remus.

What were Phoenicians doing in the ninth century before Christ? Some were trading along the West African coast and others were colonizing. It was the great-granddaughter of Eth-Baal, the young and beauteous widow Elissa, who led forth her

FIGURE 55. Deities floating in air above Ashurnasirapal, Assyrian king returning in triumph, c. 876 B.C.

loyal nobles and founded Carthage in about 825 B.C. Elissa—or Dido—was thus the grandniece of the infamous Jezebel and carried the same pernicious religion with her to Carthage. Still other Phoenicians were sailing on westward, out beyond the Pillars of Melkarth, seeking new sites for colonization. These religious zealots are known to have carried their cult practices with them out to their distant colonies.

In short, Phoenician mariners imbued with the dark religion were roaming the high seas during the very years that the Olmecs, those men of three faces, founded La Venta.

Time was, the Olmecs were thought to be early Mayas: they were using the "Maya" calendar. Now the designations of borrower and lender are in process of being reversed. How much of the lore of the Maya savants was a hand-me-down from the Olmecs is still undetermined, or precisely what the relation between these two peoples may once have been. But the link is sufficiently visible to warrant a glance at the Mayas' religion, which, being later, is somewhat more fully understood.

Perhaps "understood" is too optimistic a word. With the Mayas we have moved out of silence into the era of legend and even into the day of eyewitness reports from early Spanish observers. The first four friars on Yucatán reported that before the advent of the Spaniards the Indians of Yucatán practiced such Christian rites as baptism, confession, and penance. These are the more incongruous because the Maya religion was, like the Phoenician, a dark religion.

Discounting the Maya worship of a sun god and moon goddess, their populous pantheon, numerous priesthood, and religious orgies as less than unique, one notes many other parallelisms with the religion of ancient Phoenicia—for example, the frenzied self-infliction of bodily injury. And not only did the Mayas create both symbols and realistic portraits of their many deities, some human and others animal; they also depicted some of their gods as bearded and even with handlebar mustaches, and carved the lotus alongside their bearded gods, who, legend reports, were white men.

Here in the land of the Maya too were rites and trappings like those which Old Testament prophets once railed against.

Here was incense; quantities of it have been dredged up from the Sacred Cenote at Chichén Itzá. Here was phallus worship—here and in the Toltec domain. And here too was infant sacrifice—but more than that. Phoenician infants had been "thrown the whole height of the temple to the bottom," as Döllinger put it. Now Mayan victims were thrown down the temple steps from the summit of the pyramid to the court below.

Is this no more than the natural efflorescence of a universal religious feeling?

A frequent companion of Quetzalcoatl was Tlaloc, the rain god. In Mexico-Tenochtitlán when the Spaniards arrived, one of two Aztec high priests bore the combined title Quetzalcoatl-Tlaloc-*tlamacazquin,* the last word signifying priest. But the Aztecs came late. A thousand years before their time these deities had already been linked in the minds of the faithful. One finds them together, for instance, on the ancient temple of Quetzalcoatl at Teotihuacán (Figure 15). A curious pair, Quetzalcoatl appears on its walls as the head of a serpent in feathered ruff, and Tlaloc is only two circles or eye rings—symbols which suggest a long period of evolution.

Seen through the eyes of a native whose lot in life was to plant and harvest, pay tribute, and worship, the two gods were natural comrades, allies, Quezalcoatl as god of the winds and Tlaloc as rain god. Why, then, are both deities sometimes depicted as bearded? In the case of Quetzalcoatl the answer seems obvious, for he was also the robed and bearded bringer of civilization. But Tlaloc the rain god? Is it conceivable that Tlaloc was often depicted as bearded because as a bearded god he had been imported from out of the ancient Orient?

On the face of it this might seem an absurd conjecture. Scant need, it would seem, for an agricultural people to import a rain god. One would surmise that the various tribes had been worshiping their own rain god since those remote days when some early ancestor had planted his first seed and reaped his first harvest.

And yet, if Phoenicians arrived in Middle America, one deity in their pantheon who assuredly would have been worshiped anew in another hemisphere was their rain god, Hadad. Philo Byblius, second-century Phoenician cosmographer who drew

FIGURE 56.   Tlaloc with bolt of lightning.

upon far more ancient written sources, records that El, the original god of a monotheistic Phoenicia, had handed over most of Phoenicia to Baal and Hadad, "king of the gods." As a rain god, moreover, Hadad would have possessed an especial appeal to American Indians.

That Middle Americans worshiped a rain god signifies nothing, but if this rain god Tlaloc were ever depicted with the special attributes of the Phoenician rain god, then indeed we might be justified in suspecting outside influence.

What were the attributes of Hadad? He has been called "the most characteristic west Semitic deity." Portraits of deities always varied, but characteristically Hadad is represented as robed, bearded, and carrying a bolt of lightning in his hand.

And Tlaloc? Torquemada, the Spanish chronicler, has described the Middle American Tlaloc as the oldest deity known. "He carried a thunderbolt in his right hand, a sign of thunder and lightning; whilst his left held a tuft of variegated feathers, emblem of the different hues of our globe; his tunic was blue hemmed with gold, like the heavens after rain." This, it could be charged, was based completely on hearsay. But in the nineteenth century Torquemada's description was verified when a vase was found in the ruins of Tula, the Toltec capital. Here is Tlaloc, robed, bearded, mustached, and holding a bolt of lightning in his hand (Figure 56). Is this, one wonders, the way that American Indians, if isolated since glacial times, would have visualized their provider of rain?

The discoverer of this vase, Désiré Charnay, came later upon another Tlaloc, also mustached and bearded, also holding his bolt of lightning. And yet another Tlaloc with a walrus mustache. These two Tlalocs, shown in Figure 57, were recovered from tombs on a mountain top where, according to Torquemada,

FIGURE 57. Tlaloc with lightning (left), a conventionalized representation in permutation from man to symbol; Tlaloc mustached (center); and other vases found at Tenenepanco by Charnay.

it had earlier been the native custom to offer young children in sacrifice. The mountain-top tombs where these sacrificed children were laid to rest were, significantly, the same tombs that yielded the tiny wheeled chariots.

How far may the arm of coincidence be assumed to have reached?

14

BEARDED, BELOVED, AND BEHEADED

IN 1928, when the late George Vaillant was associate curator of Mexican archaeology at the American Museum of Natural History, a gentleman walked in one day and presented to the museum a tiny figurine which had been uncovered on his property by a peon. Only three and a quarter inches in diameter, this head of baked clay with its prominent black-painted beard (Figure 58) had been found at Balsas on the Rio Balsas, which separates the Mexican states of Michoacan and Guerrero.

For months thereafter the figurine lay on Vaillant's desk, haunting him, baffling him. At first he assumed it to be a fraud, a suspicion he later rejected. "A fake," he said, explaining why he believed this piece to be genuine, "is usually a copy of some existing specimen and embellished according to the fancy and erudition of its perpetrator. But this head was out of the run of the Nahuan and Zapotecan sculptures that the unregenerate use as models for their frauds."

Noting further that its features were "most unlike those

FIGURE 58. Vaillant's "bearded mystery" found at Balsas.

of the various American Indian physical types," Vaillant decided that the head "was either indigenous to the New World or else it came from Asia, Africa, or Europe. . . . Such a piece as this," he pointed out, "would be easily transportable, and its oddness might have caused someone to carry it with him as a pocket piece."[1]

Vaillant's next step was to try to ascertain, on the basis of artistic technique and racial type, who might have carried the figurine to the Rio Balsas. He approached the problem through a process of elimination.

First of all, he declared, the mustache and beard and the protruding eyes surmounted by heavy eyebrows were not characteristically American Indian. Nor did the face appear to be Negroid. Vaillant noted also "the distinctly un-European method of presenting the hair and beard." He further denied a Greco-Roman origin on the basis of "a lack of sophistication in modelling the expression of the face." This relative lack of sophistication suggested to him an Assyrian-Babylonian origin, as did the length of the beard also. But this in turn he ruled out because Assyrian faces are generally modeled in relief and because the Rio Balsas beard is not so "elaborately treated." The Buddhistic art of India and Indochina, he continued, rarely depicts beards. And finally, what he termed the "restlessness and staring brutality" of the Mexican specimen denied a Chinese origin.

Perhaps Vaillant considered and ruled out other possibilities too which he neglected to mention; we do not know. On the basis of what he has written, he appears to have stepped directly from Greece into Mesopotamia in the course of his global circuit, thereby overlooking all of Syria, where statues in the round are numerous, where sculptured faces wear long beards, and where the treatment, though rather skilled, is relatively unsophisticated: three criteria that Vaillant himself applied in his study.

Looking around a bit on our own, therefore, examining what remains of the art of Canaan and Cyprus when the Phoenicians were not striving to imitate Egyptian, Mesopotamian, or Grecian styles, we come to an ancient statue presumably of the Tyrian-Carthaginian god Melkarth (Figure 59). Measuring it as to type and technique by Vaillant's standards, what do we find?

First, protruding eyes surmounted by heavy eyebrows which were characteristic too of the Balsas figurine. Secondly, a drooping mustache and below it a long full beard, not two-pronged like that of Balsas but having the suggestion of a part; a curly beard, curlier than the wavy Balsas beard which seemed so un-Indian but less elaborately treated than the too-elegant beards on Assyrian faces. In general, a lack of sophistication in modeling the expression of the face. And finally, the same "restlessness and staring brutality" which Vaillant attributed to the face of the figurine found at Balsas.

The colossal figure of Melkarth stands fourteen feet high, and across its exaggerated shoulders it measures six feet eight

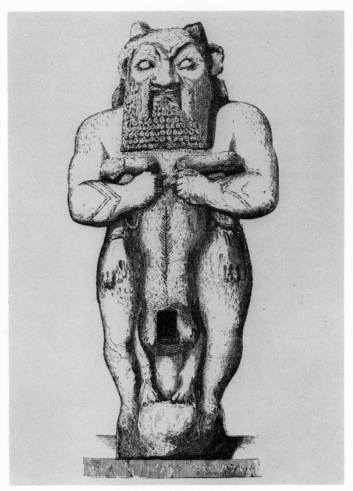

FIGURE 59. Melkarth, god of Tyre and Carthage.

inches—a far cry from a tiny figurine, but the Phoenicians were given also to making small figurines and tinting them. The god is depicted as holding a lioness whose head, now missing, once was attached by tenons.

Vaillant, having traversed the Old World to his satisfaction (or dissatisfaction), turned to the New in search of other representations of the Balsas physical type. Conducting this search more than thirty years ago, when the bearded Uncle Sam of La Venta and the Mephistophelean gentleman of Tres Zapotes still

FIGURE 60.   Clay rattle from Guatemala.

lay undreamed of beneath Olmec soil and the bearded "idol"
still reposed in a Maya sarcophagus, Vaillant nevertheless was
able to compile an impressive list of bearded faces.

On two vases from two Maya Old Empire cities, one in
central and the other in northern Guatemala, he noted representations of similar features. Studying these, he expressed dis-
belief that Mayas of the Old Empire "could have reproduced such
a figure as this, had they not seen a living prototype."

Also from Guatemala came a clay "rattle" (Figure 60) reminiscent of the small jade idol (Figure 36) which Alberto Ruz has since brought to light from beneath a pyramid in Palenque, Chiapas.

A Totonac slate mirror from southeastern Veracruz also caught Vaillant's attention; it carried the likeness of a long-eyed face with neat beard skillfully carved in low relief (Figure 61).

From Chiapas, the Mexican state which forms the webbing of the giant thumb, he listed a striking figure, the portly opera singer with Vandyke beard shown in Figure 62.

Nor was Tula unrepresented on Vaillant's list. It yielded a small jade figure with full beard. When Vaillant was writing this survey three decades ago, ancient Tula was still unidentified, and he assumed that the provenance of the easily portable bearded jade figure lay elsewhere. A similar small jade figure came from an unknown Mexican source; in his later *Aztecs of Mexico* Vaillant

FIGURE 61.   Back of a slate mirror, southeastern Veracruz.

FIGURE 62.   Figure of baked clay, Chiapas, Mexico.

assigned it to Oaxaca, the Mexican state which includes the crumbling ruins of Monte Albán.

Vaillant early abandoned his attempt to focalize this racial type, for archaeological data were at that time inadequate. He noted merely that the distribution of sculptures showing chin beards ranged from Nicaragua to the Valley of Mexico and that his list included both Mexican and Mayan material.

"We are left," he admitted, "in the perplexing position of having the same physical traits portrayed by artists of several different tribal groups, who evidently recognized a people different from themselves."[2]

Now, with additional finds bulwarking the ever-lengthening list, it begins to become apparent that most of the bearded faces lay, like the colossal "Baby-faces," in soil on which higher civilizations had flourished alongside of legends of bearded white gods. And yet, does one dare to assume that some of these bearded faces were actual portraits of the legendary bearded Fair Gods? What honors, if any, were conferred on these bearded images?

One, of course, was buried in a sarcophagus elaborately concealed beneath a pyramid. Another was sculptured larger than life and placed in the ceremonial court of the Olmec center of La Venta. Still another broods over an altar. And just south of Guatemala, in Salvador, many thin-lipped, high-nosed faces with characteristic chin beards were painted on plumbate pottery, and their eyes were then carefully circled with the eye rings of the rain god Tlaloc.

The "Baby-faces," on the other hand, though one is associated with an altar, seem more often to stand as lonely sentries, as if the head by its size alone might chill an intruder's heart. In western Guatemala, as Vaillant points out, figures with flat noses occur "as the feet of pots, indicative perhaps of a subject tribe put under submission."

In the end both types may have suffered the same fate. A sculpture from Santa Lucia Cosumalhualpa in Guatemala which may be of greater importance than is generally recognized depicts minor figures proffering severed heads to a major figure. "One suppliant offers a flat-nosed head and another presents a bearded one whose nose, however, is aquiline. In his hand the god holds a head of the same kind. Possibly here we have a people offering their hostile neighbors as a sacrifice to their gods."

This testimony is as eloquent in its way as the shattered monuments. Who knows but that both offer gruesome clues to the ultimate fate of the bearded strangers?

What happens to birds of a different feather? What befalls a band of strangers in an alien and possibly primitive land? In West Africa, so Thiercelin tells, the Phoenician colonists in time

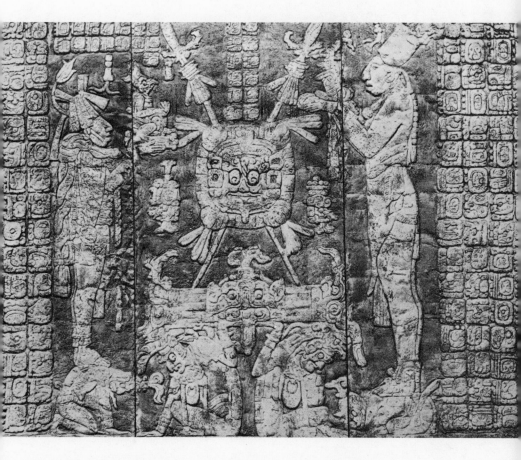

FIGURE 63.   Old Empire Maya standing on a bearded figure. From a bas-relief, Temple of the Sun, Palenque.

had to face hostility from the natives. Some of the settlers perished in fighting. Some were captured and pressed into service as slaves —an interesting reversal which provokes conjectures concerning the colossal heads and, more specifically, suggests a poignant interpretation of a Mayan relief which depicts an important-appearing Maya standing triumphantly on the back of a crouching old fellow with flowing beard (Figure 63). In West Africa some of the Phoenician colonists intermarried with natives and remained behind, while others took to the sea and sailed away. In Middle America, living families claim descent from Votan; but Quetzalcoatl vanished into the east.

FIGURE 64. Maya relief, Jonuta, Tabasco.

FIGURE 65.   Bearded figure
on a door of the Temple of
Kukulcan, Chichén Itzá.

These legends of bearded Fair Gods and the coexisting higher civilizations, temporally telescoped now in retrospect, covered a span of two thousand years. The bearded faces in pottery, stone, and jade seem likewise to cover an enormous time span: from an undetermined date centuries before the birth of Christ all the way down to the Mexican occupation of Chichén Itzá and Yucatán at the end of the first millennium of the Christian era. Bearded faces jut from edifices erected *after* that medieval conquest (Figures 64 and 65).

How does one cope with such a time span, how rationalize these continuing portraits? Three possible explanations come to mind: (1) the long, long memory of the people—although credulity is strained by the concept of nebulous memory being trans-

FIGURE 66. Funeral urn, Copán.

lated into plastic representation; (2) the conventionalization of a design (Figure 66), and of this there is ample evidence; and (3) the arrival of more bearded strangers.

Although I have departed from Vaillant's study some time since, I should like to return for a moment to his concluding remarks.

"How far primitive sculpture as a guide to race can be trusted we do not know," he admitted, "but it is apparent that in some of the higher Middle American cultures there was a recognition of the physical characteristics of several peoples besides the Mayas and the Nahuas. It is indeed unfortunate that so striking a custom as the practice of wearing a beard is not to be detected in the skeletons of people who have passed away. The tribal affinity of the head from the Rio Balsas we do not know, but in our effort to establish its authenticity, the complex character of the peoples of Middle America may be more completely understood. It probably belongs to one of those groups whose names have escaped tradition and who may have broken the civilization of the Maya or founded the high development of Zapotec or Toltec arts. The great civilizations of the Aztecs and the Mayas are like flowers, but of the stalk which bore them and gave them nutriment we have scant knowledge. Who knows what discovery awaits us that may alter our entire conception of the unfolding of Middle American civilization?"[3]

Since these prophetic lines were written, discovery has followed discovery in bewildering succession. One regrets only that George C. Vaillant, who was still a young man at the time of his death, could not have lived to see and assess them.

If the Aztec and Maya civilizations no longer are flowers without a stalk, we have now the *avant-garde* Olmecs to puzzle over. Their hieroglyphs, their calendar, their mathematical and astronomical knowledge are all as yet unaccounted for. Some archaeologists shun the name Olmec, preferring to identify them only by the sites in which they dwelt, for we cannot, at this late date, even be certain of the name by which these so-called Olmecs knew themselves. Nor can we say why, like the Phoenicians, they seemed inordinately fond of creating clay statuettes of dwarfs, or why they depicted themselves as a people with

three faces. In short, the rich and varied story of the unfolding of
Middle American civilization cannot yet be written, any more than
the votes can be safely counted before the election polls have
closed.

In the temporal elbowroom granted them by finds of recent
decades, independent inventionists are striding about. But the
shadows of bearded faces flit on the walls. . . .

As one might expect, it was that maverick American archaeologist Harold S. Gladwin who forthrightly expressed what he
called "the suspicion that a good deal of interesting evidence has
been ignored by the authors of the current version of native
American history."[4]

Among the interesting evidence ignored, as Gladwin has
pointed out, are seals—small clay seals of the "witness my hand"
variety. Gladwin, having searched the indexes of books on the
Maya and Mexico for mention of seals—almost in vain—concluded
that American archaeologists are allergic to seals. The one exception at that time was Frans Blom, who wrote:

"Again there are the small clay seals. They have been found
in irrigation ditches, on the sandy banks of the rivers washed up
by the current, and in our excavations. They are there, but we do
not know whether they were used as tribal or clan markings for
labeling property or simply for decorative purposes.

"Some of these seals are made for a single imprint, and others
are cylinders which when rolled over a surface give a band of
figures somewhat like the Babylonian roll seals. All of them are
now a puzzle to us."[5]

Now, Blom was digging in Maya territory, and, although he
mentions no specific location of these seemingly numerous seals,
one surmises that those found in irrigation ditches came from the
arid, riverless Peninsula of Yucatán and that those washed up on
the banks of rivers were in the lush country west and possibly
south of the peninsula, where rivers are many and where higher
civilizations flourished in the early years—the Olmec and Early
Maya.

Fifty years before Blom reported his findings, our old French
friend Désiré Charnay was shoveling out a house time-buried in
the hill overlooking Tula. "I picked out of the rubbish," he re-

ported, "many curious things: huge baked bricks . . . filters, straight and curved water-pipes, vases [including one depicting the mustachioed Tlaloc with lightning-bolt] . . . seals, one of which (an eagle's head) I had engraved for my personal use. . . ."[6] From which we learn that seals were known to the Toltecs too.

In the last decade, clay seals have been found in all parts of Mesoamerica—thousands of seals, in abstract, geometric, or realistic designs. Some are flat, some cylindrical, and both types seem to have been in use as far back as the Middle Preclassic period.

Seals were also known and widely used in the ancient Orient in the second and first millennia B.C.—sometimes round, often oval, often cylindrical, bearing images of animals, gods, personages, or only geometric designs. Every prominent official, it seems, had his own personal seal, and many servants had theirs. This may seem less than startling in view of the fact that official seals are still in use to this day. But the cylinder seal—or roll seal, as Blom called it—has always been specifically associated with the Tigris-Euphrates Valley, with India, and with nations that rimmed the eastern Mediterranean.

In the cylinder seal shown in Figure 67, the artist has copied the form of a Babylonian cylinder; the symbols are Egyptian, and the Akkadian cuneiform announces that Atanah-Ili of Taanach is the servant of the Babylonian pest god Nergal.

The Phoenicians themselves, ever merchants, "sealed" their bargains. For this purpose they less often took the instant of time required to roll out a cylinder than to stamp their mark with a

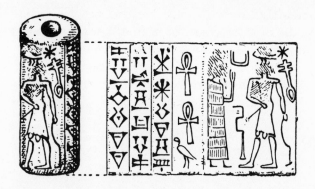

FIGURE 67.   Cylinder seal of Atanah-Ili of Taanach.

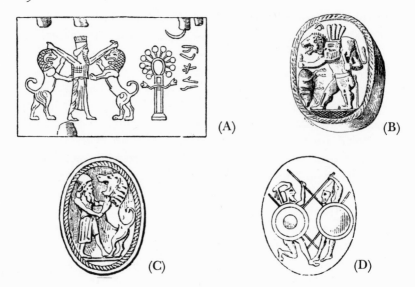

FIGURE 68.   (A) A cylinder from the north of Lebanon.
(B) The dwarf-god Bes upon a scarab of green jasper with a twisted-rope border. The Louvre.
(C) On this scarab found in Carthaginian Sardinia, the monarch wears an Assyrian tiara.
(D) Scarabaeoid depicting a Persian (left) and Cypriot (right).

seal, a scarab, or a scarabaeus. But in all these items there was profit, and Phoenicians manufactured and exported every type. The seals depicted in Figure 68 are believed to be the work of Phoenician artists.

Thus the time has come for us to follow the vanished wake of Quetzalcoatl eastward into the sunrise and walk about in lands where possibly once he walked, and Votan, and Kinich Ahau Itzamna, in the millennium before Christ.

15

THE GOLDEN
BRONZE AGE

EVEN WHILE LATE-COMING hunters out of Siberia were
paddling their skin boats from island to island en route to
Alaska, the men of the Mediterranean were maneuvering their
biremes, triremes, and longships with skill and daring. Like Odysseus in the oldest tale of the sea, they put the home port astern and
"no other land nor anything but sky and water was to be seen."
What first prodded the ancients to sail on past the Pillars of
Hercules (the Strait of Gibraltar) and commit themselves, their
ships, and their cargoes to the giant rollers of the Atlantic?

The answer lies in the mind and spirit—and commerce too—
of the Bronze Age: centuries of golden prosperity, centuries of
quickening, of surging growth. The Bronze Age looms on the chart
of man as one of the earliest peaks in human progress.

There was this about bronze which made it of paramount
importance to exploration: its raw materials—tin and copper—
had to be fetched from far places, had to be located, mined there
or traded for, and transported home. Ships had therefore to be

improved and markets and trade routes established. Thus sea trade evolved.

As the Stone Age was truly the great age of land travel, so the Bronze Age is termed the golden era of seafaring. Long before the rise of Hellenic Greece and before the Phoenicians had surged to the height of their sea power, men of the Bronze Age roamed the oceans, roamed them with joyous abandon, disdainful of distance and danger. And even as Stone Age people had ventured to cross six continents, so men of the Bronze Age accomplished great feats of navigation not equaled again till the century of Columbus.

To bound the Bronze Age neatly in dates is difficult. With the introduction of bronze, stone did not suddenly cease to be used. Stone mauls, for example, were wielded as late as the Battle of Hastings in 1066. The introduction of bronze, moreover, was staggered. Britain lagged by some five hundred years; much of America was still in the Stone Age when Columbus arrived; and Australian aborigines exist in a Stone Age culture even today. Egypt and southwestern Asia, by contrast, had climbed to the Bronze Age by about 2500 B.C.

Two thousand years before Christ was born, the galleys of Egypt and Minoan Crete crawled on the Mediterranean. The ships of Egypt, low-waisted and stumpy, designed for use on the Nile, may have sailed to Phoenicia as early as 2700 B.C. and fetched from the Lebanon the cedar logs that appeared in Egypt at about this time. Egyptians sailed on the Red Sea and just possibly also to island Crete 330 miles out in the Mediterranean. But Egypt was not, strictly speaking, a sea power, and her ships seem not to have ventured in the direction which interests us most: west.

The earliest sea travelers depicted in literature are the baffling Phaeacians of Homer, those unidentified people whose ships "know every city, every fertile land, and hidden in mist and cloud they make their swift passage over the sea's immensities with no fear of damage and no thought of wreck." Homer was clearly no stranger to seafaring. We may see in Odysseus a heroic glorification of a figure familiar to all his hearers: the Bronze Age merchant engaged in commercial travel, the "merchant prince" sailing serenely away to fabulous foreign lands. But whom shall we see in Homer's Phaeacians? Phoenicians, say some, and some say instead the men of that other great early sea power, Crete.

FIGURE 69.   Reconstruction of the palace at Knossos.

Ancient Crete stepped out of legend at the turn of the twentieth century. In 1900 archaeologist Arthur Evans, a student of hieroglyphics, looked about at the heaps of rubble at Cretan Knossos, hesitated, picked up a spade and became a "dirt" archaeologist. Almost at once he knew he had dug his way to fame, for here emerging were the skeletal ruins of the palace of Minos, legendary son of Zeus.

Months lengthened to years, and Evans continued the task of recalling prehistoric Crete from oblivion. Spending his evenings poring over thousands of artifacts, he noted that some of them seemed much older than others, and presently he divided them into three periods: Early Minoan, 3000 to 2000 B.C.; Middle Minoan, to 1600 B.C.; and Late Minoan, to 1250 B.C. Yet the word he felt justified in using to describe the ancient palace at Knossos was "modern," equipped as it was with a ventilating system, bathrooms, and drainage sumps.

Luxury and elegance, these were the earmarks of ancient Crete, bespeaking her wealth and power. Behind her wealth lay sea trade, for among the ruins of Crete were objects from Egypt, ivory from Africa, and the remains of a Cretan fleet. Seal engravings from the second millennium B.C. have been found which depict large Cretan ships propelled by both oars and sails, and the massive stones of her southern seaport still stand.

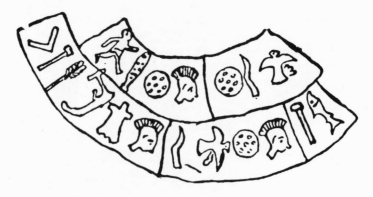

FIGURE 70. Cretan hieroglyphic writing.

The Minoans of Crete, reaching their apogee in about 1600 B.C., sailed not only south to Egypt and north to the mainland where Mycenae and Tiryns, their sister cities or colonies, lay. The Minoans dominated the Mediterranean all the way to the Pillars of Hercules. There, it was widely assumed, they halted. Latterly, however, a sparse trail of beads has suggested to several archaeologists that Cretans may have ventured outside the Pillars and up along the storm-ridden coast of western Europe. These small ribbed beads of once-brilliant blue faïence, produced in Egypt, have been found on the island of Crete and along the shores of Iberia and France, and finally in the graves of the barbaric Wessex culture not far from Britain's fabulous Stonehenge.

Stonehenge itself, that moldering megalithic mystery from the grayest past, also has recently been drawn into this consideration. One summer evening in 1953 the sinking sun lengthened the shadows on the face of one of the Stonehenge sarsens, and markings hitherto unsuspected stood forth in chiaroscuro—shallow carvings of axes and a dagger. The dagger was of a type that was strange to Bronze Age England but was used in about 1500 B.C. in the Mycenaean-Minoan culture, that remarkable Aegean culture complex of which Crete was the matrix.

Other Mediterranean touches at Stonehenge are pointed out by Geoffrey Bibby: "The fact that the technique for shaping the sarsen stones, by battery with stone mauls, is the precise technique used for the granite obelisks of Egypt raises the interesting speculation: was it an architect from the eastern Mediterranean who was commissioned some thirty-five hundred years ago to build Stonehenge in its final form? Whatever the truth of the matter, this Mycenaean dagger provides a further proof of the range of the trade routes during the peak period of the European Bronze Age."[1] To which R. J. C. Atkinson adds this comment on the architecture of Stonehenge: "It seems to me that to account for these exotic and unparalleled features [of Stonehenge III] one *must* assume the existence of influence from the only contemporary European cultures in which *architecture,* as distinct from mere construction, was already a living tradition; that is, from the Mycenaean and Minoan cultures of the central Mediterranean."[2]

To be sure, the Minoans of Crete wandered far in the Bronze Age, and being islanders they traveled largely by sea. It is tempting to visualize a Cretan sailing-ship nosing northward to Britain, encountering one of the frequent fierce storms that claw at the coast of Europe, being beaten far out to sea and then carried westward by the east winds of early spring, to ground at last on a strange North American shore. But this is sheer speculation rather than fact, and evidence of contact as early as the middle of the second millennium B.C. is as yet lacking.

Bronze Age Minoans may some day be proved to have landed on New World shores, but others who followed them traveled farther and ventured more frequently outside the Pillars onto the dark Atlantic: those greatest of ancient mariners, the enterprising Phoenicians.

16

THE ENTERPRISING
PHOENICIANS

ONCE PHOENICIA was believed to have been the first great maritime nation in the world's history. Ancient authors had testified that Phoenicians, ranging far from their shoestring land on the eastern rim of the Mediterranean, dominated that vital sea for almost a thousand years. They sailed beyond the dread Pillars of Hercules whenever it suited their purpose, and that was often. They sailed northward to Britain, southward along Africa, and westward upon the Atlantic. They discovered Atlantic islands, including the far-out, lonely Azores one-third of the way to America, islands that were lost again for nearly two thousand years and not rediscovered until the next great era of seafaring during the Renaissance.

So fabulous were the Phoenicians' nautical feats during their fifteen hundred years of seafaring that at one time each unexplained hoary oddity found in the New World was attributed to Phoenician hands. Then came the realization that other men too had been roaming the oceans during the Bronze Age, that Crete had swept to maritime might before Phoenicia.

The Phoenicians went suddenly into eclipse.

This too was unwarranted, for of Bronze Age mariners the Phoenicians were the boldest, the wisest in the ways of the sea, the most enterprising. As such they are eminently deserving of sober consideration.

Did Phoenicians reach the New World? In probing this possibility from the eastern side of the Atlantic one faces again an absence of contemporary written records. Obviously Phoenicians could write, for they have long been credited with the invention of the alphabet. Today many scholars favor the theory that the Phoenicians borrowed, probably from the Egyptians, the cardinal idea of employing symbols to express sounds instead of entire words and possibly borrowed some of the symbols too, but adapted and improved the alphabet beyond recognition and thus gave to mankind its greatest gift. Centuries later Phoenician merchants carried their alphabet into Greece, where, expanded and further improved, it formed the foundation for all European alphabets. It was also modified by the Aramaeans, who transmitted it to the Arabians, who passed it along to India.

And yet Phoenicia is what archaeologists call a "dumb" country: there are few Phoenician inscriptions, due in part to the perishable nature of their writing materials, papyrus, wood, and leather, which quickly rotted in the wet soil. Moreover, the Phoenicians were not, by and large, historians. Most importantly, they antedated the era of publicity and gave no thought to proclaiming discoveries, being less concerned with their public image than with their private profits. Theirs was, in fact, a conspiracy of silence. Although they disseminated culture along with the more profitable items of trade, they never shared information regarding trade routes, markets, or winds and currents. The routes were their road to riches, and as such were shielded from prying potential competitors.

A case in point is the story that Strabo, the ancient Greek geographer, tells.

A Phoenician shipmaster was sailing to the Cassiterides, literally the Tin Islands, to fetch a cargo of tin. Essential for the hardening of copper into bronze, tin was found in only a few places, notably northwest Spain, Ireland, and Cornwall in southwestern England. When the Phoenician captain saw that a Roman ship was following his to learn the route to the source of tin, Strabo

FIGURE 71. A Phoenician ship of the second century A.D. From a Sidon sarcophagus. (Contenau, *La Civilisation phénicienne*, Payot, Paris.)

reports, the Phoenician deliberately left his course and headed into shoal water (probably the treacherous rock-strewn waters off the fog-shrouded island of Ushant, at the western entrance to the English Channel). The Roman ship followed, and both were wrecked. The Roman shipmaster died for his curiosity, but the Phoenician escaped on a piece of wreckage and later was fully recompensed by the state for the cargo he had sacrificed to protect the secret of the route.[1]

What survives in writing today concerning Phoenician nautical achievements derives largely from later authors like Strabo—later but still so old as to be called ancient—and to a lesser extent from the Bible.

But before we delve into these, the people themselves must be brought to life and the basis laid for their explorations.

The Phoenicians called themselves Canaanites and came from that part of the world where Christ would be born. They were a Semitic people who spoke a language closely allied to Hebrew; in fact, a native of Tyre or Sidon would have had no difficulty understanding the Old Testament prophets. The Phoenicians also bore the Hebrews a striking resemblance in facial features. According to Herodotus and Justin, they had migrated westward from the thickly peopled Persian Gulf, even as other Semites had early flowed westward from Abraham's Ur of the Chaldees.

In their new home, roughly the coast of the present Lebanon, with Syria adjoining on the north and the hostile Philistines of Palestine on the south, the Phoenicians embraced whatever pleased them of the culture of earlier dwellers in the land of Canaan. The Phoenicians were superbly skillful borrowers, and chameleon-like they took on the coloration of each of their many conquerors—Egyptians, Babylonians, Assyrians, Hittites, Persians, Greeks, Romans.

A hasty glance into the tomb of one Abi-shemu, a local king of Phoenician Gebal, will demonstrate the eclectic character of Phoenician culture from an early date. Gebal—which the Greeks and Romans much later called Byblus—was an important port city north of Sidon. Like most Phoenician cities, it was a tiny pocket of soil against a backdrop of terraced hills and wooded mountains. In Gebal, within recent times, archaeologists have come upon the foundations of an unidentifiable structure long since destroyed—a common fate of Phoenician buildings. The archaeologists discovered, however, that a walled shaft had been cut down through the rock to a small room below. Inside this small room, quite dwarfing it, stood a massive stone sarcophagus oriented due north and south. When its great stone lid was lifted, the mortal remains of Abi-shemu were revealed, lying on his back in all his foreign finery.

Around his neck was a golden hawk-collar. On his feet were Egyptian sandals of silver, on his bejeweled fingers a scarab ring. By his side lay his scepter, bronze and sickle-shaped in the Babylonian style but with the gold-headed uraeus snake of Egypt crawling upon it. Nor did this Phoenician king journey into the after-world without his most prized possession. Lovingly laid inside his sarcophagus was a small vase of Nubian obsidian. It contained, according to its hieroglyphic inscription, "first quality of incense," a gift to Abi-shemu from his Egyptian overlord, Pharaoh Amenemhet III (*c.* 1840-1785 B.C.), whose cartouche appears on the cover of the vase.[2]

Almost a thousand years later, during which time other armies had tramped up and down the seacoast, the Assyrian heel came down on Phoenicia, and Phoenician ambassadors clad in the robes and shoes of Hittites, as we have noted, proffered tribute to Shalmaneser. Later probably other Phoenicians were garbed in the Assyrian fashion of Shalmaneser, and their servants in the style of his. Still later, in Phoenicia's Persian period, the Greek influence is apparent in the anthropoid sarcophagi which archaeologists have found at Sidon, laid in underground chambers beneath stone-filled shafts. On these sarcophagi, color is lavish and presumably realistic. If this be true, some of the deceased were blue-eyed and had dark red hair, from which one infers that Phoenician eclecticism extended even to physical characteristics (Figure 72).

The Hebrew prophet Ezekiel likened Jerusalem to a woman, abandoned at birth by her Amorite father and Hittite mother, tended and reared by Yahweh himself, who made her his wife; but she turned ungratefully to prostitution, taking as lovers the Egyptians, the Assyrians, and the Chaldeans, of whom she seemed never to tire. Far more than the Hebrews, the Phoenicians embraced foreign cultures. Even their temples are believed to have been patterned on those of their various conquerors. To generalize on Phoenician architecture, however, is precarious, for so little remains. Not only were the cities leveled time and again by invaders; the ruins then served as convenient quarries for the next round of building. Today archaeologists disagree as to the exact location of some of the more important Phoenician temples, even the famous temple of Melkarth in Tyre. It has been said of Phoenicia proper that its very ruins have perished.

Whether by choice or by chance, the Phoenicians dwelt in the path of trade between East and West, between the Euphrates and the Nile. Here, where conquerors sometimes trod, caravans toiled in every season. The Phoenicians have been called "the

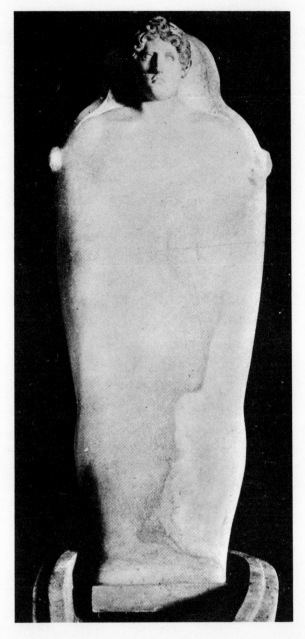

FIGURE 72.   Anthropoid sarcophagus from Sidon. Although modeled after the wooden mummy-boxes of Egypt, the sarcophagi of Phoenicia were large and deep stone troughs.

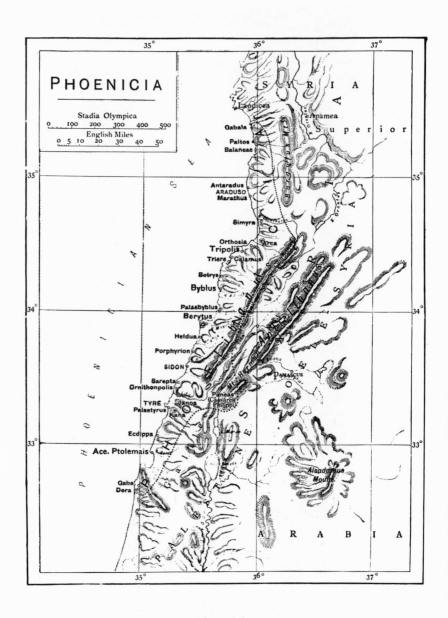

Phoenicia

greatest traders of the ancient world," their merchants "the middlemen of antiquity." Conquest, colonization, and commerce: three pairs of wings transporting culture from land to land as a bird moves a twig.

Phoenicia was a long, narrow country—like those later sea powers Norway and Portugal, but smaller than either—with less than two hundred miles of coastline facing west. At its feet lay the smiling Mediterranean; at its back rose the seemingly inexhaustible cedars of Lebanon to provide the timber for ships. It was only natural, therefore, that these practical and energetic people should develop an un-Semitic love for the sea and combine their commercial talents with navigation. As their ancestors had wandered for centuries across the North Arabian Desert, so Phoenicians continued to wander presently upon the Mediterranean and then the Atlantic.

Their earliest trade, Herodotus tells, was largely in the wares of Egypt, which seem to have been brought to Canaan rather than fetched. From the ruins of Phoenician Gebal archaeologists have recovered objects of the first Egyptian dynasty, which was flourishing before 3000 B.C. Around 2200 B.C., when nomadic Asiatics attacked both Gebal and Egypt, an Egyptian sage named Ipuwer bemoaned the fact that ships no longer were sailing to Gebal. "How now shall Egypt obtain cedarwood for her coffins?"[3]

Presently Phoenicians themselves began to sail forth, coastwise at first and then on the open sea, "freighting their vessels with the wares of Egypt and Assyria." A Theban tomb painting of the fifteenth century B.C. depicts a Phoenician ship moored at the quay. On its deck stands a Minoan jar, suggesting that the ship had just called at Crete. At about this time, too, Phoenician merchants in purple robes begin to appear in Egyptian wall-paintings, proffering their wares.

No later than 1250 B.C., and probably earlier, the thriving Mediterranean trade of the Cretans was firmly held in avid and skillful Phoenician hands. Phoenicia became, as Olmstead put it, "the one thoroughgoing exception to the general statement that the ancient oriental states were land powers."[4] Whatever was needed throughout the Mediterranean Phoenician merchants provided, whether it was spices and incense from Arabia or the salted eels of Tartessus.

Not for long were these opportunistic people content to sell only the products of others. Copying much and creating some, the Phoenicians soon were turning out wares of the highest quality. The robes of Hecuba, the wife of King Priam of Troy and mother of Hector, were woven by skillful Sidonians. Achilles' prize to the fastest runner was the world's most beautiful bowl, also fashioned in Sidon. Textiles and metallurgy were clearly Phoenician fortes.

One who in his vaunted wisdom was cognizant of Phoenician skills was King Solomon. In the two generations since Saul, the Hebrews had removed some distance away from the seminomadic life, and Solomon felt that the time had come to build a temple to Yahweh befitting the new mode of life. Solomon, who was no monotheist, had reputedly worshiped in the temple of the Tyrian god Melkarth (Baal Melkart) in Tyre and had apparently admired the temple. "Send me now therefore," he wrote to King Hiram of Tyre, "a man cunning to work in gold, and in silver, and in brass, and in iron, and in purple, and crimson, and blue."[5]

King Hiram (981-947 B.C.), as a friend of Solomon's father David and also as the father of one of Solomon's numerous wives, was pleased to comply. He sent cedars as well, and men skilled at working in wood and in stone—the massive stonework which characterized Phoenician building. When the substructure—all that remained of Solomon's temple—was uncovered in the last century, archaeologists found enormous blocks of stone—probably the work of Phoenicians.

As Solomon's temple slowly rose, there rose in it two great pillars which a Tyrian bronzeworker modeled after those in the temple of Melkarth in Tyre. Two huge winged bulls of the familiar Assyrian type were installed, and the ark of the covenant was later placed beneath their protective wings. Solomon found nothing discordant in this, and even less did the eclectic Phoenicians. The walls of the temple were plated with gold, a fact which opened another unwritten chapter of Phoenician history.

The gold was to be obtained from Ophir, the route to which lay through the Red Sea, although the exact location of Ophir is still debated. Solomon could have sent his own ships, for among his possessions was Ezion Geber, a port on the Gulf of Aqaba, an arm of the Red Sea; but the Hebrews lacked nautical skill. Under

a commercial agreement, therefore, Solomon permitted Phoenician mariners to sail from his Ezion Geber, and the sailors of
Hiram fetched the gold from Ophir. They fetched other precious
items too, including diamonds. The commercial agreement remained in effect, and both parties are said to have prospered. Thus
from about 950 B.C. Phoenician seamen sailed on the Red Sea. The
sea road to the Indian Ocean and the Pacific now lay open before
them; but, being Phoenician, they left no written record of where
they ventured.

For his assistance in building the temple, Solomon rewarded
the Tyrian king with twenty cities in Galilee. "And Hiram came
out from Tyre," the Bible tells, "to see the cities which Solomon
had given him; and they pleased him not."[6]

As a matter of fact, Hiram labeled them *Cabul*—disgusting.

Hiram could well be disdainful. For several centuries Phoenicians had been building faraway cities and colonies of their own.
Squeezed into their narrow coastal plain, the hills behind them
already terraced, they had been forced by pressure of overpopula-
tion and the encroachment of Aramaeans, Philistines, and Israelites to spill out into the Mediterranean. Of all the peoples of
Syria, only the Phoenicians thought to broaden their horizons by
overseas colonization, "their distinctive feature."[7]

Probably the first expansion was onto the island of Cyprus,
dimly visible on the horizon from northern Phoenicia. Copper
mines lured the Phoenicians, and they moved in. Greeks followed
(according to Greek tradition), and in the end a curiously blended
culture evolved in which the two elements were scarcely dis-
tinguishable.

Settlements of Phoenician merchants sprang up in Egypt during the reign of Amenophis II (1440-1415 B.C.). In Memphis the
Phoenicians reared two temples, one to their sun god, Baal, the
other to their moon goddess, Astarte. Egyptians welcomed the new
deities, and Phoenicians reciprocated by adopting elements of the
Egyptian pantheon, particularly Bast, the cat goddess; Ptah, the
god of Memphis; and Osiris, the dead god of the underworld, who
was identified with the Phoenician Adonis. All three were carried
across the Mediterranean to Phoenicia. Strictly speaking, these
Egyptian settlements were not, however, colonies: the land was

already claimed. Other Phoenicians preferred to look farther.

They spread north and then west along the coast of Asia Minor and onto Aegean islands. On the northernmost Aegean island Herodotus saw a whole mountain "turned upside down" by Phoenician mining. Beyond to the west were the "new Greeks," who as barbarian invaders had overrun the "true Greeks" of the Mycenaean-Minoan culture. At this point the Canaanite tide, deflected from the coastline of Europe, veered south toward the African shore.

Coasting wesward along Africa from Egypt, the Phoenicians searched in vain for suitable sites till they came to the Gulf of Tunis. There, at a date usually given as 1112 B.C., they founded Utica. Other colonies they planted too along the North African coast, the most active colonizers being the Tyrians.

The tide of colonization was running high and flowed on westward out past the Pillars, which they called the Pillars of Melkarth because, according to the ancient Greek writer Arrian, the towering limestone cliffs of Gibraltar seemed like colossal replicas of the pillars in the temple of Melkarth in Tyre. Beyond Gibraltar, on specific orders issued by an oracle, so Strabo reports, the Phoenicians planted a colony they named Agadir or Gadir, which the Greeks later called Gadeira and the Romans still later called Gades; it survives to this day as Cádiz, Spain. The date was traditionally 1104 B.C., or, as Strabo has it, soon after the Trojan War. (The date usually accepted for the fall of Troy is 1192 B.C.)

Phoenician colonies continued to proliferate for several centuries, primarily in Spain and Africa but also on Mediterranean islands, which the Phoenicians inspected as thoroughly as the ubiquitous Romans a millennium later examined Europe. Malta attracted because of its excellent harbors, and from there Phoenicians sailed to Sicily and established several colonies, including Palermo. Thence the route of expansion lay westward again to the mineral wealth of Sardinia and to the Balearic islands, where, as Strabo saw fit to mention, the Phoenicians clothed the natives in tunics with a broad border; and thence to the east coast of Spain. In the ninth century B.C. the tide of expansion was strong, and it continued so.

Strabo once summarized: "The Phoenicians, I say, were the

informants of Homer; and these people occupied the best of Iberia [Spain] and Libya [Africa] before the age of Homer."[8]

There was also, of course, that most famous of all Phoenician colonies, Carthage. From the day of its founding, traditionally in 825 B.C., it differed from other Phoenician colonies, partaking more of the spirit of Tyre itself. The story of that founding runs like this:

King Matten of Tyre (the same who dispatched his bearded ambassadors in their long robes and spectacular footwear to deliver his tribute to Shalmaneser) had a daughter named Elissa. This daughter he gave in marriage to his brother, the priest of Melkarth. King Matten, so the story goes, had hoped that Elissa might succeed him as ruler, but when he died in 832 B.C., the democratic element of Tyre placed Matten's nine-year-old son on the throne. When this Pumyaton or Pygmalion reached his majority, at the age of sixteen, he murdered the priest of Melkarth, Elissa's husband. Elissa thereupon swept up her husband's treasure and fled by ship. She was joined by some of the nobles of Tyre, and together they founded Carthage.[9]

It was the Roman poet Vergil, portraying her as Dido the fugitive in his *Aeneid,* who granted Elissa the immortality that eluded the city she founded, proving once again that words are more enduring than stone.

Carthage, as we know it, was named Kirjath-Hadeschath or New City by its settlers to distinguish it from older Utica about fifteen miles away. In time the Carthaginians too became ardent seafarers, and their voyages are often grouped with those of Phoenicians proper, the men of Arvad, Gebal, Sidon, and Tyre. To other ancients they were all Phoenicians, which is rather like calling Americans British. Henceforth I shall try to distinguish between them, for both achieved notable feats of exploration, stretching the known world, and possibly both reached the shores of the New.

In assessing this possibility we need to look with critical eye at their ships, their nautical skill, and their courage. How, for example, without modern instruments did they find their way by night and day across uncharted deeps?

While Phoenician ships were plying eastward from southern
Spain laden with silver or wool or the salted eels of Tartessus,
other Phoenician ships out of Spain were battling the wild Atlantic
en route to the tin of Cornwall. Sailing this stormiest ocean was a
vastly different matter from sailing the almost landlocked and
tideless Mediterranean, as Hercules emphasized when he reputedly set up the Pillars warning mariners not to trespass beyond
them.

There were, first of all, the tides. Homer could say of a Mediterranean harbor: "You need neither cast anchor nor make fast
with hawsers. All that your crew have to do is to beach their ship
and wait till the spirit moves them and the right wind blows."
But beyond the Pillars, voyagers came to Iberian estuaries where
the ocean tides swept their vessels far up into the land and out
again in a single day. A boon to a trader, Strabo called it. Off
Britain the range of the tides was even greater and, changing the
face of a harbor, constituted a peril to seamen, who found that
they needs must advance by the tedious but ever-dependable
sounding-line. There was also the greater inconvenience of awak-
ing at dawn to find one's ship stranded a mile from the water.

Less predictable than the tides were the ocean currents. Not
even the largest, the publicized Gulf Stream, once thought to be
the most clearly defined, flows neatly as if between banks. The
earliest voyagers had to contend with the great and the lesser
ocean currents, with countercurrents within them flowing the
opposite way, and sometimes with strange undercurrents—all uncharted—which could muddle the reckoning of progress at sea or
drag a small ship off its course.

And indubitably there were winds. On the Mediterranean
the Phoenicians could tell the direction of a wind by its feel; the
winds were named simply for countries or cities from which they
blew. But on the Atlantic all was changed. Seafarers had first to
discover how to use these Atlantic winds and currents.

Having sailed westward as far as what later was Sagres, Portugal, at the southwestern corner of Europe, the mariners headed
north. What they encountered is best described by one of the few
men living today who have captained sailing ships, Alan Villiers,
famed of late for bringing the *Mayflower II* across safely. "From
Norway's grim western seaboard," he writes, "round by the west
of Scotland and the Western Isles, all down the west of Ireland

and of Cornwall, of Devon, and of Wales, across the wild Bay of Biscay and past Cape Finisterre, southward down Portugal's high, rugged, and lovely coast, the waters of the North Atlantic beat at Europe. They do not 'wash' the coasts: they thrash them violently, turbulently, without end. From the Point of Sagres near Cape St. Vincent to the North Cape of Norway, the wild challenge of Atlantic gales has screamed for a billion years, and the coastline that survives the onslaught is harsh and strewn with offshore rocks, over which the sea boils in fury."[10]

A strange coast strewn with offshore rocks: nightmare of sailors through the ages. Would the Phoenicians repeatedly have battled their way up a coast such as this? More and more Bronze Age archaeologists are beginning to believe that these were not coastal but great-circle voyages.

We get a glimmer of how the Phoenicians may have reached Cornwall by consulting the sailing directions in use more than two thousand years later, when sailing had again reached a comparable state. The oldest surviving English pilot book is a copy which dates from the reign of Edward IV (1461-70, 1471-83) but is based on documents even then old, some of them probably of the fourteenth century.

"An [if] ye come out of Spain and ye be at Cape Finisterre [the northwestern corner of the Iberian peninsula]," the pilot is told, he should go his course north-northeast and by north—heading directly from Spain toward the English Channel and staying far out of sight of France—until he comes into soundings. "An ye have 100 fanthoms deep," then he would be in the latitude of Ushant (which sailors fear to this day) but well to the west of it. There he must change his course to the northeast "till ye come into 80 fathoms, and if it is streamy ground it is between Ushant and Scilly in the entrance of the Channel."[11]

Whether or not the Phoenicians followed precisely this course, they probably sailed very close to it. The belief that all ancient mariners "hugged the shore," creeping from harbor to harbor always safely in sight of land, has been effectually exploded. "Those words," as Commodore K. St. B. Collins put it, "could never have been written by a sailor. Nothing is more fraught with peril, and therefore the more assiduously avoided on a little known coast, than hugging the shore. The myth is based on the assumption that the mariner had neither the means nor the ability to find his way out of sight of land. . . . Also it takes no account of the extra sense and undoubted ability of the small-ship sailor to know where he is with remarkable accuracy without instruments or observations."[12]

Commodore Collins doubtless referred to the compass, the sextant, and other more recent instruments of observation, all of which the Phoenicians lacked. They may have had a form of astrolabe; fragments of astrolabes dating from the seventh century B.C. have been found in Mesopotamia. In any case the Phoenicians had the sun and the stars to guide them, not indeed so accurately but closely enough to lead them to port. They had also the lore accumulated in many lifetimes spent on the sea. No Phoenician records survive to tell how these men found their way on the open ocean, but we may infer a great deal from the writers of ancient Greece.

When Homer's mythical hero Odysseus wearied of life on a western island and thought to head homeward, the shrewd Calypso advised him to keep the Great Bear "on his left hand as he made across the sea." Thus for seventeen days Odysseus sailed ever eastward. Men in all ages have looked at the sky and remarked this great constellation, Ursa Major. The Egyptians knew it five thousand years before Christ. Homer wrote that the Bear "wheels round and round where it is, watching Orion [the Hunter], and alone of them all never takes a bath in the Ocean." Other men saw in it other objects and called it the Big Dipper, Charles's Wain (or Wagon), and the Plough. The ancient Greeks steered by its fiery sparks but the Phoenicians *did not*.

Both Strabo and the Alexandrian poet Kallimachos report that the Phoenicians steered instead by the Little Bear. Eudoxus of Cnidus, great Greek astronomer and mathematician, noted this fact in the fourth century B.C. His work was put into verse a century later in the *Phenomena* of Aratus, Greek court poet, who wrote that the pole "faces us in the north, high above the ocean. Encompassing it two bears wheel together. . . . It is by Helice [the Great Bear] that the Achaeans [Greeks] on the sea perceive which way to steer their ships, but in the other the Phoenicians put their trust when they cross the sea. But Helice, appearing large at earliest night, is bright and easy to mark, while the other is smaller, yet better for sailors, for in a smaller orbit wheel all her stars.

By her guidance, then, the men of Sidon steer the straightest course." This would have been news to Homer, who believed that the Great Bear "alone of them all' never bathed in the ocean. The Little Bear, as Strabo expressly stated, "did not become known as such to the Greeks until the Phoenicians so designated it for the purpose of navigation."

The Phoenicians had far to go on the sea, and their superior knowledge of the stars, their celestial beacons, served them well. Cornwall was not the most distant port of call, nor was north the only direction in which Phoenicians ventured during their fifteen hundred years of seafaring.

One of the neater Phoenician feats was to sail around the whole of Africa. Today we are taught that the circumnavigation of Africa was first accomplished by Vasco da Gama in 1497–99—a few years after Columbus reached the West Indies—and then only after some eighty years of persistent attempts by the ablest navigators of their day in the finest ships, sponsored by Prince Henry of Portugal himself and his successors. Refuting this Portuguese claim to "first" is the story Herodotus recorded in the fifth century before the Christian era:

"As for Libya [Africa]," Herodotus wrote, "we know it to be washed on all sides by the sea, except where it is attached to Asia. The discovery was first made by Necho the Egyptian King who, on desisting from the canal which he had begun between the Nile and the Arabian Gulf, sent to sea a number of ships manned by Phoenicians, with orders to make for the Pillars of Hercules, and to return to Egypt through them and through the Mediterranean. The Phoenicians took their departure from Egypt by way of the Erythraean Sea and so sailed into the Southern Ocean. When autumn came they went ashore, wherever they might happen to be, and having sown a tract of land with corn, waited until the grain was fit to cut. Having reaped it, they again set sail; and thus it came to pass that two whole years went by, and it was not until the third year that they doubled the Pillars of Hercules and made good their voyage home. On their return they declared (I for my part do not believe them, but perhaps others may) that in sailing round Libya they got the sun on their right hand. In this way was the extent of Libya first discovered."[13]

Necho reigned as pharaoh of Egypt from 609 to 593 B.C. Thus the Phoenician circumnavigation of Africa antedated the Portuguese by about 2100 years.

Whereas the Portuguese attempt was motivated by a desire to reach India, Necho, on the other hand, was building a fleet in the Red Sea and another in the Mediterranean and wished for a way to transfer ships from one fleet to the other. The old canal connecting the Red Sea with the Mediterranean (prototype of the present Suez Canal) had been rendered useless before Necho's time by silting and by the recession of the Red Sea. Necho attempted first to re-excavate the canal, but he abandoned the project when, according to Herodotus, 120,000 men perished in the work. The alternative was to do what no man had done before—to sail entirely around the Dark Continent, its extent then totally unknown, to determine whether such a voyage was feasible.

For his purpose Necho selected the sea-wise Phoenicians, whose skill and daring were then unmatched. Heart for the task was a prime requisite, and this the Phoenicians could be expected to possess. Not alone promise of profit but also zest for adventure—the challenge of danger and the unknown—had goaded them forward upon the bitter and sometimes whale-infested Atlantic.

In attempting to circle Africa clockwise the Phoenicians had much the better deal. Departing from a port on the Red Sea, they would have had fine fresh northerly winds to start them well on their way. In the lower half of the Red Sea they probably faced southerlies and had to beat their way, but after they rounded Cape Guardafui and entered the Indian Ocean, favoring winds and favoring currents must have sped them down the long eastern coast of Africa. At the crucial Cape of Good Hope the winds and currents that battered Vasco da Gama favored again an east-to-west passage, and west of the Cape the prevailing winds are from the south. But once the Phoenicians had crossed the equator a second time and were off the bulge of western Africa, there powerful trade winds and currents opposing them would have made for a nasty voyage on the last long run for the Pillars. They fetched the Pillars notwithstanding and returned to Egypt, having sailed 13,000 miles around Africa.

There was a time when the majority of orthodox historians arbitrarily dismissed the entire story as fiction. Herodotus was

Africa

not above telling tall tales, and this one was labeled impossible. That time is past. Historians now recognize that the ancient Phoenicians possessed not only the ships but also the skill, a point that a practical seaman has aptly stated in these words: "If they could sail across the Bay of Biscay with heavy cargoes, they could also round the Cape of Good Hope; there is no doubt of that."[14]

The proof of the feat seems to lie in the only statement that Herodotus sniffed at, saying: "I for my part do not believe . . . that in sailing round Libya they got the sun on their right hand" —that is, on the north. True son of the Northern Hemisphere, Herodotus knew that for him the sun stood south of the zenith. No man before the Phoenicians had ever reported seeing the sun in the north or even, apparently, conceived that that might be. More than half of Africa, as we sometimes find it hard to remember, lies north of the equator. Many generations were to pass away before theoreticians first perceived that in the Southern Hemisphere the sun would stand to the north; but this single Phoenician observation, which also emphasizes the unsuspected length of Africa, gives credibility to the entire account.

Our concern with the circumnavigation of Africa is not the digression it might seem. For although it by no means places Phoenicians in America, it helps to establish a fact long suspected: that Phoenician nautical prowess and daring attained a level not again reached until the century of Columbus.

What other Phoenician achievements escaped the record because no Egyptian pharaoh sponsored and proudly announced them we can only conjecture. As Vilhjalmur Stefansson wryly remarked of the African jaunt: "If the Phoenicians had been left to tell it, they probably would have reported failure due to one or more of the stock explanations—that the sea was muddy, that it was full of rocks and whirlpools, that the water was full of serpents and the air full of dragons, that the sun did not shine."[15]

Chances are, the circumnavigating Phoenicians who found themselves blown and buffeted off the West African coast were not in utterly strange waters. Over a long period Phoenician traders, leaving the Pillars far behind, had sometimes turned, not to the north and Cornwall, but south along Africa.

These voyages to the south are of the utmost importance, for inherent in them is the combination of circumstances that could have carried Phoenician mariners inadvertently to Middle America from as early as the tenth or twelfth century B.C.

The earliest Phoenician traders and colonists had found more than enough within the convenient Mediterranean to occupy even their boundless energy. But soon they began to make long-sighted plans. Having founded Utica in North Africa and Gades beyond the Pillars in about the twelfth century B.C., Phoenician merchants presently moved along the African coast outside the Pillars, founding more colonies.

According to Strabo, "To the south of Lixus and the Coteis [western spur of the Atlas Mountains] lies a gulf called the Emporicus, which contains the settlements of Phoenician merchants." He cites the authority of older historians that "on the gulfs which come next after the Emporicus Gulf there were ancient settlements of Tyrians, now deserted, no fewer than three hundred cities, which were destroyed by the Pharusians and the Nigritae; and those people, they say, are at a distance of a thirty days' journey from Lynx."[16]

Strabo's estimate of three hundred colonies has been ridiculed by later scholars, and the distance of "thirty days' journey from Lynx" is difficult to pinpoint on a map; but both are matters of only secondary importance in the present consideration if we may safely assume that Phoenician colonies were planted prolifically, well down the coast of Africa. It was Alexander von Humboldt who pointed out that the presence of the Nigritae would indicate "a very southern locality." This view is shared by the English historian George Rawlinson, who wrote that the early Phoenicians' "frail and small vessels, scarcely bigger than modern fishing-smacks, proceeded southwards along the West African coast, as far as the tract watered by the Gambia and Senegal."[17]

In other words, the Phoenicians passed the present Morocco, passed Spanish Sahara and Mauritania, and sailed on south to the site of modern Dakar, the westernmost point of Africa, before turning about for the long voyage home.

It is *off this bulge of Africa*, significantly, that powerful head winds and currents first batter a ship sailing north.

Phoenician vessels of this early period, small and shallow-draft, were undecked or at best only partially decked and thus

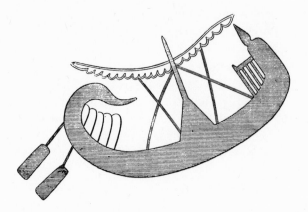

FIGURE 73. Early Phoenician trading vessel, from a painting on a Cypriot vase.

easily swamped. The stern soared high and was curved like the flicking tail of a giant fish (Figure 73). Some, if we may judge by extant representations, were propelled by manpower (Figure 74), some by both oars and sails, and some were fitted only with sails —always a single mast and a single sail. The crucial fact is that many of the larger merchant vessels are thought to have been totally wind-propelled.

No doubt these experienced seamen could beat to windward if need be, tacking and clawing and inching along. But the better way, when it offered, was to find a more favorable wind. On the return voyage from Africa the Phoenicians must have learned— as the Portuguese too learned so many centuries later—that if they

FIGURE 74. Early Phoenician merchant galley.

hoped to make northing they must first turn their prows to the northwest: they must take to the high seas in order to avoid both the northeast trades and the Canaries current. Phoenician inscriptions, incidentally, have been found on the Canary Islands.

So the returning ship, standing well out to sea, passes between the Canaries and Madeira, a "belt of calms and variable winds." What would happen if at this point a storm arose?

In reply to this question the eminent Portuguese geographer Armando Cortesão points out that between these two archipelagos the prevailing winds blow from the northeast. "If such a ship," he states, "had no other means of propulsion but her round sails, she would stand every chance of being impelled southwestwards until reaching the belt south of the Sargasso Sea, where the trades that blow exclusively from the eastern quarter of the compass and the northern equatorial current, which becomes strong as from longitude 40° W, would thrust her irresistibly toward the Antilles."[18] From the Antilles, as we noted earlier, the current is known to have carried an Indian canoe westward to beach on the east coast of Yucatán.

Given long centuries of Phoenician traffic up and down the West African coast, it follows that one or possibly many Phoenician ships must have met with a sudden storm between the Canaries and Madeira. Thus one or probably several Phoenician ships might have been impelled to a point south of the Sargasso Sea, from whence, according to Cortesão, they would have been "thrust irresistibly toward the Antilles," the West Indies.

For such an achievement to have been recorded, the ship must needs have found its way back to a home port, where, however, the Odyssean wanderers bursting with tales of the voyage of the ages would have faced the Phoenicians' muzzling rule of silence. The passion for secrecy notwithstanding, it would seem counter to human nature that news of such moment could be totally suppressed; and so, lacking written records from Phoenicia itself, we turn to the writings of other ancients.

17

TESTIMONY OF
THE GREEKS

IN 1934 A. W. BRØGGER, director of the Norwegian Museum in Oslo, stood before the second International Congress of Archaeologists and in his role of president expressed opinions which were little short of heresy for that time and place.

"It could also very well be believed," said Brøgger, "that the route to *America* was discovered during the Bronze Age, at the time when sea voyaging was at its height. It could perhaps help to explain why the American peoples were living in a Bronze Age when Europeans reached them in the next great era of voyaging. It must be remembered that the prevailing winds and currents almost compel the discovery of Central America from Spanish and Portuguese harbors, when once open-sea voyages are begun. The *story of Atlantis* found in Plato would thereby gain a new and natural explanation: the great discoveries of the Bronze Age mariners, which were made and lost again. But the Greek written sources show only the end phase, the period when geography was in transition from the *maritime* world-picture of the Bronze Age to the *continental* one of the Early Iron Age."[1]

There is more than Plato's Atlantis to go on, which is all to the good, for evidence based on Atlantis alone would probably sink like the island itself. This is not to say categorically that Plato's tremendous island somewhere west of the Pillars never existed. Plato heard of this island—"larger than Asia Minor and Libya together"—indirectly through Egyptian priests, preservers of ancient learning.

Indeed, the tradition of land to the west has been so persistent that it cries for an explanation. The explanation is certainly *not* that the ocean has widened. As a matter of fact, the Atlantic has widened by at least a thousand miles, but this was a gradual process that began when the earth was young and was largely completed thirty million years before the first ancestor of early man climbed down from the trees. And still there are Homer, Plato, Theopompus, Aristotle, Diodorus Siculus, Strabo, and other ancients writing of lands beyond the known world.

Some of these islands undoubtedly were only the Canaries, Madeira, and the Azores; but ancient mariners had sailed farther west, for ancient writers also wrote of a terrible sea of seaweed, where the seaweed growing upon the waves "holds the ship back like bushes." Though it may seem the figment of a disordered imagination, there *is* such a sea of seaweed, the Sargasso Sea, lying in mid-Atlantic farther west than the westernmost Old World island—in fact, approximately midway between the coast of West Africa and Florida. The words of the ancient writer seem to echo the awe of an eyewitness, strongly suggesting that mariners had already ventured or strayed as far as this midway sea.

This far—and how much farther? Were they indeed then "thrust irresistibly," as Cortesão contends would happen to such a ship, from the belt south of the Sargasso Sea toward the West Indies? Again, ancient records suggest that they were.

In the fourth century B.C. Theopompus wrote of an island "of immense extent" somewhere in the ocean beyond the known world. Patently the Canaries, Madeira, and the Azores fail to meet Theopompus' specifications, being tiny to moderate in size. This island, moreover, was "inhabited by strange people quite different from ours." How strange? As strange as the natives of the Cassiterides, the Tin Islands? Much stranger than this, one surmises, for the inhabitants of the Cassiterides are described by another ancient writer, Avienus, merely as "enterprising people who occupy themselves with commerce," a description which would admirably fit the Phoenicians also. As strange, then, as American Indians? . . .

If we admit the evidence of Theopompus, we must concede that someone not only hove in sight of but also landed and went ashore on this "island of immense extent" and had some acquaintance, however slight, with its strange and different inhabitants.

Thus far these tantalizing tidbits have all been descriptive. Three centuries after Theopompus, however, another ancient writer explained graphically how one such discovery came to be made. The author of the account was Diodorus Siculus, who regrettably was not distinguished for accuracy. He lived, however, as his name implies, in Sicily, where Carthaginian colonies once flourished, and he may conceivably have had access to information otherwise little known.

Diodorus recorded this incident in the century before Christ, but even then the event was old beyond date:

"There lies out in the deep off Libya an island of considerable size," wrote Diodorus, "and situated as it is in the ocean it is distant from Libya a voyage of a number of days to the west. Its land is fruitful, much of it being mountainous and not a little being a level plain of surpassing beauty. Through it flow navigable rivers. . . .

"In ancient times this island remained undiscovered because of its distance from the entire inhabited world, but it was discovered at a later period for the following reason. The Phoenicians, who from ancient times on made voyages continually for purposes of trade, planted many colonies throughout Libya and not a few as well in the western parts of Europe. And since their ventures turned out according to their expectations, they amassed great wealth and essayed to voyage beyond the Pillars of Heracles into the sea which men call the ocean. And, first of all, upon the Strait itself by the Pillars they founded a city on the shores of Europe, and since the land formed a peninsula they called the city Gadeira; in the city they built many works appropriate to the nature of the region, among them a costly temple of Heracles [Melkarth], and they instituted magnificent sacrifices which were conducted after the manner of the Phoenicians. . . .

"The Phoenicians, then, while exploring the coast outside the Pillars for the reasons we have stated and while sailing along the shores of Libya, were driven by strong winds a great distance out into the ocean. And after being storm-tossed for many days they were carried ashore on the island we mentioned above, and when they had observed its felicity and nature they caused it to be known to all men."[2]

Here, almost uncannily, is two-thousand-year-old confirmation of Cortesão's contention that a sail-propelled vessel off the west coast of Africa would, if caught in a storm at a critical point, stand every chance of being impelled far to the west. Toward the West Indies, says Cortesão. But where was Diodorus' island?

This large island "distant from Libya a voyage of a number of days to the west" could scarcely have been the Canaries, Madeira, or Cape Verde, none of which lies that far west or possesses the navigable rivers specified by Diodorus. The Azores, though many days to the west, lie off Portugal rather than Africa and are not only small but also far north of the probable path of a ship storm-driven from Africa. West of Libya (in its broad ancient meaning, Africa, rather than the present-day country) lie the islands mentioned, then a vast and islandless expanse of Atlantic, as Columbus learned when sailing westward from the Canaries, and the next land sighted would be one of the green islands of the Antilles, better known as the West Indies. And here—in Haiti, Cuba, and of course on the mainland of North and South America —one finds the first navigable rivers west of Africa.

As to size, Diodorus mentioned only that the island was "of considerable size." Now, the island described by Theopompus as inhabited by a strange and different people was "of immense extent." Plato's island was said to be larger than Asia Minor and Africa lumped together. When is an island not an island but instead a land? To the astronaut every continent seems an island; to the canoeist every large island seems a land. For the early explorer too the answer was difficult and possibly sometimes arbitrary. One suspects that the term "island" was, in such usage, not necessarily significant and cannot be declared positively to rule out a land mass.

Diodorus added one extremely provocative item concerning the island whose discovery he attributed to Phoenicians:

"Consequently the Tyrians," he continued, "at the time when they were masters of the sea, purposed to dispatch a colony to it; but the Carthaginians prevented their doing so, partly out of concern lest many inhabitants of Carthage should remove there because of the excellence of the island, and partly in order to have ready in it a place in which to seek refuge against an incalculable turn of fortune, in case some total disaster should overtake Carthage. For it was their thought that, since they were masters of the sea, they would thus be able to move, households and all, to an island which was unknown to their conquerors."

Here, as in the earlier passage, Diodorus offers titillating clues which together enable us to reckon the date of the discovery —tentatively, of course—within three centuries.

First, he moves directly into the account of the discovery from a brief discussion of the founding of Cádiz. From this we would place the discovery—at the earliest—in the eleventh century B.C. Alexander von Humboldt believed that Diodorus referred to an epoch "far more ancient" than that of Carthage, and indeed an early date would account for Diodorus' startling statement that the Phoenicians "caused [the island] to be known to all men." Such incaution on the part of Phoenicians suggests not only total mastery of the seas, which Phoenicians could claim until the ships of Hellenic Greece began to pose a threat in, say, the seventh century B.C.; it suggests further that Phoenician city-states were enjoying a period of independence and peace so extensive that it seemed interminable and they harbored no fear of some day needing a distant refuge. This was their sanguine situation from the time the Egyptian leash was removed in approximately 1300 B.C. until the Assyrian noose dropped over Phoenician heads in about 876 B.C. and very slowly tightened. From that time forward, with occasional important intervals of successful rebellion and subsequent respite, the story of Phoenicia is studded with strife. Consequently some time during the ninth century B.C., possibly down toward 800 B.C., might be taken as a terminal date, the end of those halcyon days when the Phoenicians, having discovered their island, would have made it known to all men. Who knows?— perhaps the glowing reports of this island inflamed the imagination of Homer.

Then comes a second phase, the era of silence, during which

the island that was known to all men becomes instead "unknown."
It seems likely that the canny Phoenicians surveyed their worsen-
ing situation and deemed it politic to make no further mention
of the island. Perhaps they even reported that it had sunk?

The third and final phase can be dated with a fair degree of
accuracy because of an apparent but not, I believe, an actual
inconsistency on the part of Diodorus. The Tyrians "at the time
when they were masters of the sea," says Diodorus, purposed to
dispatch a colony to the island, but the Carthaginians prevented
it, preferring, "since they were masters of the sea," to retain for
themselves this excellent place of refuge.

It was during the years 587-574 B.C. that the mastery of the
Mediterranean passed from Tyre to Carthage, and with it the
control of the gates to the Outer Ocean, the nine-miles-wide neck
just west of Ceuta. Before that time it is doubtful whether Carthage possessed the power to thwart the plans of her mother city.
But in 587 B.C. Nebuchadnezzar, that rampaging Babylonian,
began his thirteen-year siege of Island Tyre and blackened the
opposite shore with his host of balding warriors camped amid
the smoking ruins of Mainland Tyre. For thirteen years the
Tyrians stubbornly resisted conquest—years of frustration, fear,
and want; years when a distant and by that time secret island
would have seemed Elysian. And ships lay at anchor in the harbor.

Supremacy at the Pillars the length of the Mediterranean
away probably did not change hands in an instant. Ships from the
mainland and ships from the island city of Tyre might well have
sailed through en route to their distant and peaceful island before Carthaginians perceived that their hand was now the upper.
And these were the crucial years, as we noted some time back, in
which Herbert J. Spinden believes from internal evidence that
the Maya calendrical system was devised.

Tyre was to rise once more to maritime might, but the day
of her undisputed supremacy was past. In the western Mediterranean it was Carthage that thenceforth patrolled the gates to
the Outer Ocean, Carthage that sent its ships up and down the
West African coast, and Carthage—if we may accept the statements of Diodorus—that held the key to the future of that large
island far to the west of Libya.

Diodorus Siculus was not the only ancient author who attributed to Carthaginians the knowledge of such an island. Another was Aristotle, who described the island as fertile, wooded, fruitful, traversed by navigable rivers, and lying a sail of many days' distance outside the Pillars. So attractive was the island, according to Aristotle, that many Carthaginian traders and "other men" visited it and some remained—till the Senate of Carthage, fearful lest other nations should learn of this land, issued a decree that thereafter no one should sail there, under penalty of death.

Still another was Claudius Aelianus, who reported in the second century A.D. that knowledge of the existence of such an island was a continuing tradition among the "Carthaginians or Phoenicians" of Gades. And who would be more likely to know of the island than those who dwelt near the port of embarkation or the last European port of call and the first port visited by any who returned? Gades, on the Atlantic Ocean, had even then been a nursery of sailors for hundreds of years.

Only the naïve accept as gospel every word penned by every ancient historian. Equally unjustifiable, however, is the "everlasting No."

Did the enterprising Phoenicians stumble upon the New World? There is no documentary proof except what has here been cited: pre-Christian written references to an island "of immense extent" somewhere out in the ocean beyond the known world, inhabited by a strange and different people; a sea of seaweed; the story of a storm-tossed Phoenician ship driven many days westward across the ocean from Africa, grounding at last on a large and fruitful island with mountains and navigable rivers; a distant island that was ruled off limits by the Senate of Carthage; and above all the persistence of the ancients' belief in land far to the west upon the great ocean. These are at best indications, albeit indications that yield to no other satisfactory explanation.

Add to these written records the account of a Phoenician navigational feat not achieved again till the age of Columbus: the circumnavigation of Africa. Add, too, the fact that Phoenician ships were sailing outside the Pillars for centuries, sailing on a treacherous ocean where winds and currents might drive them west.

And to these add that single most potent of forces: the spirit of man. It would be inconsistent with human nature if no early mariner ever pointed his prow deliberately toward the challenging ocean—for the selfsame reason that men through the ages have dreamed that an earthling would some day visit the moon; the reason which George Leigh-Mallory once stated so simply and truly when asked why he had climbed a mountain: "Because it is there."

As Cortesão sums up: "Once we realize that in ancient times there were considerable means and possibilities of high-seas navigation, probably no less developed than in the last quarter of the fifteenth century of our era, it will be easier to understand some other problems of history still obscured or shrouded in mystery." He adds that "the discovery or rediscovery of the Atlantic archipelagos, and very likely of the American continent itself, at an interval of about two thousand years or more, is indeed one of the most remarkable facts of the history of geography."[3]

§◊§◊§◊§

18

§◊§◊§◊§

PHOENICIAN CARTHAGE

RISING IN THE IMAGE of her mother city, Carthage flourished from the outset. The Carthagians introduced advanced methods of agriculture that had been in use on the Syrian
coast; they set up markets in the city to which the natives of the
interior carried their produce. Carthaginians intermarried with the
native Berbers; and Carthage grew. With elbowroom, Carthage
erected magnificent buildings, grander than Tyre itself could ac-
commodate. Presently Carthage became the most important out-
post of Asiatic civilization in the western Mediterranean. And
still it grew. "Periodically," so Aristotle wrote in his *Politics,*
"Carthage sends colonies made up from her own citizens into the
countries round about, and insures them an easy existence."

Like her mother city, too, Carthage sent forth her ships in all
directions and traded in the products of many lands—even in
amber from the Baltic. Wealth in every ancient form rode into
her mammoth harbors, and no source of trade was overlooked.
Carthaginian merchants sailed down along the West African coast
for hundreds of miles and lighted signal fires to summon the
natives to trade. Herodotus labeled it "dumb commerce" and has
left us a graphic description.

Promptly after landing, Herodotus wrote, the Carthaginians unload their wares, lay them neatly along the beach, and leave them. Returning to their ships, they raise a great smoke. The natives, seeing the smoke, come down to the shore, lay out as much gold as they deem the goods to be worth, and withdraw, leaving the wares. The Carthaginians come ashore and look. If the gold seems to them sufficient, they take it and sail away. If not, they return to their ships and wait. The natives return and add to their gold. "Neither party deals unfairly by the other; for the Carthaginians never touch the gold till it comes up to the estimated worth of their goods, nor do the natives ever carry off the goods till the gold has been taken away."[1]

Historians long regarded this tale as beyond credibility. But in 1877 R. Bosworth Smith pointed out that it had been "proved by the concurrent testimony of modern travelers to be an accurate account of the dumb trade which still exists in many parts of Africa." He added, "It proves also that the gold-fields of the Niger, so imperfectly known to us even now, were well known to the Carthaginians.[2]

Carthage seems always to have had an abundant supply of gold. But another product of Africa was important to the Carthaginians second only to gold: people.

The amicable arrangement described by Herodotus must have suffered occasional lapses or certain tribes must have proved reluctant customers, for Carthage had a ready supply of slaves for the market. Some of these slaves were obtained from the north; Corsican slaves, for example, were highly valued. But many of the slaves Carthage offered were Negroes. If one may judge by methods in use as recently as the nineteenth century, they were probably captured in raids on African villages. It seems likely that the forays were made, not by land-based groups, but, in the interest of safe retreat, by Carthaginian sea-traders who plied the West African coast.

And theirs, of course, were the ships that battled the head winds and currents, the ships that on every return voyage north to Gibraltar ran the calculated risk of encountering a storm and being wind-driven far to the west.

We might do worse than to follow such a hypothetical ship, bearing its captured African slaves, on its hypothetical voyage. We first scud southwest, driven by the northeast trades and the

Canaries current. After many days the wind slackens and our speed declines. Now we are slowly skirting the southeastern edge of the mammoth Sargasso Sea, where, far off, golden seaweed floats on the motionless indigo water. At 40° west longitude the sail swells again and begins to thrum, and from that point on the trades drive us steadily west to the West Indies. We enter the Caribbean riding the Equatorial Current and, still with the Equatorial Current, enter the Gulf of Mexico. On the southeastern coast of Mexico we make our landfall, but after a long look at Yucatán we round the peninsula and sail slowly south, then west, till we come to a lush green land whose rivers beckon.

And there, within our own lifetime, archaeologists have discovered long-buried colossal stone heads that look like portraits of Negroes—perhaps because they are.

If in the account of this hypothetical voyage I have inadvertently conveyed the impression that Carthaginians were inept or feckless mariners, I hasten to correct it by quoting in full the actual and contemporary record of a major Carthaginian expedition for colonization and exploration. Of Carthaginian literature, the text of only this one document has survived, but by happy chance it gives us tremendous insight into their nautical capabilities. The text is unique, too, in the manner of its preservation.

When the leader of the expedition, Admiral Hanno, returned safely to Carthage, he personally posted this account in the temple of Baal as a thank-offering. There, apparently, a visiting Greek with notebook in hand noticed and copied it, for it is preserved in a Greek translation only. It is cited in *Marvellous Narratives,* a work of the third century B.C. ascribed to Arstotle, and cited again later by Pliny and others.

To banish whatever odor may attach to "Marvellous," it should be noted that the Periplus of Hanno is widely regarded as authentic. As Bunbury put it, "The authenticity of the work may be considered as unquestionable. The internal evidence is conclusive upon that point."[3]

"It pleased the Carthaginians," wrote Hanno, "that Hanno should voyage outside the Pillars of Hercules [undoubtedly Hanno called them the Pillars of Melkarth], and found cities of the Libyphoenicians. And he set forth with sixty ships of fifty oars, and a multitude of men and women, to the number of thirty thousand, and with wheat and other provisions.

"After passing through the Pillars we went on and sailed for two days' journey beyond, where we founded the first city, which we called Thymiaterium [identified by Müller as Mehedia at the mouth of the Sbou River at about 34° 20′ N]. It lay in the midst of a great plain.

"Sailing thence toward the west we came to Solois [probably the modern Cape Cantin], a promontory of Libya, bristling with trees. Having set up an altar here to Neptune, we proceeded again, going toward the east for half a day, until we reached a marsh lying no great way from the sea, thickly grown with tall reeds [probably the marshes bordering Cape Safi]. Here also were elephants and other wild beasts feeding, in great numbers. Going beyond the marsh a day's journey, we settled cities by the sea, which we called Caricus Murus, Gytta, Acra, Melitta and Arambys.

"Sailing thence we came to the Lixus, a great river flowing from Libya [the Wadi Draa, which flows into the Atlantic at 28° 30′]. By it a wandering people, the Lixitae, were pasturing their flocks; with whom we remained some time, becoming friends. Above these folk lived unfriendly Ethiopians, dwelling in a land full of wild beasts, and shut off by great mountains, from which they say the Lixus flows, and on the mountains live men of various shapes, cave-dwellers, who, so the Lixitae say, are fleeter of foot than horses.

"Taking interpreters from them, we sailed twelve days toward the south along a desert, turning thence toward the east one day's sail. There, within the recess of a bay we found a small island, having a circuit of fifteen stadia; which we settled, and called it Cerne [now Herne Island, in the mouth of the Rio de Oro at about 23° 45′]. From our journey we judged it to be situated opposite Carthage; for the voyage from Carthage to the Pillars and thence to Cerne was the same. [Very nearly accurate.]

"Thence, sailing by a great river whose name was Chretes, we came to a lake, which had three islands, larger than Cerne."

(To interrupt here, Müller identifies the Chretes River with the modern St. Jean, at 19° 25′, which has three islands at its mouth. The fact that the Chretes was not, apparently, named by Hanno suggests that Carthaginian traders had traveled this way before him. Hanno specifically mentions assigning names to the colonies he planted and to one small island because he settled a colony on it, but the capes and rivers down to this point seem to have borne names previously. The following paragraph suggests that the Chretes River at 19° 25′ was close to the southern terminus of previous Carthaginian sailing. This terminus, if such it was, is far south of the Canary Islands—the length of the desert and more to the south of them. It is also, however, considerably *north* of trading points which Phoenicians of Tyre are believed to have reached.)

"Running a day's sail beyond these [islands]," Hanno continued, "we came to the end of the lake, above which rose great mountains, peopled by savage men wearing skins of wild beasts, who threw stones at us and prevented us from landing our ships. Sailing thence, we came to another river, very great and broad [the Senegal, approximately 16° 30′ N], which was full of crocodiles and hippopotami. And then we turned about and went back to Cerne.

"Thence we sailed toward the south twelve days, following the shore, which was peopled by Ethiopians who fled from us and would not wait. And their speech the Lixitae who were with us could not understand. But on the last day we came to great wooded mountains [Cape Verde]. The wood of the trees was fragrant, and of various kinds.

"Sailing around these mountains for two days, we came to an immense opening of the sea [the mouth of the Gambia River,

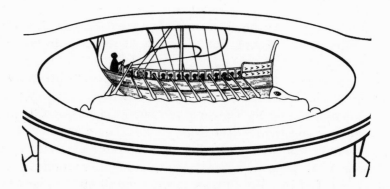

FIGURE 75.   Mediterranean galley of the period of Hanno's Periplus. From a vase in the Metropolitan Museum, New York.

13° 30'], from either side of which there was level ground inland; from which at night we saw fire leaping up on every side at intervals, now greater, now less."

(To interrupt again, what Hanno here describes in understatement was doubtless the annual burning of the grass, still practiced in the region of the Senegal and Gambia Rivers. When the rainy season has passed, the grass becomes parched by winds blowing off the Sahara Desert, and the Negroes set it afire to clear the land for fresh verdure. An English traveler described it in 1799 as a scene of terrific grandeur. "In the middle of the night, I could see the plains and mountains, as far as my eye could reach, variegated with lines of fire; and the light reflected on the sky made the heavens appear in a blaze."[4])

"Having taken in water there," Hanno went on, "we sailed along the shore for five days, until we came to a great bay, which our interpreters said was called Horn of the West. In it there was a large island, and within the island a lake of the sea, in which there was another island [the Bissagos off Portuguese Guinea]. Landing there during the day, we saw nothing but forests, but by night many burning fires, and we heard the sound of pipes and cymbals, and the noise of drums and a great uproar. Then fear possessed us, and the soothsayers commanded us to leave the island. And then quickly sailing forth, we passed by a burning country full of fragrance, from which great torrents of fire flowed down to the sea. But the land could not be come at for the heat. And we sailed along with all speed, being stricken by fear.

"After a journey of four days, we saw the land at night covered with flames. And in the midst there was one lofty fire, greater than the rest, which seemed to touch the stars. By day this was seen to be a very high mountain, called Chariot of the Gods. [Müller identifies it as Mt. Kakulima, 9° 30' N.]

"Thence, sailing along by the fiery torrents for three days, we came to a bay, called Horn of the South. In the recess of this bay there was an island [Sherbro Island off Sierra Leone at about 7° 30' N], like the former one, having a lake, in which there was another island, full of savage men. There were women, too, in even greater number. They had hairy bodies, and the interpreters called them *Gorillæ*. When we pursued them we were unable to take any of the men; for they all escaped by climbing the steep places and defending themselves with stones; but we took three of the women, who bit and scratched their leaders and would not follow us. So we killed them and flayed them, and brought their skins to Carthage. For we did not voyage further, provisions failing us."[5]

Concerning this last episode, several historians contend that the hairy men and women were not gorillas. Instead, they were probably pygmies, the primeval dwarfish people of equatorial Africa whose bodies are hairy and whose head hair is a woolly reddish brown. Livingstone's Stanley, describing a full-grown pygmy who stood four feet tall, wrote: "His color was coppery, the fell over his body was almost feathery, being nearly half an inch in length."[6]

All of which may seem less than tangential to the restless reader who rightly believes that the Carthaginians chasing pygmies on Sherbro Island were still a long way from the New World. The periplus of Hanno is not, however, digressive. This abbreviated, elliptic logbook throws light on the Carthaginian character and *modus operandi* and serves as a basis on which to compare Carthaginian navigation with that of the Portuguese over the same route in the fifteenth century, "the century of discovery."

In the 1420's the mariners of Prince Henry the Navigator were feeling their way apprehensively along the West African coast. Prince Henry's training, equipment, and methods were already paying dividends, for in 1420 Madeira had been "discovered." But now as his men advanced farther south they found that the set of wind and current was steadily away from home. The prospect of rounding Cape Bojador (26° N) filled them with terror. "Suicidal," they called it. But Henry kept urging his captains on. And finally eleven years later, in 1434, Gil Eannes doubled Cape Bojador.

This is a stretch of African coast which Hanno refers to casually: "Taking interpreters from them, we sailed twelve days toward the south along a desert, turning thence to the east one day's sail." The Carthaginian colony of Cerne was planted *beyond* it, suggesting that in the fifth century B.C. other voyages there were contemplated.

After a lapse of several years because of Moroccan and domestic difficulties, Prince Henry of Portugal continued to send his

men forth in better ships with the latest in navigational instruments. In 1441 the Portuguese sailed past Cape Blanco. This was
still north of the Chretes River, which, it would seem, both
Phoenicians and other Carthaginians had reached before Hanno.

At this time the Portuguese took two products which Hanno
must also have found but does not mention: slaves and gold.
These gave a considerable push to Portuguese efforts, and four
years later one Portuguese captain had sailed as far as the Senegal
(Hanno's great and broad river teeming with crocodiles and
hippopotami) and another had rounded Cape Verde (Hanno's
great, wooded, fragrant mountains).

The following year, 1446, another of Henry's captains became the first known in the Christian era to reach Sierra Leone
(where the men of Hanno had pursued the hairy wild natives).
Though Portuguese efforts to push on southward continued, it
has not been established that any point farther south was reached
before the death of Prince Henry in 1460.

Compared with this forty-year struggle by the ablest mariners of the age in the finest ships, Hanno's voyage over the same
route with sixty ships seems like an afternoon's sail.

We learn much from the periplus also concerning the Carthaginians themselves as explorers and colonists. For example,
their religiosity: they tarried to set up an altar to Neptune. Their
adaptability with natives, specifically the Lixitae, "with whom
we remained some time, becoming friends." Their use of interpreters. Their matter-of-fact acceptance of the presence of elephants, crocodiles, hippopotami, "and other wild beasts" of the
land. Their absence of fear in the face of the unknown. Their
courage when finally fear possessed them: they "sailed along by
the fiery torrents"—sailing *south,* not turning about to flee for
home. And finally, we are reminded that the day of firearms lay
far in the future, for the Carthaginian fleet was deterred "by
savage men wearing skins of wild beasts, who threw stones at us
and prevented us from landing our ships."

Concerning their secrets of navigation Hanno tells nothing.
But we learn that Carthaginians could estimate accurately the
length of a day's sail despite winds and currents, for the distance
from Carthage to the Pillars of Hercules and from the Pillars to
the island of Cerne (or Herne) is approximately the same, just

as Hanno estimated it to be. We infer that Carthaginians had mastered logistics, for thirty thousand people (if the number is not an exaggeration) could scarcely have hoped to live off the land. The point at which provisions failed was 2600 miles beyond the Pillars of Hercules and more than 3500 miles from Carthage. And then there was still the 3500-mile voyage home for those who were not left behind in the seven new colonies.

The seven colonies, incidentally, would doubtless have given rise to still further voyages along the West African coast, voyages that would have been undertaken largely by merchant ships totally wind-propelled. That follow-up voyages were made in sufficient number to sustain at least some of the colonies is suggested by Saint Augustine's statement. Saint Augustine, who was bishop of Hippo from 396 to 430 A.D., declared that in his day Phoenician was spoken on the west coast of Africa as far as Cape Noun.[7]

If the Carthaginians ever emulated their Phoenician forefathers to the extent of circumnavigating Africa, no record of the feat has survived, but Herodotus may have intended to imply such a voyage when he wrote: "The Carthaginians, too, have said that Libya is surrounded by water."

The date of Hanno's periplus is uncertain, for the name Hanno was common in Carthage. This Hanno is believed to have been either the father or the son of the Hamilcar who led an invasion of Sicily in 480 B.C. Those who hold that Hanno was the father of Hamilcar assign to the periplus the date of about 520 B.C. The other group of scholars believes that the periplus was made by the son of Hamilcar in about 470 B.C.[8]

At that time Carthage was the wealthiest city of antiquity, approaching the height of her power. The native Berbers, to whom Carthage had once paid ground rent, had been pushed back and forced to pay heavy tribute. Carthage had ceased her payments of tribute to Tyre. Instead, the other Phoenician colonies along the North African coast, with the single exception of Utica fifteen miles distant, were now forced to render tribute to Carthage to help defray the expenses of her exploration and colonization and her huge armies of mercenaries. The armies were necessitated by the rise of twin stars along the Mediterranean: Hellenic Greece and the still faint star of Rome.

The population of Carthage in about 470 B.C. is unknown, but in about 150 B.C., when two Punic wars had greatly reduced her, 700,000 people were computed to be living within her walls. There is probably no greater stimulus to colonization than over-population. Carthage actively followed the policy of relieving herself of excess population in this manner, as the sixty-ship colo-nizing expedition of Hanno indicates. The 30,000 said to have been dispatched to West Africa with Hanno is possibly no enor-mous exaggeration, for in his day ships were distinctly larger than the first frail Phoenician vessels.

While Hanno was coasting southward along Africa looking for suitable sites for colonies, another Carthaginian, Himilco, was leading a similar expedition northward, according to Pliny. In-stead of a firsthand, precise report of this expedition, however, we have only the late and confusing account of Avienus, from which Fridtjof Nansen concluded that Himilco probably sailed as far as Britain. Himilco seems to have been much concerned that others—probably Greeks—would follow, for Avienus' ac-count is studded with perils: a ship becalmed, a sea so shallow that its muddy floor is scarcely puddled with water, sea monsters endlessly circling the slow-moving ships. . . .

It might also well be that at this time the Carthaginians, capable and foresighted as they were, saw fit to investigate those attractive lands across the Atlantic, not perhaps for immediate colonization but, as Diodorus Siculus put it, "in order to have ready in it a place in which to seek refuge against an incalculable turn of fortune, in case some total disaster should overtake Car-thage."

Total disaster first befell the mother city of Carthage, indom-itable Tyre, when, alone of Phoenician cities, Tyre chose to make a stand against the triumphal surge of Alexander the Great. The story of how the Tyrians matched their will and their wits against Alexander's is one of the strangest ever recorded.

Ancient Tyre, many centuries older than city-states one usually speaks of as ancient, by about 1200 B.C. had already spilled out onto an offshore island, and before the time of the Biblical King David it had surpassed Gebal and Sidon as the foremost city of Phoenicia. Island Tyre had an area of approximately 125 acres, covered with closely packed houses many stories high—"more

stories than in Rome," as Strabo put it. Perrot and Chipiez estimated that its population could not have exceeded 25,000, but
probably the mainland city was at least equally populous, and
the surrounding cultivated plain supported a large population of
peasants and slaves. The importance of maritime cities, furthermore, particularly those built on islands, is not to be measured in
area and population.

Island Tyre represented an enormous engineering project.
By a vast earth-moving operation the Tyrians had filled in the
eastern border and formed the Broad Square, where they built a
temple to Melkarth facing Mount Hermon. The old harbor to
the south they improved, and they also created a second harbor.
When Island Tyre too proved inadequate for the growing population, they added adjacent islands to it by filling the intervening
channels and then constructed a massive stone wall around the
the entire "city of perfect beauty" till it stood as a mammoth fort-
ress in the sea, there to endure forever.

It was here that Alexander appeared in 332 B.C. Before his
massed might Gebal and Sidon had already surrendered. Now
Alexander requested permission to enter the walls of Island Tyre
and worship in the famous temple of Melkarth. But the Tyrians,
suspecting a Trojan-horse maneuver, refused; they suggested
politely that he worship instead in the older temple of Melkarth
in mainland Tyre.

Alexander was adamant. Tyre was obdurate. When it became
apparent that neither would yield, the Tyrians put their old
men and their women and children aboard ship and sent them
to Carthage, and girded themselves for war.

Alexander's initial strategy stunned the Tyrians. In order to
bring his army and his engines of war to the city half a mile out
in the sea, he began to construct a mole. To form a sturdy stone
foundation for it, the Macedonians hurled the debris of mainland
Tyre into the channel.

Soon Alexander was out where the sea was deep and the
current strong. Tyrians sailed forth from their island in triremes
and attacked the workers and later brought up a fire ship. The
Macedonians could accomplish little, and that little the sea undid.

Alexander needed a fleet, and quickly he summoned one—
ships from Phoenician Gebal, Arvad, and Sidon, and more from

Cyprus—224 ships in all. While they kept the Tyrian fleet bottled up in its harbors, the mole grew swiftly. A tremendous thing 200 feet wide rising to a height of 150 feet because of the towering city wall, it shouldered through the sea until, half a mile out, it connected at last with the island city. And now Alexander drew up his engines of war.

At this point the Tyrians attempted to escape their island-prison by a mass attack against the fleet blockading one harbor. They very nearly succeeded, and for minutes history hung in the balance. But when freedom seemed almost in sight, still another fleet appeared to bolster the forces of Alexander. The Tyrians retreated behind their wall, and the siege began in earnest.

Alexander attacked with battering rams, but the Tyrians, equally resourceful, broke the force of the rams with bags of sea-weed. Alexander hurled missiles, but the Tyrians had erected whirling wheels on the walls which caught the missiles. With long scythes the Tyrians parted the ropes that operated the battering rams. With grappling hooks the Tyrians swept the attackers away, or scalded them by pouring down molten metal, or scorched them with blistering sand. When the walls began to crumble despite all their efforts, the Tyrians hastily erected an inner wall. But the walls were finally breached at their weakest points, near the harbors, by battering rams placed aboard ships.

The Tyrians were even yet not ready to yield. They fought in the streets, in the houses, on rooftops. In the end two thousand Tyrian bodies could be seen hanging from the walls, an undetermined number of Tyrians escaped by concealing themselves aboard Sidonian ships, and thirty thousand were placed on the auction block and sold into slavery.

At last Alexander entered the temple of Melkarth, whom he identified with Heracles, and gave thanks for his victory over Tyre.

Once again Tyre was to rise from its ruins, but its part in our consideration has come to an end.

The year was 332 B.C. At that time Carthage, "the Queen of the Mediterranean" and only a few decades past her zenith, had less than two centuries left to live.

The Carthaginians were not clairvoyant, but they were amply

endowed with Phoenician foresight. Beholding the awesome destruction of Tyre, they could scarcely have failed to ponder the fickleness of fate and to take a long look directly north across the Mediterranean, where already the Romans were flexing their muscles. Thus 332 B.C. or shortly thereafter marks another propitious moment in history when prudent Carthage might well have sent forth a test group of colonists to try the new land across the Atlantic—colonists, incidentally, whose art and architecture were now more sophisticated than those of Phoenicia in the ninth century B.C., who admired and copied much that was Greek, and who, coming from populous Carthage, might have arrived in greater numbers.

Those who were young when Tyre was smashed lived to see the outbreak of the series of wars with Rome—the Punic wars, as they are called, Punic meaning Phoenician, for most of the extant accounts are written from the Roman point of view and none from the Carthaginian. The first Punic war lasted twenty-three years (264–241 B.C.) and cost Carthage her possessions in Sicily. The second Punic war, termed one of the titanic struggles of history, lasted seventeen years (218–201 B.C.) and cost Carthage her possessions in Spain, Sardinia, and Corsica. Stripped of all but her African holdings, she had to surrender her war fleet.

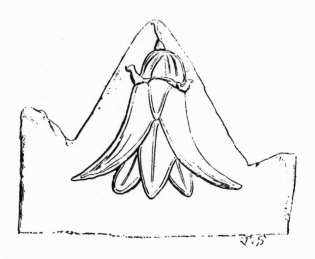

FIGURE 76.   Lotus design on a Carthaginian stela. The double outline, dimly recognizable here, was a favorite device of Carthaginian artists and was also employed in Middle America.

The star of Carthage was setting swiftly. Her lands, her wealth, and her commerce had shrunk. Her citizens (700,000 fifty years later) were divided politically, a large group favoring alliance with Rome.

Once in the dim but still not forgotten past, Tyrians distressed by the political situation in Tyre had broken away and founded distant Carthage. Now indeed was the time for Carthaginians too to move on, to seek refuge beyond the terrible reach of Rome, to search out that island which once long ago had been cause for concern "lest many inhabitants of Carthage should remove there because of the excellence of the island." That a major emigration occurred seems highly doubtful, but that some of the doughtier Carthaginians followed the ancient sea road west to constitute another "small descent" is distinctly a possibility.

This hypothesis, like its predecessors, is based upon an assumption challenged by many: that in ancient times a ship could have sailed as far as the New World and *could also have found its way safely back* to the Old, there to report the discovery. From the writings of various ancients we have read of distant discoveries in the Atlantic; we have seen how a ship *could* have reached the New World. But how could that first ship, single-sailed, probably small, probably lost, ever have found its way back to the Pillars of Hercules?

What would a sailing-ship captain today do in this situation, anchored along an American shore, without any prior knowledge of local winds or currents? He would know only that to attempt to retrace his route would be folly, for his ship would be fighting every mile against the winds and currents that had made his voyage across to the New World so delightful. He would know that he had to head north or south in the hope of finding a favoring wind to carry him east. Chances are, from southern Mexico he would turn his prow to the north, knowing that he was already very far south of the latitude of Gibraltar.

A Phoenician or Carthaginian navigator would have arrived at the same decision, and for the same reason, for he too could estimate latitude. Had he been unable to gauge his position, he would scarcely have voyaged regularly to Cornwall; or again, heading north on the open Atlantic off Africa he would not have known where to turn east toward the Pillars. For the ancients had no accurate means of gauging longitude; they had first to make the latitude and then sail east or west till they fetched their goal.

Today we can only surmise how, out on the open unmarked ocean so long before the day of the sextant, they could ascertain when they had reached the latitude of Gibraltar. They knew because they had learned it through generations of seafaring. They knew because the Phoenicians were collectors as well as purveyors of knowledge: from the Egyptians they had long ago learned astronomy, and from the Babylonians astronomy and mathematics and perhaps even the use of the gnomon, an instrument which measures the length of the sun's shadow, just as the Greeks learned its use from the Babylonians later. This is precisely the type of information that eager Phoenicians might have sought while gleaning so much from Babylon.

The night sky served as well as the sun. Perhaps the Phoenicians measured the height of the polestar above the horizon as the Arabs did centuries later—by extending an arm and gauging the distance with their fingers spread, thumb down. When the polestar stood as high in the sky as it had stood at the Pillars, and no higher, the ship had arrived at the same distance north of the equator. This was not the polestar we know as Polaris today, for the pole has been shifting slowly throughout the centuries. In Homer's day Polaris was twelve degrees or more from the pole. Kochab, the nearest bright star in the Lesser Bear, was seven, and inching farther away. But to an ancient measuring its altitude with his fingers or using the mast or the height of a man as his yardstick—and all this aboard a rolling ship—a star so close to the pole would appear to be motionless, fixed at the pole, as Eudoxus, the founder of Greek astronomy (who himself had studied in Egypt), once described Kochab. The ancient seafarer probably never thought in terms of degrees. His calculations were at best imprecise; and yet they served.

A homeward-bound Carthaginian captain off what is now Middle America, seeing Kochab too low in the sky and seeing the Great Bear dip his feet nightly into the ocean, would have steered to the north. Soon he would have been swept along by the outflowing Gulf Stream, propelling him east around Florida, then north along the Atlantic seaboard past what are now the Carolinas and Virginia, and presently again to the east.

The clear blue Gulf Stream is part of a vast meandering mass of warm water which swirls incessantly, generally clockwise, round and round the North Atlantic, carrying more water than all of the world's great rivers poured together. By the time it is off Cape Hatteras, North Carolina, the Gulf Stream is still forty miles wide, its sharp western edge of indigo blue a dramatic contrast alongside the gray-green inshore waters flowing south. Soon the Gulf Stream veers eastward, slows its pace, changes its name, widens further and begins to separate, one large branch ambling on east along the thirty-ninth parallel. Here the current, slowed to a drift, joins with prevailing westerly winds to carry the voyager eastward toward the Azores.

Is there any tangible indication that a Carthaginian ship might once have followed this route when homeward bound from America? By merest chance, there is.

In 1749 a storm that clawed at the western coast of Corvo Island in the Azores uncovered in the sand a broken black cask. Inside the cask was a caked mass of ancient coins. The mass was pried apart and the coins studied by numismatists, who reported that these were Carthaginian coins of the fourth and third centuries B.C.!

Now, the easternmost island of the Azores lies more than eight hundred miles from Europe, which accounts for the fact that the Azores were lost and not rediscovered until the next great age of discovery so many centuries later. ("These islands," reads the legend on a time-yellowed map, "were found by Diogo de Silve, pilot of the King of Portugal, in the year 1427.") But Corvo is not the easternmost. It is instead the *northwesternmost* island of the Azores, the first in the path of a ship sailing eastward along the course of the ocean drift from North America. It is the Old World island lying closest to North America, is in fact only 1,054 miles from Cape Race, Newfoundland.

The first Portuguese who landed on Corvo reported finding on a headland a statue with its right hand pointing dramatically west. Today this is only hearsay; the statue, if it ever existed, has long since disappeared. But for a discoverer to fabricate evidence of predecessors seems contrary to human nature.

As for Carthage herself, the sands had almost run through

her glass. The third Punic war (149–146 B.C.) was brief and final. Carthage, like Tyre, never surrendered, and her annihilation at the hands of the Romans was complete. Scipio Africanus Minor "conquered it, house by house, and sold the surviving inhabitants into slavery." Plundering followed, and then burning. When Carthage was only a bed of reeking cinders, of blackened stones and charred bones, even these poor vestiges of her mortal glory were plowed under.

And now what adventurers from the Old World would sail forth in search of distant shores? It would be incorrect to imply that among the ancients only Phoenicians and Carthaginians ever ventured upon the Atlantic. The Romans were less able mariners but willing to learn, as Strabo demonstrated in his account of the Roman captain who thought to follow a Phoenician ship to the Tin Islands and paid instead with his life. Fragments of ancient Roman pottery that have been dredged up from the Porcupine, a fishing bank far off the coast of Ireland, suggest that another Roman captain dared to investigate distant waters, only to meet a similar fate. In the twentieth century wind erosion has partially denuded a lowland in southeastern Iceland, laying bare several Roman coins of the third and fourth centuries A.D.

Insufficient evidence on which to base important conclusions, perhaps, but surely enough to give pause to those who contend, as some still do, that every ancient mariner hugged the coastline and no man dared to sail westward over the dragon-infested abysmal Atlantic before the century of Columbus.

Nor can one assume that, of the seven seas, only the Atlantic beckoned to the stout of heart. That maverick archaeologist Harold S. Gladwin has advanced a startling theory which also deserves an unprejudiced hearing, even at the cost of dimming the outlines of the hypothesis sketched in the foregoing chapters.

19

THE LOST FLEET
OF ALEXANDER

HAROLD S. GLADWIN, that thorn in the flesh of orthodox
archaeologists, has propounded a theory of contact which
accounts in a different manner for the presence in the New World
of certain remains that appear to bear the stamp of the Old.
Gladwin's gaudy conjecture, though not widely shared, is nonetheless worthy of note, partly because it jostles the mind from
routine acceptation and gives wings to the imagination, and
partly because it starts with an established historical fact and finds
cause therein for a migration from the Old World into the New.

Gladwin opens with a modest plea. "I do not know of anyone," he writes, "who has yet been rash enough to try to connect
the origins of American civilizations with definite causes, at
definite dates, in the progress of Old World history, and it is for
this reason that I have said that this tale will need support and
will undoubtedly need to be changed. This, however, is the way
that every theory should be treated, and no harm will be done if

when a new idea is launched it is regarded with due reserve, but also without prejudice."[1]

These words from Gladwin instantly call to mind R. J. C. Atkinson's observation on the changing concept and purpose of archaeology. Atkinson's comment, it must be stressed, is quoted quite out of context in juxtaposition to Gladwin's, for Atkinson was hypothesizing on Stonehenge; but his words seem too eminently pertinent to be shunted aside for that reason.

"I make no pretence," Atkinson admitted, "that these speculations are anything but the purest fancy. Nevertheless I rehearse them quite unrepentantly, for it seems to me that this is the *kind* of information that archaeology should seek to collect, if only the evidence is available. Even fifty years ago, most modern archaeological doctrine would have been unthinkable, and archaeologists would have protested that the nature of the evidence was such that it could not permit such interpretations as are now drawn from it. The change is not due to the development of scientific techniques of research, but simply to the growth of ideas about what archaeology is *for*. The wildest fancies of today may thus well become the commonplace orthodoxies of tomorrow."[2]

Gladwin's theory must indeed be placed in this category of "wildest fancies," but who is to say that it or another equally startling might not become "the commonplace orthodoxy of tomorrow"?

Go back, says Gladwin. Go back to 323 B.C., when Alexander the Great had just conquered most of the known world. Beginning with Greece, Alexander had swept through Asia Minor, Syria, Phoenicia, Palestine, Egypt, Persia, and part of India. In his wake lay dozens of cities, perhaps as many as seventy, not ravaged or smashed like Tyre but newly sprung from the plains and valleys: cities which Alexander had founded. For the fiery Macedonian was no mere conqueror; he was a colonizer dreaming grandiose dreams. Was he weeping now for more worlds to conquer? On the contrary, says Gladwin. Having recently built a magnificent fleet, Alexander was too busy planning further exploration and colonization.

This fleet, which forms the basis of Gladwin's hypothesis, is said to have boasted eight hundred ships, some so large that they carried crews of five or six hundred men. The crews, like the ship-wrights and carpenters, had been recruited from the entire eastern end of the Mediterranean. The mariners who comprise Gladwin's cast of characters were "the most experienced seamen of their day—Phoenicians from the coast of Syria, Greeks, Cyprians, Cretans, Egyptians. . . ."

Admiral Nearchus reported that the ships were fully equipped, manned, and provisioned. The fleet, harbored in the Gulf of Persia, was ready to sail. And at that fateful moment, the great Alexander died.

Pandemonium broke loose in the patchwork empire. Admiral Nearchus decided that his duty or his opportunity lay with Antigonus, and he left the fleet to join the general. What then became of the fleet, provisioned and ready to sail? History's only comment is one vast silence.

Into this breach steps Harold S. Gladwin. It was June, he points out, with the monsoon blowing steadily from the west. Westward into the wind lay barren, waterless Arabia. Beyond, if ever they reached it, lay home and probably chaos. Eastward lay lands to colonize. Therefore—and here Gladwin launches his giant conjecture—the fleet sailed eastward.

As we pause a moment to scrutinize Gladwin's assumption, counterindications immediately leap to mind. Two years earlier Alexander's Indian campaign had been curtailed when the army had balked at going farther. At the time of his sudden death Alexander was planning a voyage westward around Arabia. At the end of a war, moreover—if one may measure the ancient war-rior by the modern soldier—most fighting men are abruptly transferred into homing pigeons. But in 323 B.C. there were other considerations: the difficult circumnavigation of Arabia, a voyage of several thousand miles, to be followed by the chancy business of traversing conquered Egypt via the ancient canal (on which, since Pharaoh Necho's time, Darius the Great and Alex-ander himself had bent their efforts), before emerging at last into the Mediterranean and whatever might then prevail there. Add to this that restless element who never choose to go back. It is even conceivable that, in the general upheaval following the death of Alexander compounded by the defection of Nearchus and prob-

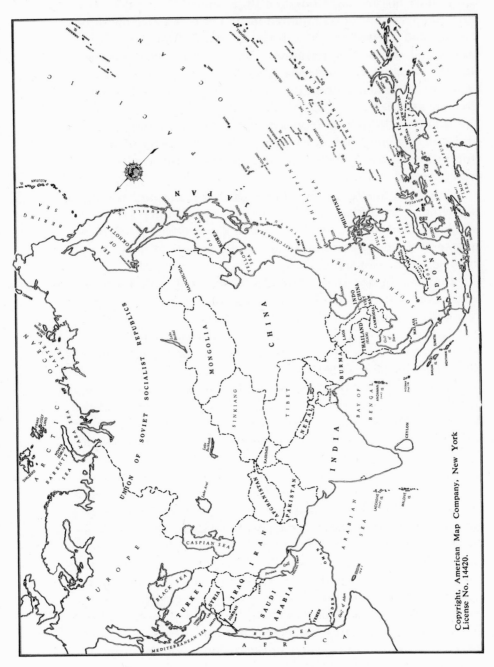

Asia

ably others, it was no longer possible to hold the huge fleet together, that ships turned sterns one to another and sailed off in opposite directions.

Granting Gladwin, therefore, at least a partial fleet to maneuver, we shall see where he takes them.

Setting out from the Gulf of Persia, Gladwin theorizes, the great fleet sailed eastward, following the shoreline of southern Asia. They sailed down the west coast of India, around the tip, and up along the east coast, stopping from time to time and no doubt picking up native recruits. From India the fleet went its leisurely way to Burma, then southward along the Malay Peninsula. At its tip the wanderers turned again east, sailing along the northern shore of Sumatra, out through the Straits of Malacca, out to the East Indies. Here and there others joined them; here and there men dropped off. "We will begin," says Gladwin, "by leaving some of the Greek contingent on Sumatra in order to account for the line of native princes who claim direct descent from Alexander."

East of Sumatra lay other islands: Java, Borneo, and—farther along—New Guinea. The natives of New Guinea today are Negroes, but some have noses which Gladwin calls "very large, convex . . . best described as a caricature of the Armenoid or Jewish nose." This nose has puzzled many an anthropologist. "Why this exaggerated imitation of an Armenoid nose should appear in New Guinea is a mystery," wrote Earnest A. Hooton.[3] To Gladwin, however, the explanation is as obvious as the nose. "This nose," he states, "is not an imitation at all. It is the real thing, because Negroids in New Guinea acquired their Armenoid noses directly from the producer. You need only to cast your eye over some of the boats of our fleet to see the simon-pure article adorning the faces of the Armenians, Syrians, Phoenicians, Cyprians and Egyptians who make up a large part of the crews."

Satisfied that the lost fleet of Alexander got at least as far as New Guinea, Gladwin continues to move them along. In about 300 B.C., he believes, they were working eastward through the Carolines, Marshall, and Gilbert Islands, ready to push out into mid-Pacific. The many islands that dot the mid-Pacific like beads of a broken necklace are, though scattered over thousands of miles, terminologically one large group: Polynesia. Thus Polynesia becomes the next conjectural stop.

Alexander's maritime band as it arrived in Polynesia was a far cry from the fleet that had upped anchor in the Gulf of Persia more than a quarter of a century before. The men were older, the ships were older, and probably many of both had been left or lost along the way. Supplementing the Levantine crews were natives, a motley group from the Ganges and Burma, Malaya, Sumatra, Java. Supplementing the fleet were canoes—canoes which were not only seaworthy but freighted with significance for Gladwin.

These canoes, as Gladwin visualizes them on the basis of later Polynesian canoes, were often a hundred feet long or longer. They were equipped with lateen sails, rows of paddles along each side—sometimes thirty paddles or more—and high prows which "seem to have been copied from the Greek ships," according to Gladwin. "It should help to reassure you," he adds, "to tell you that canoes of this kind are known on the Malabar coast of south-western India, in Madras on the east coast and in Burma and Siam —exactly along the route we have been tracing." Some of the smaller canoes had outriggers, "a cigar-shaped wooden float held parallel to the hull by horizontal booms. In the larger craft this had been carried a step further by substituting another canoe for the float, the result being two parallel canoes, spaced and held in position by spars on which a deck has been laid, and on which food, women, children and supplies have been stowed. There is usually some sort of awning over the deck."[4] That such a craft could sail the Pacific has been demonstrated many times over. These giant canoes were certainly no less seaworthy than the Kon-Tiki, a raft of balsa logs which carried six Scandinavians across four thousand miles of Pacific from Peru to Polynesia in 1947.

And now the strange fleet that had once been Alexander's and its heterogeneous crew are presumed to be somewhere in Polynesia, ready to start the last long leg of the journey. The picture fogs a bit here; but, as Gladwin and others have pointed out, Brigham Young led the Mormons from Illinois to Utah as recently as 1847, and were it not for the written records (including Mormon inscriptions on headstones) it would be impossible to trace their trail across the prairies today.

The fleet or parts of it reached the Americas, Gladwin believes. They landed on the west coast near the waspish waist of the western hemisphere, no farther north than Mexico, no farther south than the northern bulge of South America. And the Spaniards who arrived some eighteen centuries later found civilization far more advanced in these very sections than anywhere else in the New World.

There was more than one landing, in Gladwin's opinion. In fact, he suggests that probably many such caravans crossed the Pacific over a period of centuries. He dates this migration as having occurred likely between 300 B.C. and 500 A.D. Some of the men of Alexander, some of their children's children, and descendants dozens of generations removed took the last long step, he believes, landing at various points of Middle and South America.

This contention he bulwarks with a hundred pages of reasons. Choosing among them arbitrarily for the sake of brevity, I shall limit this recapitulation to six.

First, the helmets, which point to the sailors of Alexander themselves. Going ashore, Gladwin theorizes, the men anticipated a fight and donned their Grecian helmets. No such helmet seems to have survived these twenty-two centuries, but ancient Mochica pottery found in Peru carries illustrations of crested helmets, from which Gladwin infers that Peruvian Indians made their own copies. "They were tight-fitting caps of wickerwork, surmounted by a curved crest, the whole covered with feathers and exactly the same shape as the Greek helmet of the days of Alexander. The resemblance is so perfect," Gladwin says, "that the question has been raised as to whether they were not copies from late European models, but this idea was scotched by Captain Cook who found them in fashion in Hawaii when this first European contact with Polynesia was made."[5]

From helmets we turn our attention to Panpipes. The Panpipe is a primitive wind instrument not only played by but also invented by the goat-footed Greek god Pan—or so the myth has it. But here were Panpipes in Panama, Colombia, and Peru—

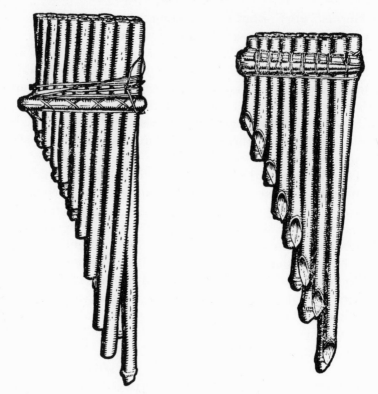

FIGURE 77. Panpipes from the Solomon Islands (left) and Bolivia (right).

before Columbus—and Panpipes in the Solomon Islands, those Pacific islands lying just east of New Guinea. Coincidence? Independently invented? Perhaps; but a fairly complicated coincidence and a distinctive instrument. Some may regard it as significant, Gladwin adds, that the pipes in the Solomon Islands and those in South America "have been shown by Hornbostel to have tonal identity and the same pitch."[6]

Exhibit three is the game of parchesi, which comes to us from India and appears to have been a popular pastime also in prehistoric Mexico. "Parchesi, as you probably know," Gladwin explains, "is played on a board laid out like a cross, each arm ruled off into spaces to make ladders. Each player has four colored disks or men, and, by casts of the dice, these climb the ladders or are sent home. The game called parchesi is ancient beyond memory in India, but the same game, called patolli, was known in prehistoric Mexico. Such similarity in minor details is often more convincing than the more spectacular contraptions."[7]

A more spectacular contraption he mentions is the vertical loom, in use from the American Southwest down to Peru, "exactly the same as that found in Egypt." (Kenneth Macgowan has pointed out further that pre-Colombian looms found in the New World "have the same eleven working parts" as those found in the Old.[8])

By way of spectacular processes Gladwin offers metallurgy. Not only smelting, plating, sintering, welding, soldering, forging, and filigree—with gold, silver, platinum, copper, and lead—but also the intricate process of casting by the lost-wax method. All of these techniques were known and all of these metals used by the South American Indians of Colombia and Peru hundreds of years before Columbus. Before that, all of these techniques and metals were known in the Near and Middle East. Gladwin finds it both strange and significant that, whereas progress in metallurgy was painfully slow in the Old World, in the "isolated" New World there is no evidence of an experimental period. From the first use of copper anywhere—probably in Armenia in about 5500 B.C, he indicates—thousands of years were required for the development of the techniques listed above. But in America metallurgy seems to have burst forth suddenly in fullest flower—at a level, moreover, which has never again been achieved by American Indians in post-Columbian times.

And finally, there is the weird practice of head deformation. To Gladwin it seems far more than coincidental that, in three widely separated parts of the globe, people with prominent convex noses have tried to improve upon nature by changing the shape of the human head. He begins in the Near East with the Armenoids, whose noses "first appeared on frescoes depicting ancient Hittites, later becoming the hallmark of all peoples of the eastern Mediterranean." In the Levant these Armenoids intentionally flattened the heads of their children until they "have sometimes been classed as sugarloaf." Jumping to the Pacific, he finds the same practice in Samoa, Tonga, the Marquesas, Fiji, and throughout Polynesia. There too parents shaped the heads of their infants to their taste by pressing flat stones or pieces of wood against the top or sides of the infant's head or by flattening the forehead and occasionally the nose with the palm of the hand. Again in the New World—in Peru, Central America, Mexico— cranial deformation appeared. Even the Mayas practiced it, they of the advanced culture and the great hooked noses which they carved "in stone on their steles with such emphasis that it looks as if they were trying to out-nose the Armenoids."9

Gladwin does not rest his case here, but I shall. The reader who wishes to study Gladwin's full reconstruction should consult his *Men out of Asia,* a fresh and provocative book.

To attempt an evaluation of Gladwin's hypothesis on the basis of the six reasons cited above, hand-picked at that, would be manifestly unjust. These are, I might add, not straw men set up to be knocked down with a flourish. On the contrary, I deliberately selected his arguments which seemed to me most persuasive. Now, looking back over them, I see that they serve to illustrate several different aspects of this involute problem of contact.

To begin with an aspect illustrated by the Hindu game of parchesi: the time element. The more enlightened cultures of Middle America did indeed bear marks of pre-Columbian Hindu contact. Parchesi is a prime example, but there are several others almost as close. One may tell himself that the resemblances are purely accidental; but I at least tried it and failed. How, then, did these Hindu influences cross the Pacific? They *could* have come in the ships of Alexander. Or they could have been carried across in those native canoes quite without Alexander's assistance: crumbs of culture passing from hand to hand, from mainland to island to island to mainland. This would have been later, possibly much later—not before the central and eastern Pacific islands were peopled, and probably not before the era of the great Polynesian voyages of approximately 500-1200 A.D. For this reason we need to know more. If cultural duplications which could have come only across the Pacific can be pinned down to a period *after* 323 B.C. but *before* the era of Polynesian seafaring, then Gladwin's Alexandrian conjecture will take on considerable weight.

The helmets illustrate another facet: the gradual diffusion of an idea from a focal point. These large crested wicker helmets are astonishingly suggestive of those we have seen depicted on

FIGURE 78. Helmeted Hittite warriors. Carchemish, *c.* 9th century B.C.

ancient Greeks. To hear that such a helmet was adorning the head of a native when the first white man stepped ashore in Polynesia is surely to wonder. The time differential of some two thousand years fades into unimportance, given the ultraconservatism of less highly developed civilizations. There *must* be an answer, and possibly Gladwin has it. But helmets were neither a Grecian invention nor a Grecian monopoly. The Grecian helmet, like much that was Greek, was borrowed from earlier cultures. It seems to have been modeled after those of the ancient Hittites (Figure 78); and other Mediterranean people had borrowed it too before the Greeks.

On the southern coast of Cyprus, early colonized by Phoenicians, rose the city of Amathus, where the Phoenician language, religion, and political supremacy are believed to have survived down to the time of Alexander. Here in the nineteenth century General di Cesnola came upon the necropolis, the unmolested tombs and sarcophagi of the rulers and high priests of Amathus, now lying some forty to fifty feet underground, which yielded archaeological treasure far richer than any found in the oft-pillaged tombs of Phoenicia proper. Among his finds was the so-called cup of Amathus, actually a silver plate. This plate, a portion of which is shown in Figure 79, interests us at the mo-

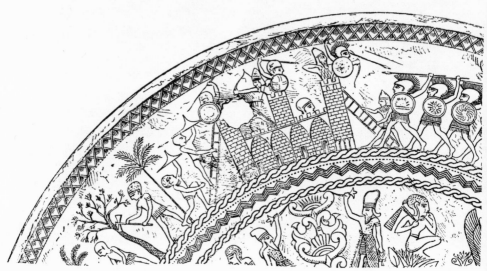

FIGURE 79. Detail from the Amathus cup.

ment because of the variety of helmets it displays. The assailants on the right are thought by some to represent Greeks, specifically the Greeks who attacked Amathus in 500 B.C. Strangely, however, one of the defenders wears the same type of helmet and carries a similar shield. Another wears a conical helmet. And the defender in the center of the Assyrian-looking fortification and the defender on the extreme left wear helmets which resemble present-day football helmets or the helmets carved on Olmec "Baby-faces" in Middle America in about 500 B.C. If the artist was striving for realism in this little scene, then the Cypriot Phoenicians availed themselves of many models, in helmets as in sculpture, architecture, religion, and other matters.

In America, helmets were known in Peru and Mexico: the gods of Mexico were said to have worn them. And Montezuma, whose mother was a Toltec princess from Tula, told Cortés that the gods had come from the east. It is possible that similar helmets were dreamed up by the natives in these various places quite independently of each other, or of Europe, or of Asia. Possible but unlikely. How, then, to reconcile helmets putatively on the east coast of Mexico, depicted on pottery in Peru, and actually gracing the heads of Pacific islanders? One may choose from several explanations:

(1) The seamen of Alexander did indeed cross the Pacific and wade ashore prepared for a fight. This conjecture is supported by tangible evidence—paintings and helmets—but leaves the legendary gods who landed on the east coast of Mexico quite unexplained.

(2) Helmeted men from the Mediterranean crossed the Atlantic, not the Pacific, and came ashore in eastern Mexico. In due time helmeted men from Middle America ventured south to Peru. Much later, the sea-roving Polynesians found their way to this scarcely avoidable coastline and sailed back home with a helmet. Fantastic, you say. And yet there is strong archaeological support for the very part which sounds most preposterous: the round-trip visits of Polynesians to Peru and Middle America before the era of Columbus, a matter to be considered in the final chapter. This contact could also have been made in the opposite direction, from Peru to Polynesia, as Thor Heyerdahl dramatically demonstrated.

(3) Both might have occurred, a Macedonian ship arriving from across the Pacific and a Phoenician ship from across the Atlantic, between them circling the globe with crews who had much in common—including helmets. The fact that one group of ancients might have reached the New World does not *ipso facto* rule out the arrival of others. If anything, it enhances the possibility.

Finally, the gruesome practice of head deformation and the early American skill in metallurgy are of especial interest because now we can tag them with radiocarbon dates.

Along the arid coast of Peru, bodies and objects buried deeply—below the reach of occasional rainfall—have been astonishingly well preserved for more than two thousand years. Here, in a culture radiocarbon-dated as having flourished in about 700 B.C., are corpses whose heads were manually deformed in infancy. Ascribed to this period also are objects of gold and silver and copper which early metallurgists had welded or soldered or filigreed. These are believed to be the oldest examples of metallurgy in America.

In short, both head deformation and metallurgy were practiced in America several centuries before Alexander the Great ordered shipwrights of the eastern Mediterranean to build him a fleet.

This fact does not of necessity negate Gladwin's hypothesis. It does, however, remove two of his sturdier props. Gladwin's *Men out of Asia* was published in 1947—a comparatively recent work. Since then much has been learned and much that was previously known has been radiocarbon-dated. This may have been what Gladwin had in mind when he said that his tale would "undoubtedly need to be changed." Every archaeologist who deals with the recrudescent past confronts the same possibility. No one may cherish dogmas—though many do.

What *did* become of the fleet of Alexander? Who can say? The farther Gladwin leads it away from the home port, the fainter its wake; or so it seems to me. Gladwin argues persuasively, and one follows along entranced past India, Burma, Sumatra, even out to New Guinea. This part of his theory alone would answer several questions, as he himself pointed out.

Having voyaged this far, however, Alexander's ragged band

might well have been weary of wandering; and ahead lay the whole vast empty Pacific. Gladwin himself looked beyond, saw the Americas, noted the numerous artifacts bearing the thumbprint of just such people as made up his crews: men "from the eastern end of the Mediterranean . . . Phoenicians, Greeks, Cypriots, Cretans, Egyptians. . . ."

But one eclectic seafaring people from the eastern end of the Mediterranean had helped themselves freely to the cultures of all these: the Phoenicians.

And now, having followed the lost fleet of Alexander a long distance, we leave it and enter the lost civilizations of South America.

20

STRANGERS IN
SOUTH AMERICA

O N THE COAST of Venezuela, where the waves of the
Caribbean wash the northern bulge of South America, a
most unusual find was made: a jar containing several hundred
Roman coins. The coins date from the reign of Augustus down to
about 350 A.D. and cover every intervening period. Now in the
possession of Mendel L. Peterson of the Smithsonian Institution,
the coins include many duplicates, from which it has been inferred
that they were not the misplaced collection of a numismatist but
were probably once a Roman trader's ready cash, carefully buried
in the sand by their owner or washed ashore after a shipwreck.

The picture that flashes unsummoned on the screen of
the mind—of Roman seamen splashing ashore in Venezuela in the
fourth century—is unsupported by documentary proof, but the
coins alone might give pause to those who too quickly voice their
thunderous "No."

The sprawling continent of South America must here receive
inadequate treatment. Despite the army of archaeologists who
have dug and delved there in recent years, too little is known of

its preconquest past—and at the same time too much. To read all that has been published on the Incas alone would be the major work of a lifetime. And yet the people who concern us most are not the Incas but rather their nebulous predecessors who are only now emerging as nameless enigmas.

In this and following chapters I propose to treat of those earlier cultures that nurtured the Inca and, insofar as data permits, of the people who shaped them, limiting the discussion to the western coastal and Andean regions because there where extensive work has been done the picture, though still sketchy, is beginning to assume an outline. To be sure, it is far from complete as yet, and far from consistent. Here and there one sees indications that Peruvian Indians lifted themselves by their own bootstraps without any boosts from a bearded Fair God; and here and there in juxtaposition stand strong implications of early contact with the ancient Near East or with Europe.

The pathway into the past of the southern continent is tortuous, endlessly bifurcated, and leads at last only to the aspirin bottle. Rather than attempt to follow it mile by wearying mile, we shall touch down upon it now and again at points of especial interest.

It was 1527 when Francisco Pizarro, sailing down the Pacific in a small Spanish caravel, skirted and cased the Peruvian coast. What he saw he deemed worthy of taking, and so he returned to Spain to plan and prepare. It was May 13, 1532, when he returned to conquer.

Stepping ashore near Tumbez, the northernmost coastal city of the Inca realm and its first city south of the jungle, Pizarro and his audacious band of only 180 soldiers found themselves in a flourishing empire, an empire of absolute and despotic power, a militaristic welfare-state which controlled the destiny of every citizen from womb to tomb—quite unlike the loosely-knit Aztec confederation that Cortés had smashed eleven years earlier. The Inca Empire, stretching 2,500 miles along the Pacific, included most of what are now Ecuador, Peru, and Bolivia and part of Chile. In area it was roughly equivalent to the American colonies at the time of the Revolution. Its population, as estimated by Steward, was three and a half million.

Not only its size impressed the handful of Spanish conquistadors. They marched to conquest on wide and well-engineered Peruvian roads, roads which led them beside the sea, across the desert, and over great walls of mountains. On their southward march they passed truncated temple-pyramids, swarming cities, and vast irrigation projects. An anonymous conquistador recording his impression of Pachacamac, a mecca near Lima, wrote: "This town is larger than Rome."[1]

Six months after they had disembarked, the conquistadors came to Cajamarca. There they captured the last Lord Inca, Atahualpa, held him for the fabulous golden ransom, watched golden art works come pouring in by the hundreds of llama-loads, and saw the large treasure room filling with gold to the high white line "above the reach of a man." Having received their millions in golden ransom, the Spaniards declared Atahualpa free; then presently in brutal treachery they tried him on trumped-up charges and graciously granted him the choice of being burned alive or, if he accepted Christianity, death by garroting.

This bloody-black tale has been told long since by Prescott in his *History of the Conquest of Peru*. High tragedy though it is, this is scarcely the place to rehearse it. Rather, one wishes to peer behind it into the mind of Atahualpa, for this forceful young emperor was no vacillating Montezuma, nor was he poorly informed, nor did he mistake the Spaniards for gods—except at first.

Within hours after the Spaniards had disembarked, native couriers were speeding up the Andes in relays with a full report for Atahualpa. The number of men and nameless animals was correct. The creatures were reported to have "feet of silver," and beast and rider were one. Later couriers corrected this misinformation: the beast was a kind of sheep.

At the moment he received this startling intelligence Atahualpa was resting at Cajamarca, having just completed five years of murderous warfare to establish his claim to the Inca-ship over that of his brother. Soon he would enter the capital, Cuzco, in triumph. And now when he heard that bearded white men had arrived from over the sea, he who had conquered all envisioned one further triumph. Only the gods were white and bearded. These must be the envoys of Viracocha himself, the god of civilization, who, in ages past, had gone off over the waters. There would never be so triumphal an entry as Atahualpa's!

So he lingered at Cajamarca, awaiting the gods and the demigods who were coming to conduct him to Cuzco.

But while he was waiting, the gods en route were behaving strangely like men. Atahualpha, informed of their deeds along with their progress, began to entertain doubts. When word reached him that the bearded strangers had stopped at Caxas in northern Peru and raped his five hundred sacrosanct Virgins of the Sun who were vowed to perpetual chastity, he knew for a certainty that these were no gods and that this was not Viracocha.

He let them come on nonetheless, innocent as he was of firearms. The invaders were few in number, and surely no more would be coming from over the sea. Let them come on to Cajamarca where Atahualpa was waiting, surrounded by his thousands of veteran warriors. Let them come on to Cajamarca and enter his trap. . . .

The great Alexander von Humbolt, who visited Peru in the late eighteenth century, once remarked that it was indeed a peculiar circumstance among the American Indian nations that, in no less than three remarkable instances, superior civilization had been attributed by ancient traditions and records to the sudden presence among the natives of "persons differing from themselves in appearance and descent."

The conquering Spaniards who followed Columbus had traveled widely in this strange Stone Age world of tepees and tomahawks, observing life as it might have existed aeons before. Till at length—in Mexico, in Central America, and again in Peru —they had come upon people of more advanced cultures; and in each case preconquest native legends attributed this higher culture to bearded white gods. The story of Quetzalcoatl is not unique, and in repetition it gathers strength.

For although culture gods are common creations of primitive man, culture gods who were bearded and white, created moreover by Indians who were beardless and tawny and had presumably never set eyes on a white man, are indeed a different matter. Found in association not only with higher civilizations but also with traces of Old World culture, these legends begin to seem more than the figments of three overactive and oddly repetitive imaginations.

Kon-Tiki Viracocha, the Peruvian Fair God, was said to have been a white man—"extremely white" like the Spaniards, so they were told—with a long, flowing beard. A gentleman of imposing mien, of medium height or sometimes described as tall, he wore a long robe. That these details were not invented on sight to please the Spaniards is evidenced by pre-Hispanic statues depicting Viracocha as robed and bearded, and by the fact that the natives addressed the first Spaniards they saw as Viracocha.

This Fair God, whose name means "foam of the sea," told the natives that he was a son of the sun. According to legend, he and his people lived on an island in a huge lake (probably Titicaca). Later they moved to Tiahuanaco, where they erected large stone structures. Viracocha was not only an architect but also a sculptor and engineer. "He caused terraces and fields to be formed on the steep sides of ravines, and sustaining walls to rise up and support them. He also made irrigating channels to flow . . . and he went in various directions, arranging many things."[2] Till at length, still long before the day of the Incas, he sailed away over the Pacific, first telling the natives that in time to come he would send his envoys to teach and protect them.

The similarity of the various versions suggest the possibility of a single source. But it also suggests most persuasively that somewhere in Mexico, Central, or South America countless centuries before Columbus a bearded white man did indeed walk among the natives as teacher and leader.

Viracocha was not the only culture god worshiped in South America. There was also Bohica (or sometimes Bochica), who is said to have appeared in Colombia. Legend relates that Bohica, described like the others as bearded and white, "appeared to the Mozca Indians in the plains of Bogota, taught them how to build and to sow, formed them into communities, gave them an outlet to the waters of the great lake, and . . . settled the government."[3]

For perhaps a thousand years before the Spaniards arrived, historians aver, while neighboring tribes lived as savages these Mozca or Muysca Indians possessed a higher though mixed culture. Semibarbaric, they nevertheless used coins—round tiles of gold without any stamp or marking. They lived in large timber houses, often shaped like a pyramid and cemented with adobe clay. They carried their chiefs on wooden litters, and their distinguished dead they mummified.

Last in the cavalcade of South American strangers is a flamboyant creature called Naymlap. Different in tone, the legend of Naymlap serves as an antidote to an excess of sweetness and light and provides also a glittering picture of an immigration in process, as the natives believed that their forefathers had actually witnessed it in Lambayeque, a Peruvian province which lies along the Pacific. The Lambayeque legend, as it is called, has broad archaeological support. It was recorded thus by the early Jesuit father, Miguel Cabello de Balboa:

"The people of Lambayeque say—and with them agree all the folk living in the vicinity of this valley—that in times so very ancient that they do not know how to express them, there came from the northerly part of this Piru, with a great fleet of balsas, a father of Families, a man of much valor and quality named Naymlap; and with him he brought many concubines, but the chief wife is said to have been named Ceterni.

"He brought in his company many people who followed him as their Captain and leader. But those among them who were of the greatest bravery were their officials, who were forty in number, including such men as Pita Zofi, who was the trumpeter or player upon certain great shells that are much esteemed among the Indians. Another was Ninacola, who was in charge of the litter and Throne; another was Ninagintue, in whose care was the drink of that Lord, after the fashion of a Butler; another was called Fonga Sigde, whose duty it was to scatter the dust of seashells upon the ground where his Lord was to Tread; another, Occhocalo, was his cook; another had charge of the ointments and color with which the Lord was wont to adorn his countenance, this official being Xam Muchec. Ollopcopoc supervised the bathing of the Lord. Another very important official, much esteemed by his Prince, was called Llapchillulli, and he wrought shirts and clothing of feathers. With this retinue, and with an infinite number of other officials and men of importance, he [Naymlap] brought his person and house, already adorned and established.

"With all his possessions this Lord, Naymlap, made port and landed at the mouth of a River which is today called Paquisllanga, and having there abandoned their *balsas,* they went inland, desirous of making a settlement, and having advanced half a league, they built certain Palaces after their fashion to which they gave the name of Chot."[4]

All of which smacks of the gaudy splendor of Montezuma or of the Maya love of display and face-paints. Indeed some archaeologists, offering the balsas as evidence that the Naymlap party had come from no very great distance, select Central America as the starting point of the expedition. The Spaniards, one recalls, also reached Peru by sailing from the Pacific coast of Central America, where the overland distance between the oceans is minimal.

Others have detected, in Naymlap's elegant entourage, echoes of ancient Oriental pomp. David had his list of royal officials, and Solomon his, modeled on the courts of Babylon, Thebes, and Ashur. Sennacherib of Assyria in the eighth century B.C. counted among his administrators a grand vizier, chief cupbearer, chief cellarer, chamberlain of the palace, lotion-maker, and chief cook.

Naymlap—and this is what gives him especial interest—lived many centuries before the Aztecs, possibly back in the earliest days of the Maya Old Empire. The Lambayeque legend continues by listing the rulers who followed Naymlap. Except for an interregnum of indeterminate length, it brings us all the way down to the time of the Spanish conquest. On the basis of this dynastic history, the late Philip Ainsworth Means, outstanding Peruvianist and one-time director of the National Museum of Archaeology at Lima, Peru, estimated that "we may reasonably assume that the Naymlap dynasty flourished some time during the first six centuries or so of our Era or, in other words, during the Early Chimu period."[5]

Now, the Early Chimú period, exemplifying the fluid state of Peruvian archaeology, has undergone one and possibly two name changes since Means wrote these lines. First, to distinguish it from the Chimú period which came later, it was renamed Mochica after the language spoken in this area when the Spaniards arrived. Recently Peruvianists have suggested that Moche, the name of a site, might be a preferable name for the period, for it is not known what language these people spoke in the early centuries of the Christian era.

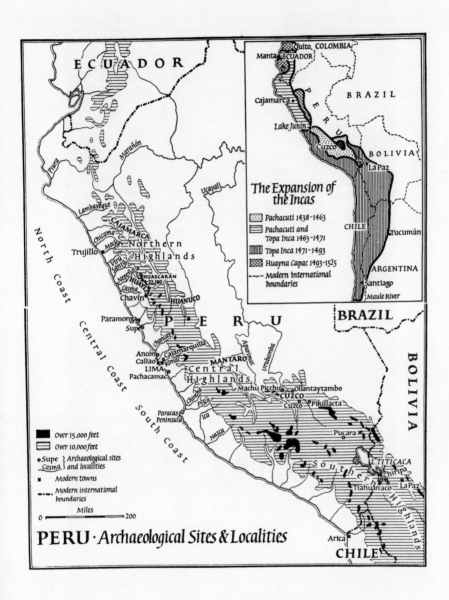

The Expansion of
the Incas

▦ Pachacuti 1438-1463
▥ Pachacuti and
   Topa Inca 1463-1471
▨ Topa Inca 1471-1493
▩ Huayna Capac 1493-1525
--- Modern international
   boundaries

■ Over 15,000 feet
▥ Over 10,000 feet
● Supe ⎫ Archaeological sites
Casma ⎭ and localities
× Modern towns
--- Modern international
   boundaries

Miles
0 ⟞━━━━━▸ 200

PERU · Archaeological Sites & Localities

Archaeological sites of Peru

FIGURE 80.   Mochica warrior, Trujillo.
A. Folkwang-Museum, Hagen i. W.

FIGURE 80. Mochica warrior, Trujillo.
B. Museo Nacional de Antropología y Arqueología, Lima.

All this to explain why I use the standardized term "Mochica" rather than the discarded "Early Chimú" in referring to the realistic pictorial pottery which dates from the period to which Means has assigned the legend of Naymlap and roughly to the same geographical area, the northern coastal region just south of the westernmost bulge of South America. Here native artists depicted on pottery the scenes they saw about them in daily life. Mochica pottery comprises an incredible picture-album of people going about their mundane business more than a thousand years ago.

If a stranger called Naymlap arrived from afar, what did he and his entourage look like? It would be presumptuous and perhaps erroneous to assume that they looked like the people found on Mochica pottery. And yet these are the people closest in time and place whose likenesses may still be seen today. So, with these reservations, we might glance at two Mochica warriors depicted on stirrup-spout bottles (Figure 80).

The Mochica warrior in Figure 80B wears a cone-shaped helmet and a knee-length tunic with short sleeves. He carries a spear-thrower and two javelins, and from his waist hangs a large ax head which, as Means observed, "must have jabbed him cruelly now and then as he walked." His face, as Means also saw fit to mention, "is heavily painted with dark pigment save around the eyes, in which we see an interesting corroboration of what Father Cabello de Balboa has to say concerning Xam Muchec, guardian of the royal face-paints." This soldier's feet and legs, we note too, were painted as if to give the appearance of boots.

Face paint seems also to adorn the visage of an important personage depicted, on another Mochica pottery vessel, receiving litter-borne visitors. Class consciousness, indicated by a wide range

FIGURE 81.   Mochica chief receiving litter-borne visitors.

FIGURE 82.   Huaca del Sol, Moche.

of distinctive costumes, marked the Mochica world; the litter
bearers in this gay scene appear to be attired in their birthday
suits (Figure 81).

When these Mochicas gazed about, their glance fell upon a
burgeoning culture: first upon enormous pyramids, the outstanding example being the Huaca del Sol, a terraced platform 750 by
450 feet surmounted by a stepped pyramid, constructed of some
130,000,000 sun-dried bricks (Figure 82). Nearby in this coastal
desert were vast irrigation projects, canals, and aqueducts. One
huge aqueduct in the Chicama Valley was almost a mile long.

Aqueducts at once suggest Rome and the splendid Roman
examples still standing today; yet aqueducts were invented long
before Roman times. One of earlier construction was an aqueduct that carried water three miles to the original village of
Mainland Tyre in the second millennium B.C., when the inhabitants, few in number, still dwelt atop a huge rock that jutted

Figure 83. Coastal road and Mochica pyramid near Trujillo.

some fifty feet above the surrounding plain. There were aqueducts in Mexico too; a double one conducted a large stream of water to the fountains and reservoirs of Mexico-Tenochtitlán.

In the territory of the Mochicas there were also roads—roads of a seemingly standard width of thirty-three feet, wider than many a modern highway, though Mochica roads were used only for foot traffic. Wide roads, anciently paved, have been found too in the coastal swamps of Mexico and Central America.

Roads, like aqueducts, at once suggest Rome, and surely the world's two great early road systems were those of the Incas and the Romans, both constructed for the same purpose: control of an empire (Figure 83). But the idea of roads originated with

neither Incas nor Romans. Before the Incas, the Chimús, the Tiahuanacos, and the Mochicas had roads; before the Romans, the
Persians and the Assyrians. The royal road built by King Sargon
of Assyria in the eighth century B.C. was paved, forty feet wide,
and marked by milestones. But his son exceeded him. Sennacherib's road was seventy-eight feet wide, and alongside it he set up
a stone with this warning: "Royal Road, let no man decrease it."
Anyone, Sennacherib added, who should encroach on the width
of the road by restoring his home was to be impaled on a pole
before it. Width, it seems, was a point of pride.

The royal roads of the Persians which the Phoenicians found
so convenient for their land trade also had stone mile markers,
as did the royal roads of the Romans and Incas. And another important adjunct: couriers who raced up and down the roads bearing messages written or oral. Herodotus in the fifth century B.C.
described the Persian relay system and the post houses set at intervals along the roads. "The whole idea," he says, "is a Persian
invention." And now we see, along the Mochica roads, platforms
at intervals suggesting a relay system. And more than that; we
learn from Mochica pottery that couriers went speeding along the
roads with messages, even as Roman couriers shortly before had
hurried along the roads to Rome and a millennium later the Inca
couriers hastened to Cuzco.

Mochica couriers are depicted as carrying small sacks; along
with these, small objects are shown which seem to be lima beans
incised or painted with strange markings. The Peruvianist Ra-
phael Larco Hoyle sees in these symbols a close resemblance to
Maya glyphs. On still other Mochica pottery, persons are portrayed
as studying such beans, and these men, Larco Hoyle believes, are
decoders. Other Peruvianists are not convinced that Mochica beans
carried glyphic writing, though the question remains at this
moment open.[6]

Other Mochica feats are accepted without question. Mochica
doctors are known to have performed circumcision (that important ancient Semitic rite which originated, so tradition has it,
in Phoenicia when the god El circumcised himself). Mochica
doctors also performed more intricate operations, including the
amputations so naturalistically portrayed on Mochica pottery.

Here weaving was done on a "shop" basis, the overseer sitting
beneath his sunshade while rows of women worked at their looms

FIGURE 84.   Amputee depicted on Mochica pottery.

—again according to Mochica pottery. And gold was being cast.

Is this what Naymlap wrought? Perhaps. Perhaps some of these concepts, inventions, and cultural appurtenances were brought in by outsiders from a source as yet undetermined. But some were doubtless inherited from earlier Peruvians, for the Mochicas were not the first in Peru to attain a higher culture.

Before the Mochicas the Gallinazo, in the Virú Valley of this northern coast, had also had pyramids, irrigation, metallurgy. The Gallinazo culture was recently radiocarbon-dated as of, roughly, 450 B.C.

And there were others before the Gallinazo. . . .

All that the Spaniards saw and heard in Peru they called Inca. In this they were only parroting an error of the Incas themselves, whose error, however, stemmed not from honest ignorance but from intent to deceive. A deliberate campaign for Inca aggrandizement not unlike that which has emanated in recent years from Moscow was achieved by what Harold Osborne has termed the "selective manipulation of history"—that is, by "editing" the memories of the people and by "selective distortion."[7]

For the Incas, like the Aztecs, "arrived" late. The first Inca ruler, the legendary Manco Capac, may have flourished in about 1200 A.D., though the date is still in dispute. The amazing expansion of the Inca empire, however, came later, beginning in about 1438. In less than one century the Incas not only overran all neighboring Andean tribes but, extending their domination farther and ever farther, well into Ecuador and Chile, soon were ruling an area of about 350,000 square miles. In order to mold the scattered peoples whom they had conquered into one vast cohesive empire, the Inca government deliberately undertook an empire-wide sponging of memory. All earlier cultures must be forgotten, along with the fact that from these cultures the Incas had inherited or appropriated almost everything they possessed— except organization.

In this effort the Inca "historians" were aided by an absence of written records, for no pre-Columbian South American ever learned to write. (To this there are dissenting opinions but as yet no widely acceptable proof.) The only Peruvian "book" was a system of knotted cords called a *quipu,* the only "written" words a series of knots—knots in strings of different colors, knots of varying shapes and sizes.

And yet on these simple quipus the Inca government, ruling a far-flung empire, kept all its records: its tax records "with such accuracy," as Pedro de Cieza de León described them, "that not so much as a pair of sandals would be missing." There was even a "symbol" for zero: appropriately, an empty space, no knot where one might have been expected. For zero was an essential concept in the Peruvian mathematical system, a decimal system involving place value. There was also a method of recording historic names and events. And always, of course, an interpreter, for quipus were no more than mnemonic devices. It has, in fact, been said that the Incas kept their records in "human files"—professional rememberers who knew the meaning of every knot.

Today the few quipus that survived the evangelistic zeal of the Spanish fathers and those recovered from tombs hang limp and mute and meaningless. Many of the memorizers were eliminated by the Spanish conquest, and presently time erased the rest.

FIGURE 85. Inca quipu-camoyoc, quipu, and counting device. From Poma de Ayala, Inca-Spanish chronicler, *c.* 1565.

The first hiatus in the study of early South America, then, is the absence of written records; the last, the loss of quipus and rememberers. Between, in a gap as wide, stand the Incas themselves, manipulating history, twisting the facts as nimbly as the *quipu-camayoc* knotted the strings. For the official rememberers were trained by the Incas to forget, if ever they knew, that important cultures had flourished and died here before the Inca civilization. The official Inca line was that all culture had sprung from the deeply fertile creative genius of the Incas, who had found the land culturally sterile, peopled only by savages.

Nothing, of course, was further from truth. One recalls the honest perplexity of that reliable reporter Pedro de Cieza de León, a Spanish soldier who rode down the length of the Inca highway. Coming in 1549 to Tiahuanaco, he wrote, "Tiahuanaco is not a very large village, but it is celebrated for the great edifices near it, which are certainly things worth seeing . . . vast foundations . . . which must have been standing for many ages. . . . For myself I fail to understand with what instruments or tools it could have been done; for it is very certain that before these great stones could be brought to perfection and left as we see them, the tools must have been much better than those now used by the Indians."[8]

Not only did the Incas, when they built their capital centuries later, borrow to some extent the architectural style of these already-ancient structures. It is believed that the Incas also borrowed the Fair God Viracocha from these same Tiahuanacos. (Or so the people are called today because the name by which they knew themselves has long been forgotten.) The larger-than-life-size head carved atop the great monolithic gateway at Tiahuanaco is said to be a representation of Viracocha, with forty-eight little figures running toward him (Figure 86).

Three decades ago Ronald L. Olson labeled the larger development of the Andean cultures "one of retrogression from the superior to the inferior." Olson added, "We can dismiss the retrogressive evolution of the culture of Peru by stating that evolution does not always result in progress. But we must still account for the appearance of the Early Chimu and Nazca cultures. Spontaneous and sudden generation does not take place in the cultural sphere any more than in the biological. It must be, therefore, that back of the Early Chimu and Early Nazca periods lie long epochs of growth and development. The search for remains from these preceding periods has so far proved fruitless. . . ."[9]

But this was three decades ago. Since that not-so-distant date an enormous amount of archaeological research has been carried on in South America. Layer after layer has been peeled back, and

FIGURE 86. Monolithic gateway, Tiahuanaco, Bolivia.

in many places the spade has bitten down to the empty earth. Now the prehistory of South America is in process of being told once more, not by empire-cementing Incas but by fact-dredging archaeologists.

That story, still sketchy and not yet fully assessed, will be recounted briefly in the following chapter.

UP FROM SAVAGERY

SOUTH AMERICA was discovered, obviously, from North America. The discoverer was a simple fellow, a hunter, a fisherman, a gatherer rather than a grower of food: a Stone-Ager. He was a dolicocephalic Asiatic who had, in all likelihood, crossed into Alaska at Bering Strait and had wandered down the length of the northern continent armed with his spear and spear-thrower, for the bow and arrow were still far in the future. In due time he filtered through the bottleneck of Panama and arrived at another great continent.

How long ago? Who can say? Perhaps shortly before 8000 B.C., give or take a millennium. The refuse of human occupation found in a cave near the southernmost tip of South America has been tested and dated as of approximately 6700 B.C.

Thus South American man arrived and in this same condition he lived for many millennia—and some still do, notably the aborigines of Tierra del Fuego. But farther north in South America, where other Protomongoloids meanwhile were drifting in, things at length began to stir.

Just when the idea of planting and thus to some extent controlling his food supply rather than merely gathering whatever grew wild first occurred to a South American is still undetermined. "The idea is a perfectly natural one," as J. Alden Mason pointed out, "that might have presented itself to any people, and possibly it occurred to several independent groups at more or less the same time; on the other hand, the suggestion may have come from across the Pacific."[1]

There can be little doubt that Alaska was still a port of entry long after the Old World invention of agriculture, but whether any of the immigrants who wandered into South America during this period were agriculturalists is a moot question. The farmer is not a nomad; but through the ages nomads have gazed upon the farmer toiling among his crops and have gone their way with mixed emotions of longing and revulsion.

The invention of agriculture—probably the most important discovery in the long history of mankind—is believed to have occurred originally in the Old World's Fertile Crescent before 5000 B.C. From there the idea of growing one's food was passed along or borrowed. V. Gordon Childe in his *Dawn of European Civilization* and *New Light on the Most Ancient East* has traced its slow spread from southwestern Asia through Europe without a break till it reached the subarctic forests of northern Europe three thousand years later. At the same time and from the same source, the Fertile Crescent, agriculture was also spreading gradually in other directions. Which is not to say categorically that it was carried into South America but rather that the Old World pattern suggests that this may have happened.

The earliest known agricultural site in South America, as these lines are being written, is Huaca Prieta on the northern coast of Peru. The oldest C14-datable material from this oldest site—charcoal which lay upon bedrock at the lowermost level of the mound—has yielded the radiocarbon date of 2347 B.C. plus or minus a possible error of 230 years. This date for the charcoal, representing the earliest human habitation of the site, was acceptable to the veteran archaeologist who uncovered Huaca Prieta, Junius Bird. So we might step back and scrutinize this milestone.

By this date, 2347 B.C., the Old Kingdom of Egypt was nearing its close and the great pyramid of Khufu had already weathered the sands of three centuries. In the Sumerian-Assyrian-Babylonian world, Sargon I, having been set adrift on a stream in infancy like the later Moses and having been fetched from the stream for a purpose, was about to unite the fragments of Mesopotamia under his scepter. At the same time a large part of Europe was virgin forest; but it was one day to carry the mark of both these early civilizations, particularly the Mesopotamian.

The year 2347 B.C., however, should not be construed as marking the beginning of South American agriculture. As such the date could be challenged on two counts: earlier evidence of agriculture may yet be found elsewhere in South America; on the other hand and equally important, the first experiments in simple agriculture made at Huaca Prieta seem to have postdated by many centuries the sample of charcoal left by the earliest residents of the long-occupied site.

The simple paleolithic people who settled here in about 2347 B.C. lived largely by fishing, supplementing their diet by gathering foods that grew wild. At this distance in time it is difficult to say what may have been wild and what cultivated. There was no corn (maize), that later staple of the Indian diet which cannot survive unless tended by the hand of man, for when an ear of corn drops to the ground all of the seeds germinate, and the thickly massed seedlings soon die. Presently the people of Huaca Prieta had, however, other food plants which seem to have been cultivated: squash of a species believed to be of American origin; beans; and bottle gourds almost identical with those grown on the islands of Polynesia. There was also cotton—of which more in a moment.

A radiocarbon test (#L-116B) has ascribed the date 1699 B.C. plus or minus four hundred years to the first agricultural efforts at Huaca Prieta, the earliest agricultural site known thus far in South America. Again, this date is open to question but must serve at the moment.

"We scarcely give a thought to the very surprising fact," observed Geoffrey Bibby in his survey of prehistoric Europe, "that the time lag between the introduction of agriculture and the introduction of bronze remains practically constant."[2]

Agriculture was invented in southwestern Asia before 5000 B.C.; copper came into use in Mesopotamia and Egypt about a thousand years later; and bronze followed not long after. Regarded in this light, it is not surprising that copper and even bronze were in use in parts of the Western Hemisphere when the Spanish conquistadors arrived. But there were other surprises.

The residents of Huaca Prieta had no pottery[3] but instead used bottle gourds as utensils. They had no metals, of course, no ground stone tools. They lacked even tools made by pressure flaking, a technique which other American Indians had mastered thousands of years before. And yet the people of Huaca Prieta wove cloth. About three thousand fragments were found, all small—approximately eight by sixteen inches, a large percentage of them made by the primitive twining process; and most of the cloth was of cotton, none of wool.

Cotton exemplifies a new and exciting key to prehistory, the botanical approach, which may unlock the unwritten record of forgotten voyages even as radiocarbon dating is assigning calendrical dates to objects which only a few years ago were mutely timeless. At the moment, however, cotton is a botanist's nightmare, for when this ancient cotton from Huaca Prieta was examined, it was found to be an *Old World-New World hybrid*.

In the distant days before man domesticated plants, cotton grew wild in both hemispheres. The two wild types were, however, quite distinct: Old World cotton had thirteen large chromosomes, and wild American cotton had thirteen small chromosomes. But the cotton found at Huaca Prieta had twenty-six chromosomes, thirteen large and thirteen small. Botanists concluded that at one time some Old World cultivated cotton *must* have appeared in America and, growing side by side with American wild cotton, produced this strange new type.[4]

But how? One botanist suggested that this may have occurred by means of a Pacific land bridge in late Cretaceous or early Tertiary times. His theory was rejected on several grounds. From New Guinea to Peru the Pacific is almost 10,000 miles wide, and not much narrower in any latitude where cotton would thrive. And even if a land bridge once existed there, it had vanished before the origin of agriculture and, in fact, of man himself.[5] Cotton, in short, did not spread naturally to America; it was carried.

If cotton seeds were carried to America from Asia in the second millennium B.C., who were the carriers? Not birds, who won't touch the things. Not the west wind—not across the Pacific near the latitude of its greatest width. Not even the footsore Stone Age traveler whose time in transit up the length of Asia and down the length of the North American wilds far exceeded the germinative life of the seed. Which leaves only an unidentified man in a vessel.

We know a few facts about him. He was no primitive nomad who lived solely by hunting and gathering food. The cotton he carried aboard ship was cultivated rather than wild, and it was linted and therefore provided the raw material for weaving fabrics as other cottons did not. Before his time someone had perceived that cotton could be useful for more than its oily seeds and had developed a linted cotton. We know that the voyager's ship was probably sail propelled rather than merely adrift on the ocean, for, as Carter has pointed out, cotton seeds "rapidly lose their power to germinate when exposed to moist air."[6] His ship must have traveled on tropical or subtropical waters and landed on a tropical or subtropical American shore—probably the West Indies, Mexico, or Peru, for in these three areas tetraploid (26-chromosomed) cotton was cultivated in pre-Columbian times. Whether he crossed the Pacific or the Atlantic is a question still under discussion. At any rate, one need not postulate two very early and separate transoceanic voyages. A simpler exchange would have been between Middle and South American Indians, though which of them first grew cotton and possibly passed it along is not as yet clearly established.

Who the Old World voyager was remains a puzzle. But this much is certain: he came; civilized man from the Old World sailed across an ocean and landed somewhere in that general area where the higher American cultures flourished in pre-Columbian times.

Here is an embarrassment par excellence, not only to the botanists whose scientific acumen has treacherously flung them onto a battlefield but also to those archaeologists who find the word "contact" cacophonous.

Our panning gaze returns for a moment to the mouth of the Chicama Valley, where the sedentary people of Huaca Prieta lived on, potteryless and maizeless, raising their beans, their squash, and their cotton, and using their gourds as utensils. A thousand years after their arrival in about 2347 B.C., their descendants still dwelt on the site in much the same fashion.

But elsewhere in South America there were incipient stir-
rings.

In due time, probably more than a thousand years after early
settlers had located at Huaca Prieta, residents of the Virú Valley
on the north coast of Peru began to domesticate the llama. There
was apparently no pastoral stage as such in South America (if
indeed there was one in the Old World, for this is another theory
in process of being discredited). America had, as has been mentioned, no bovines of any form, no domesticated goats or pigs.
Only in Peru were there domesticated animals: the llama (that
stylized and humpless miniature cousin to the camel) and its
sheep-sized next of kin, the alpaca. These cameloids the Peruvians
now began to domesticate, obtaining wool from both.

The llama was presently pressed into service as the continent's only nonhuman beast of burden. It was never used as a
draft animal (is not even today used for wheeled drayage, being
unsuited to such chores) and was rarely ridden, perhaps because
it is small and balky.

Around 1200 B.C., fishermen-farmers or their women in the
little village of Guañape began to make crude pottery, the earliest
known to date in South America.

Slower than the steps of an infant, these faltering first steps
up the long, steep road toward civilization. Indeed, they leave one
quite unprepared for the dramatic leap about to follow.

Some thirty years ago a Peruvian archaeologist, Dr. Julio C.
Tello, listened with open ears and mind to the lore of his native
land. The trail of legend (acknowledged in retrospect by the desig-
nation of "oral history") led him deep into the past, led him, in
fact, to archaeological treasures not only unheard of but even undreamed of by his soberer colleagues. It led him into the northern
highlands, into a narrow river valley, into crumbling Chavín de
Huántar, where he came upon the ruins of an ancient ceremonial
center.

Here, neither covered by shifting desert sands nor laced in
the tentacles of a jungle, loomed a complex of terraces, plazas,
courts, mounds, and well-constructed stone buildings, oriented to
the cardinal points of the compass and covering an area approximately eight hundred feet square. This ceremonial center, be-

FIGURE 87.   The Castillo, Chavín de Huántar.

speaking a civilization far higher than archaeologists had had any
reason to believe existed in South America at so early a date, was
constructed only a few hundred years after the first crude pottery
vessel was molded at Guañape.

The largest building at Chavín de Huántar, the immense
"Castillo," epitomizes this baffling spurt. The Castillo is the earliest great stone structure found to date in Peru; yet the architect
who planned it was clearly no novice. He incorporated in it such
advanced features as an efficient system of horizontal and vertical
ventilating shafts. The well-laid stone walls of dry masonry rose
to three floors—a height rarely attempted by Peruvians during the
ensuing two thousand years. These floors, set back by narrow terraces, were accessible by ramps and stairs. Below a cornice, un-
Mongoloid carved-stone human heads jutted from the walls and
were held in position by tenons (Figure 87).

Distressingly, before this amazing structure had received anything approaching adequate study it was buried by a landslide

FIGURE 88.   Stone feline, Chavín.

in 1945. The long and expensive task of digging out was begun in 1956 by the Dirección de Arqueología.

The Castillo at Chavín de Huántar may epitomize, but it by no means embraces, the enigmas of the Chavín-Cupisnique horizon. The Chavín art style spread widely through northern Peru and also left traces farther south. *Terraced pyramids* mark such sites. It may have been a religious movement, for a feline god reminiscent of the Olmec jaguar seems to have moved along with the art and architectural style (Figure 88).

Coastal graves of this period have added greatly to the fund of archaeological knowledge, for the arid desert has preserved the bodies buried deeply within its sands. Those bodies today reveal that skull deformation was practiced during the Chavín-Cupisnique period, and this practice—like so much that appeared at this time—carried down into later periods (Figure 89).

From Cupisnique graves comes also a relatively sophisticated pottery, although the beginning of the Cupisnique period, according to radiocarbon dating, was 848 B.C. plus or minus 167 years, only about 350 years after the first crude efforts at pottery were made in Guañape. Some Cupisnique pottery even bears the mark of the mold, indicating quantity production at a surprisingly early stage.

Even more interesting (except to the myriad archaeologists whose first love is always pottery) is the jewelry. Metallurgy had previously been unknown in South America, but metal jewelry has been ascribed to the Chavín period. As J. Alden Mason describes these pieces, "Some are of pure gold, one is seventy-four per cent silver, and the others consist of a large proportion of gold, a small proportion of silver, and a little copper; the three metals were probably not intentionally mixed. Most of them were made of thin hammered gold, for casting, later the principal metallurgical technique, had apparently not yet been invented. The techniques employed, however, represent the rapid advance of the goldsmith's art, for they include hammering, embossing, anneal-

FIGURE 89.   Deformed skulls.

ing, welding, soldering, strap joining, incising, champleve, cut-out designs, and the manufacture of bimetallic objects. One pin has a gold head and a silver shaft. For all that we know to the contrary, metallurgy and all the above goldsmithing techniques may have been invented in this northern coastal Peruvian region—or they may have been introduced from we know not where."[7]

It may well be that corn (maize) also was introduced at this time—conceivably, as Robert Wauchope suggests, from Middle America. Wauchope, a careful scholar who worked out parallelisms between radiocarbon dates from Middle and South America, writes significantly:

"It is at this point that maize first appears in the Andean sequence. I pick the earliest one-sigma date [714 B.C. ± 200] in order to reduce the priority of maize in Middle America to a minimum, although with this priority already a matter of over three centuries one might not be too concerned over the point. However, I have in mind one possibility, which seems rather remote but I am really in no position to evaluate it properly. Several authorities have called attention to very generalized similarities between the Chavin and Olmec cults. An early stage of Olmec art was already well under way in Middle America. Drucker has called attention to the interesting, but not necessarily significant, fact that both cults featured feline attributes.[8] Thus, when I read Steward's list of Chavin-Cupisnique and Middle American Formative features and found 'Inter-American culture exchange'[9] it occurred to me that perhaps this was the explanation of maize's sudden appearance in South America."[10]

Wauchope's cautious suggestion warrants consideration. It is indeed conceivable that—even as the legendary Naymlap and his entourage reputedly tootled into Lambayeque—so Mesoamericans, possibly Olmecs, had ventured down to Peru bearing not only maize but also less tangible cultural gifts: architectural skill, some knowledge of astronomy, a feline deity, and possibly even an account of a bearded Fair God. For what it is worth we might note that the crosses adorning the cat god shown in Figure 88 are of the same equilateral form as the crosses which are believed to have decorated the robe of Quetzalcoatl. It is even conceivable that these early cultural ambassadors were the Fair Gods themselves, who had voyaged down the Pacific as Pizarro did later.

An ancient writer characterized the Phoenician thus: "He dwells not in a single place, but his legs are ever driven wandering."

In connection with the Olmecs we might cast a hasty side-wise glance at another Peruvian site.

In the Casma Valley at no very great distance from Chavín lies the coastal site of Cerro Sechín. Here stands a line of erect stone slabs on which a forgotten artist long ago outlined large human figures. Archaeologists—or those of them who agree on this important but anomalous site—find these dynamic figures similar to the "dancers" outlined on large stone slabs at Monte Albán, Mexico.

But just at this point we meet a blank wall, one of the many odd contradictions of South America. For Cerro Sechín, although it seems to be roughly contemporaneous with the Chavín culture, bears little resemblance to the Chavín-Cupisnique art style.

It was that dean of Peruvianists Dr. Julio C. Tello, the discoverer of Chavín de Huántar, who propounded the theory that the Chavín culture had originated in the Amazon region. The tremendous Amazon River, pouring into the Atlantic from northern Brazil, traverses South American from west to east, almost severing the continent at its greatest breadth. The westernmost tributary, the Marañón, rises in the Andes. Chavín de Huántar lies on a small tributary of the Marañón River, just east of the continental divide.

If (and here clearly I leave the dry land of fact to set sail on the sea of conjecture)—if early mariners were, like later ones, seeking a westward passage, the Amazon would surely have beckoned, luring the traveler westward ever farther, until at last he reached its unnavigable headwaters, not far from Chavín de Huántar.

Brazil, jutting far eastward into the Atlantic and reaching out toward the westward bulge of Africa, has long been regarded the potential or actual landfall of various pre-Columbians. But that is another book, another story.

South America remains an enigma.

The people who in time learned to weave the world's most beautiful fabrics, the people who developed tapioca from a poisonous root called manioc and who gave to the world the misnamed

Irish potato, that benevolent member of the treacherous night-shade family, might also have been capable of developing, again in due time, almost any phase of their culture. Man is, as every man himself knows, a creative animal; and creative he will remain until by his very creativity he extinguishes life on this planet or until by his eventual failure to create—and thus to adapt to an inimical environment—all life is extinguished by forces he has not mastered.

But in South America as in North, "the trap of time" gives one cause to doubt that all was homemade. The doubts expand when one looks upon other riddles: "identity in complexity," cotton, and so on.

In order that we may examine a few of these individual South American riddles, I shall here abandon this sketchy chronological survey of early South American cultures; for having glanced at Chavín we have seen the foundation of the succeeding higher Peruvian cultures. We have seen, before the midpoint of the first millennium B.C., terraced pyramids, maize culture, irrigation, metallurgy, skull deformation, and numerous other practices which marked the succeeding periods of higher Peruvian cultures, even down to the time of the Incas and the arrival of Francisco Pizarro. Whether the old, old "myth" of the Fair God also dates back to the Chavín horizon there is no way of knowing.

So, noting only that another flurry of new techniques, another dynamic bound up the ladder of civilization seems to have occurred in the period immediately following 400 B.C., we turn to a few of Peru's more obstinate puzzles.

ENIGMAS OF PERU

WHETHER OR NOT the only element, Asiatic Protomongoloids were ancestral to the vast bulk of the Andean peoples. The stamp of the Protomongoloidal American aborigine is large and deep on *almost* every Peruvian product. It is this very fact which makes the seemingly alien products or skills stand out. Were they happenstance, "sports," or the thumbprints of strangers?

For example, in the field of medicine. The Peruvian medicine man, like his counterpart throughout the preconquest Americas, diagnosed by divination. If his diagnosis revealed—as it often did —that a "foreign substance" in the patient's body was the cause of illness, the "doctor" sucked at the source of pain and always, miraculously, managed to pull forth the offending object: a needle, a pebble, a pin. This sleight-of-hand was practiced by Indians throughout the Americas. And yet in Peru the medicine men performed not only such primitive magic but also surgical operations—operations on the frontal sinus, amputations of legs or arms, excisions, trepanning.

Trepanning or trephining involves the removal of a section of the skull to alleviate pressure on the brain. More than ten thousand trepanned skulls have been found in Peruvian graves, and in many of these the renewed bone tissue is eloquent proof that the patient survived. A particularly high percentage of trepanned skulls have been found at coastal Paracas Cavernas and date from, roughly, 400 B.C.

Before that time, trepanning was a popular operation in various countries of the eastern Mediterranean world—perhaps too popular. Modern surgeons look askance at the sweeping manner in which Hippocrates (born *c.* 465 B.C.) recommended the trepanning operation in his essay *On Injuries of the Head.*

As with medicine, so with mummification. In the Old World process as described by Herodotus, the Egyptians removed the brain and viscera, preserved them in "canopic jars," cleansed the cavity with spices and wine, dried out the body, and wrapped it in cloths. No South American note-taker recorded the Peruvian practice, and the royal mummies, the mummies of the Inca emperors, were looted by the conquistadors and have disappeared. But hundreds of "lesser" mummies are available for examination; in one four-year period the Spaniards collected 1,365. At one pre-Christian site, Paracas Necropolis (close to the trepanning center of Paracas Cavernas), archaeologists found 429 mummies. These reveal that the Peruvian process of mummification, although considerably cruder, was similar to the Egyptian. The viscera were removed and preserved in a container, the body was dried and swathed in the finest cloths.

In Phoenicia mummification was practiced occasionally, in a form similar to but considerably cruder than the Egyptian.

If the general similarity in mummification did not bemuse its discoverers, certain Peruvian mummies must have. For strands of wavy auburn hair still clung to some of the skulls, and others had ash-blond hair.

Medicine, mummies—and golden masks. Back in the nineteenth century the ebullient Heinrich Schliemann, having found Troy by following Homer, had proceeded along the trail of tradition to golden Mycenae. There he had come upon royal graves and royal treasure. Down on his knees he was scraping the clay from the face of a corpse when his fingers touched metal: a golden mask. Here were five corpses, each with a golden mask—"unquestionably," he said, "a facsimile of the dead person's actual appearance"—to protect the deceased from forces of evil after death.

FIGURE 90. Golden mask: Chimú.

Golden masks in ancient Mycenae; in Phoenicia, as mentioned earlier; and golden masks have been found in Peru (Figure 90). Coincidence?

But too many elements seem to be crowding in—Phoenician, Egyptian, Mycenaean. Surely not all (if any) of these ever reached Peru.

Heinrich Schliemann, curiously, noted the same phenomenon in Greece. In the ruins of Mycenae he found traces of Egyptian culture. In the ruins of Tiryns (where archaeologists had tried to dissuade him from digging in the "medieval" remains) he found the Phoenician geometric pattern. Schliemann recognized in this apparent confusion the interaction of cultures—Asian, African, and European—and sensed that from these a cultural complex had evolved.

The apparent parallelisms between Peruvian and too many other cultures might possibly be a reflection, in part, of just such cultural interaction within the Old World. This is one complication, one obstinate knot beneath the fingers of those who would disentangle the past. Another, unquestionably, is the fact that man in his steep climb upward tends to follow a given path.

Primitive man, turned primitive peasant, shared certain methods in common with other peasants, whatever small plot they dug with their digging sticks in whatever far corner of the fertile earth. As their skill increased, their methods improved. In arid regions these early farmers presently learned the secret of irrigation. Irrigation was early practiced in Mesopotamia and adjacent countries under Babylonian influence, including Phoenicia; in Egypt; in parts of Mexico and Peru. The methods of irrigation and terracing and of water conduction in general were everywhere almost identical. The "Water Code" which Hammurabi promulgated for Babylon in the second millennium B.C. sounds, as Victor W. von Hagen (an uncompromising independent-inventionist) noted, "like an Inca text";[1] and Peruvian and Old World terraces rise in the same majestic patterns (Figures 91 and 92).

The flow of water being subject to immutable natural laws, these similar methods of water conduction might be in each case another independent manifestation of man's inventiveness. Or, on the other hand, the *idea* of irrigation and terracing may one day

FIGURE 91. Ancient terraces still in use: Pisac, Peru.

FIGURE 92.   Ancient terraces still in use: the Lebanon.

be traced to a single source, even as the idea of agriculture and of the wheel have been traced across millennia and continents back to a single source in the Fertile Crescent.

For whatever light it may cast on this puzzle, when was irrigation first practiced in Peru?

Not by the Incas, who in this as in other matters were the able inheritors. Tracing the concept backward, one comes, in the early centuries of the Christian era, to the valleys of the arid northern coast and the civilization of the Mochicas, makers of the picture-book pottery. Here sprawling irrigation works, including a mile-long aqueduct and a canal still in use to this day, watered every cultivatable acre. But the Mochicas, like the later Incas, may only have expanded what they inherited. The Mochica civilization centered in the Chicama, Moche, Virú, and Santa valleys. In the Virú Valley the earlier Gallinazo civilization, too, had multiplied agricultural production—and hence population—by irrigation and terracing. In about 550–350 B.C. the Gallinazos achieved a cultural level almost equal to that of the Mochicas, marked by large pyramids and advanced techniques of weaving and metallurgy. But again they were not the first in Peru to practice irrigation. For that we must turn to the still earlier Chavín-Cupisnique horizon, when beginnings of irrigation seem to have been undertaken alongside the earliest South American pyramids, the earliest South American metallurgy, the first appearance in the southern continent of the feline deity, and the first known appearance of skull deformation.

What significance, if any, attaches to the simultaneous appearance of pyramids, metallurgy, irrigation, and skull deformation? One must align himself by his answer, joining forces with either diffusionists or independent inventionists.

"Pyramid" is perhaps an ambiguous term. The Peruvian pyramid, rising in northern Peru in early periods, was stepped or terraced, with a wide external staircase leading up to the truncated top and its crowning temple—in short, a structure resembling the ziggurats of Mesopotamia and, even more, the Mexican pyramids.

True it is, as C. W. Ceram asserted, that "once the cultural soul has been awakened, a tendency to heaven-storming monumentality consistently appears. Despite all differences, there is a basic relationship linking the Babylonian ziggurat, Romanesque-

FIGURE 93.   Pyramid of Vilcashuaman, Peru.

Gothic churches, and the pyramids of Egypt."[2] But the urge to storm heaven via monumentality does not of necessity produce the terraced pyramidal form, meticulous orientation to the cardinal points of the compass, and other such features duplicated east and west.

In their heaven-storming construction the Incas, at least, used tools and techniques almost identical with those of Mediterranean masons. (The means by which earlier Peruvians reared their great structures, although not precisely known, seem to have been the same.) Conveniently, Egyptian artists in about 1500 B.C. saw fit to depict Egyptian stonemasons at work. These low-relief sculptures at Thebes show Egyptians using the same type of stone celts which the Incas used, and handling them in the same way.

Quarrying likewise. Seton Lloyd's study of quarrying methods revealed that stone was quarried in the New World identically as in the Old—by driving wooden wedges into natural faults in the stone, which cracked when the wedges swelled with water. Thus the Egyptians quarried stone, thus Eurasians and other early

Mediterranean peoples including the Romans, and thus too the pre-Hispanic Mexicans and Peruvians.

Identity in methods of quarrying, identity in stonemasonry tools and techniques, identity in irrigation and terracing: how significant is each of these? It might strain credulity somewhat to label them all coincidental, that is, the precise solutions which any man anywhere would sooner or later stumble upon in his groping search; but one would scarcely label them all "identity in complexity."

For examples of identity in complex devices and processes we turn instead to weaving and metallurgy.

Our earliest glimpse of Peruvians was back at Huaca Prieta, on the northern coast at the mouth of the Chicama Valley. Here the simple farmers, without pottery, without maize, without llamas, nevertheless wove cloth. As the earliest craft yet recognized in Peru, weaving would therefore seem the least likely to point toward contact. And yet—

Of the three thousand pieces of woven cloth found at Huaca Prieta, about 78 per cent were twined and most of the others were netted—two of the simplest methods of producing fabrics and everywhere two of the oldest. What occurred in Peru thereafter is best described by J. Alden Mason, who has devoted particular attention to weaving techniques.

"According to radiocarbon datings," writes Mason, "about a thousand years elapsed between the time of the last potteryless fishermen-farmers of Huaca Prieta and that of the men who deposited the burials in the Paracas Necropolis, and technology had made tremendous advances in this period. From then on up to the time of Pizzaro no great technical advancement was made in the textile industry. The tools used by the 'Chosen Women' who made Atahualpa's vestments were practically the same as those used by the women who made the Paracas mantles. . . . The earliest known weavers of the southern coast, those of the Paracas period, as well as those of the later Nazca Valley, practiced every important fundamental technique known in the latest periods."[3]

This thousand-year period during which such tremendous strides were made had ended before the Christian era. Tools introduced into use in Peru during that period duplicated,

strangely enough, those of the Old World. Spindle whorls excavated in Palestine, Egypt, Troy, in the Toltec capital of Tula,
and in Peru can be laid side by side, and even an expert can
scarcely tell them apart.

As with spindle whorls, so with looms. Not only were back-
strap looms widely used in both worlds. Peruvian *horizontal* looms
were identical with a horizontal loom depicted in an Egyptian
tomb of about 1900 B.C. Peruvian *vertical* looms were identical
with those found in a tomb at Thebes. Certain pre-Columbian
Old World and New World looms had the same eleven working
parts. Coincidence?

Such technicalities quickly weary the nonspecialist, and
many a technical explanation is interred between uncut pages.
For which reason I hesitate to launch into lengthy exegesis of
such examples of identity in complexity as *mise en couleur* and
cire perdue. Both techniques were employed in the Old World,
and both were practiced in quite the same way in Middle and
South America.

Briefly, *mise en couleur* involves casting an object of an alloy
of gold and copper, then treating the surface with acid to dissolve
the copper, leaving a pure gold surface.

Cire perdue is frequently called the "lost wax" method. The
ancient metallurgist, whether in the New or the Old World,
first modeled his object in clay, then dusted it with finely ground
charcoal. Over this he applied the crucial layer, the wax, being
certain that the object retained or achieved the shape he desired.
Then he covered the whole thing thickly with clay, leaving, however, an orifice. When the thick clay casing had hardened, he
heated the object and drained out the melted wax through the
hole. Into the clay model he poured molten gold or silver, thus
replacing the lost wax with metal. When the metal had cooled
and hardened, the outer casing was broken away, destroying the
the mold, and the job was finished.

Thus metal was cast in the New World long before Columbus. And thus the Phoenicians too had cast objects in bronze and
in precious metals. Coincidence?

There is always the other side of the coin.

A legion of archaeologists still believe that the aeons-long
isolation of the American Indian was uninterrupted until Octo-

ber 12, 1492, when the lookout aboard the *Pinta* peered out across the moonlit white lace of the Caribbean and shouted, *"Tierra! Tierra!"* and Captain Martín Alonso Pinzón fired a gun to announce the landfall. So profound is the gratitude of the American people to Christopher Columbus that many laymen sincerely believe that the voyage *could not have been achieved* before the Genoese pointed the way.

Archaeologists, eschewing this emotional approach, for the most part deny transatlantic contact on two other grounds: first, an absence of positive proof, particularly documentary; and secondly, certain strong counterindications.

The counterindication usually mentioned first is the wheel. Until the discovery of the pottery toys with axles and eight clay disks at Tres Zapotes, Mexico, it was asserted that the wheel was totally unknown in the Americas in any form. One frequently reads that pre-Columbian America lacked the vehicular wheel, the spinning wheel, and the potter's wheel. Now it is uncertain whether the vehicular wheel was unknown or merely of little use in a world without draft animals; if there were large wooden counterparts of the small clay wheels in the millennium before Christ, they would long since have rotted away.

The spinning wheel, on the other hand, is a comparatively recent and short-lived invention unknown in the Old World until about the fourteenth century A.D. If one had been found in previous use in Peru, that would indeed have been news! But the lack of a potter's wheel, in use from most ancient times in Egypt, is as baffling as the absence of writing in South America.

Language is also sometimes mentioned in this connection, and the lack of resemblance to Old World tongues is dwelt upon. But language seems scarcely the proper gauge in this situation. When Pizarro arrived, the Incas were waging an aggressive campaign to mold together their enormous empire. They had early imposed their Quechua language on all conquered peoples, a task that was hastened by their program of resettlement and colonization which called for the shuffling about of recalcitrant peoples. But even if the Spaniards had arrived a century earlier—before the Inca expansion got under way—it is doubtful whether much to this point could have been learned from the tongues of the various Peruvian tribes.

This bald assertion, at odds with some widely held views

about language, is based on the loss of the mother tongue by small groups of invaders within historic times. It was not the 180 men of Pizarro—three shiploads of men—who imposed the Spanish language upon Peru, but the many who followed after to colonize and administer. A closer parallel therefore to a "small descent," predominantly male, is General Almagro's "vanished army."

General Diego de Almagro, Pizarro's partner, plunged from glory as quickly as Lucifer. After conquering mighty Cuzco, he entangled himself in a feud with Pizarro's brother the upshot of which was battle. While the Indians stood on the hills and marveled, thirteen hundred Spanish soldiers armored and armed in the style of Europe clashed in bloodiest slaughter. Almagro was captured and summarily executed in 1538. The remnants of his shattered army not only fled but vanished. Four centuries passed, and the fate of the vanished army remained a riddle—till, only a few years ago, explorer Ken Krippene happened upon their descendants. Living on the high pampas of Peru and now numbering 18,000, these people still maintain certain Spanish customs and habits. Their religious practices are a curious blend of Roman Catholic and pagan rites. But they have forgotten the Spanish language utterly.

Another enigma is disease. In this "cultural" exchange, it is popularly said, the white man brought the Indian smallpox and the Indian reciprocated with the gift of syphilis. At the risk of spoiling a good story, however, not all physicians agree that syphilis was of American origin. To their long-standing doubts another was added recently when a cemetery dating back to about the time of Christ was discovered near York, in northern England. Scientists who have thus far studied several hundred of the skeletons, which date from the Roman occupation, report that the appearance of some of the bones definitely suggests syphilis. The disease might also have been frambesia, however, better known as yaws, a related disease still common in Africa.

Nor do all archaeologists agree that American Indians earlier knew no smallpox. Mochica pottery depicts an Indian scarred with pockmarks, and at a distance of more than a millennium there is understandable disagreement as to their cause. There is also the unhappy scratcher depicted in Figure 94, who appears to be in the acute stage of some eruptive disease. There is some

FIGURE 94. The unhappy scratcher. From the Chimú area of Pacific
North Peru.

indication, too, that yellow fever, transmitted by the *Aëdes aegypti* or yellow-fever mosquito, was present in both the Old and the New World.

In short, the subject of pre-Hispanic diseases which afflicted American Indians cries for further research by qualified personnel. It is true that wave after wave of "civilized" diseases —presumably measles, smallpox, mumps, tuberculosis—swept through the American populace after the Spaniards arrived: strong implication that there had been no extensive contact for a very long time, if ever. It is also true, however, that in 1962 a terrific epidemic of measles swept through remote Greenland and afflicted a high percentage of the population, despite the fact that Greenland is in continuous, though slight, contact. If Middle and South America were visited by no outsiders between the two great eras of exploration, a gap of some fifteen centuries, could one not logically expect a wave of disease to arrive with the Spaniards?

The final and clinching argument of the isolationist school is usually the compilation of two lengthy lists: plants cultivated in the Old World, plants cultivated in the New. The two lists are almost mutually exclusive, almost completely different, thus establishing most convincingly that the two worlds were botanically oceans apart. Apparently no common wild ancestor for any food or industrial plant was indigeneous to both hemispheres. But such a list can be of disservice to its compiler. For when one reads that sweet potatoes, gourds, and cotton were known and grown in *both* worlds *before* Columbus, there would seem to be only one explanation for such a phenomenon: a man in a ship.

A MUTED RUMBLE

THE MUTED RUMBLE one hears today afar off, like the distant grinding and crunching of a winter-long ice jam breaking up, is the echo of archaeological opinion slowly splitting asunder.

A generation has passed since Baron Erland Nordenskiöld listed forty-nine items or cultural traits found in South America and also on Pacific islands. Extending his tabulation, Nordenskiöld listed numerous other locales scattered across both American continents and indicated which items reappeared in each. Then, analyzing his imposing array of plus and minus signs, he could find no telltale trail leading down from Alaska.

How to account for the duplications? Nordenskiöld offered three hypotheses. First, these Oceanic culture elements may have derived from weather-driven vessels that landed on the coasts of America—"a possibility not to be entirely disregarded," as he put it. Or, continued Nordenskiöld, some of these items "may also originate from actual immigrations into South America from directly across the ocean, of exceedingly remote date. Or, with one or two exceptions, these culture elements may simply have been invented independently both in America and in the Old World."[1] He himself seemed to favor the third view.

Nordenskiöld's conclusions at first roused scant comment, perhaps because independent inventionists were satisfied to accept his third premise and diffusionists his first or second. History repeats, the independent inventionists observed, prehistory repeats, and human beings repeat one another endlessly. Diffusionists, on the other hand, interpreted the evidence thus: A ship on an ocean leaves no enduring wake, and at least thirty-eight of Nordenskiöld's forty-nine duplicate items were found in Colombia and Panama—precisely where the crew of an eastbound ship out of Polynesia, if drifting with the Equatorial Counter-Current, would first sight land. It is in the Bay of Panama that this east-flowing Equatorial Counter-Current, shunted aside by land, turns to the northwest and follows the slanting coastline of Central America till it reaches the Revillagigedo Islands off the coast of Mexico, where it joins the west-flowing North Equatorial Current and turns back across the Pacific.

To a few archaeologists thirty-eight Oceanic items duplicated in Panama and Colombia seemed quite too many to dismiss with a shrug as accidental parallelism, and presently they expressed this heresy openly. Whereupon independent inventionists reiterated that the American Indian had existed in absolute isolation, inventing what sometimes proved to be duplicate items out of his own fertile creative imagination. And the battle was joined.

Thus far our gaze has focused largely upon the Atlantic, *the* ocean in the thinking of a nation whose roots extend from Europe. But the Americas are flanked by two great oceans. From the islands that dot the vast Pacific, men were also going down to the sea in ships—could not in fact have arrived at their far-flung islands by other means.

The major peopling of the central and eastern Pacific islands called Polynesia, although not yet fully understood, is generally thought to have been achieved from the west because the cultural, linguistic, and racial affinities of the Polynesians seem to be largely with Southeast Asia. Anthropologists agree that Polynesia was the last large habitable area of the globe to be populated. Radiocarbon dates indicate that the first voyagers may have reached some of the northern fringe islands of Melanesia several centuries B.C., but Hawaii, New Zealand, and the islands to the east are believed to have lain uninhabited for centuries thereafter. Today the Polynesians—that is, the people of Hawaii, Tahiti, Pitcairn, the Marquesas, and Easter Island, to name but a few— are a hybrid people, part white, part Negro, and part Mongolian, with the white element usually predominant; tall, lithe, coffee-with-cream-colored men and sinuous, tawny women. We know these comely creatures best through the paintings of Gauguin.

This is the place where one might expect to find expert seamanship, and here indeed one finds it. The "ships" of the Polynesians were mammoth double canoes, and in these canoes the islanders traversed incredible distances. Since paddling across the Pacific would be dreary business, they mounted a triangular sail and with a good stiff favoring wind could do seven knots. At a time when the Vikings were sweeping the northern seas in their longships, the Polynesians in their long canoes were ranging

FIGURE 95.   A Polynesian double canoe.

thousands of miles across the Pacific, roaming that ocean as freely as earlier Stone Age men roamed across continents.

In about the year 950 A.D., to cite an example, a Tahitian named Kupe sailed almost two thousand miles to New Zealand—in itself a remarkable feat of navigation, but Kupe exceeded himself; he then turned around and found his way back to tiny Tahiti, a mere speck on the ocean.

The Tahitians had no writing. They possessed, however, prodigious memories, weird but reliable charts made of sinews and shells, seaworthy canoes, and courage unlimited. Thus two hundred years after Kupe's feat other Tahitians, *following Kupe's verbal sailing directions* preserved by professional memorizers, successfully migrated to New Zealand.

Another two hundred years later a large fleet set out from Tahiti for the same destination. The middle group had not returned, so the emigrants of 1350 had only Kupe's four-hundred-year-old oral directions. If some of these people doubted the nautical skill of an ancestor so remote or questioned the sailing directions repeated but never recorded for four hundred years, the doubts were not weighty enough to stay them. The group embarked, followed Kupe's directions, and arrived in New Zealand.

New Zealand was not, of course, the only Polynesian port of call. Another known voyage was the 2,000-mile sail from Hawaii to Tahiti—*and back*. According to local tradition, on the voyage south they steered by the polestar until they came to the navel of space (the equator), and thereafter they steered by the star that was new in the south.[2] On the precarious return voyage northward from Tahiti to Hawaii the Polynesians again had to cross the South Equatorial Current flowing westward and the east-flowing Equatorial Counter-Current, both of which might have dragged them off course and upset their reckoning, before they reached the west-flowing North Equatorial Current. If the voyagers missed the Hawaiian Islands nothing lay north of them but Alaska. And yet such a voyage was successfully completed in about 950 A.D.

If other peregrinations carried them far to the east, the Polynesians could scarcely have missed the 10,000-mile-long coastline of the Americas. In fact, a study conducted by Walter Lehmann, the results of which were published in the *Orientalische*

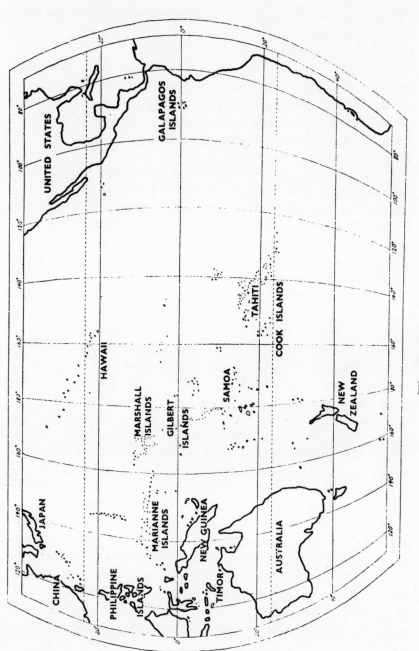

The Pacific Ocean

Literaturzeitung in 1930, shows that traditions of such landings
had been handed down by the Indians themselves. And the Polynesians' uncanny ability to find their way back to their tiny
Pacific islands has already been demonstrated.

This is the nautical background, but what of the items that
served as the battering iceboat which rammed the first wedge in
the ice jam of isolationism? We need glance at the merest handful.
Actually, the existence of some had been known for three hundred
years, while the ice jam of isolationism expanded and thickened.

The first modern explorers who reached Anaa in the Tuamotu
Archipelago, in 1606, noticed a gold ring on the hand of the first
woman they saw. The nearest gold was in Peru, some three thousand miles away, or in Australia, still farther distant. The gold
might well have come from the west, but these Spanish explorers
saw something else which almost certainly had come from America: the sweet potato.

The first European known to have looked on a sweet potato
was Columbus, who saw it in the West Indies on November 4,
1492, and learned that the natives there planted it in small
mounds. But the sweet potato was not apparently indigenous to
the Antilles. It had been depicted a thousand years earlier on
Mochica pottery. Before that, as Julio Tello discovered, it was
placed in prehistoric graves along the coast of Peru, the graves
of Paracas, which have been radiocarbon-dated as of the last
centuries B.C. And then it was discovered in the Society Islands
of Polynesia, which include Tahiti, planted, just as Columbus
saw it, "in small mounds."

Botanists now believe that the sweet potato is a plant of
American origin, that it is not indigenous to Polynesia but was
transported there by human hands, for the sweet potato is trans-
planted as a tuber, tender and easily bruised. Sir Peter H. Buck,
himself a Maori on his mother's side, even named the place of
origin: "The Peruvian coast is specified because in the Kechua
dialect of north Peru, the name of the sweet potato is *Kumar.*
As the general Polynesian name for the plant is *Kumara,* the tuber
must have been obtained from an area that used the name
Kumar."[3]

If one were to select a single feature of American Indian

culture as unique, he might possibly name the quipu. And yet the quipu has also been found in Polynesia. On strikingly similar quipus, Hawaiian tax collectors who could neither read nor write kept "very exact accounts of all the articles, of all kinds, collected from the inhabitants throughout the island"[4]—just as their counterparts did in Peru. Found by the earliest European visitors, quipus were still in use in Hawaii as late as 1830.

Thus far the indications of Polynesian contact point toward Peru, but we encounter another interesting situation in the Northeast Pacific, where an arm of the east-flowing Kuroshiwo Current sweeps past British Columbia. Among the various American Indian tribes that make up this so-called Northwest Coast culture, sealed off from the inland tribes by high mountain ranges, are many who from the time of their first contact with Europeans were observed to bear a strong physical resemblance to Polynesians. Certain elements of their culture, too, seemed more Polynesian than American Indian. They sailed about in large, deep-sea canoes that have been described as having "a great resemblance to the Maori canoes,"[5] and sometimes they voyaged in double canoes—two canoes lashed together in the Maori-Polynesian manner. Also like certain Polynesians, the Indians of the Northwest American coast hammered copper, donned wooden helmets for fighting, and indulged in head deformation. The significance of each of these cultural similarities and many others found in this same Northwest Coast culture have been debated endlessly. Although there are dissenters, various archaeologists have gone on record as believing that Polynesians did, in fact, reach this fringe of the North American continent, and that they reached it not by land but by sea.

No claim has been or is likely to be advanced that the Polynesians had any profound effect on American Indian cultures in general. The Polynesians, if they came, arrived comparatively late, when certain of the Middle and South American higher cultures had long been flourishing. The significance of such similarities in our present consideration is rather this:

Belief in the utter and complete isolation of the American Indian from the day when he wandered a Stone Age half-brute out of Asia down to the day when Christopher Columbus stepped proudly ashore is no longer sacrosanct. A belief that is still oft repeated and hotly defended whenever challenged, it nevertheless *is* challenged by men of science whose reasons stem from neither whim nor fantasy but from tangible facts and an earnest desire to learn the unfettered truth.

Double canoes and quipus, sweet potatoes and gold. Even those who grant that these and various other items must surely have traveled across the Pacific, even those who agree that pre-Columbian contact *occurred*, disagree as to the manner. Were the hands that carried the sweet potato to distant Pacific islands Polynesian or American Indian?

Once it was thought that, excepting only the tribes of the Northwest Coast, the American Indian was never a deep-sea sailor. As recently as 1942 Philip Ainsworth Means referred to the Incas and their predecessors as "those singularly unmarine-minded people, the ancient Andeans." He went further, averring that neither Quechua nor pre-Inca coastal languages had adequate terms for sailing, and this he regarded as "a reflection of the general ineptitude of the people for seamanship as a whole."[6] Only five years later Thor Heyerdahl and his colleagues, having constructed the balsa raft *Kon-Tiki* according to old Peruvian specifications, demonstrated that such a craft could sail 4,300 nautical miles to Polynesia, a distance equal to a flight from Chicago to Moscow.

Heyerdahl learned much more than that such a voyage was a physical possibility in ages past. He learned that on certain downwind Pacific islands old men still repeated ancient legends concerning the founder of their race, reputedly a bearded white chief-god named Kon-Tiki. Now, the name Kon-Tiki was the older form of a name already familiar to us in its Inca or Quechua version: Viracocha. In Peru, according to South American legend, the bearded white men who built the enormous stone edifices were in time attacked by a chief named Cari. Most of the white men were massacred, but Kon-Tiki Viracocha and some of his friends escaped, fled to the coast, and presently disappeared westward over the sea. Thor Heyerdahl believes that Polynesian legends even yet extant are living proof that the bearded white men who fled Peru arrived safely in Polynesia.

His theory is founded on evidence more substantial than

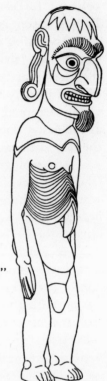

FIGURE 96.   An Easter Island "long-eared ghost-man."

legend, for here on certain Pacific islands and atolls where Kon-
Tiki is still revered are other appurtenances of his culture: pyramids, for example; also Panpipes and helmets; and proof that
irrigation, trepanning, and head deformation were practiced. Also,
these same Pacific islanders knew that the earth was round.
"Whence," asks Heyerdahl, "had the Polynesians obtained their
vast astronomical knowledge and their calendar, which was calculated with astonishing thoroughness? Certainly not from Mela-
nesian or Malayan peoples to the westward. But the same old
vanished civilized race, the 'white and bearded men,' who had
taught Aztecs, Mayas, and Incas their amazing culture in America,
had evolved a curiously similar calendar and a similar astronomical knowledge which Europe in those times could not match."[7]

Those times. And what were those times? When he was
writing *Kon-Tiki,* Heyerdahl believed that the date of this westward migration into the Pacific was approximately 500 A.D. He

believed further that the landfall was made on Easter Island. Lonely Easter Island, only twice the size of Manhattan, lies two thousand miles west of Chile at 27° S latitude. Today the natives call Easter Island "the navel of the Islands," and Heyerdahl theorizes that from that point some of the cultural items were carried spottily farther. Heyerdahl's estimate of the date was not widely accepted, for the commoner view was that Easter Island, as the easternmost island of Polynesia, must therefore have been the last to be peopled—probably in about the fourteenth century A.D. Archaeologists who later accompanied Heyerdahl to Easter Island, however, obtained a radiocarbon date of 380 A.D. ± 100 years,[8] and there is as yet no way of knowing that the man-made defense ditch which yielded the material tested was constructed during the earliest years of the island's occupation.

Heyerdahl learned also that Easter Island was honeycombed with caves—hidden and secret caves, each belonging to a single family. Only one representative of a family in each generation was permitted to know the location of the cave and to enter it and tend the ancient family treasures secreted within. These treasures consisted primarily of small stone statues carved in the round, some depicting fantastic creatures and some representing perhaps —who knows?—some early ancestor. Figure 96 depicts a *moai-kava-kava* found on Easter Island, "a long-eared ghost-man," for the earliest inhabitants of the island were said to have worn heavy earrings that stretched their ear lobes to excessive length.

Little more than a generation ago the merest suggestion of pre-Columbian transoceanic contact was anathema. Now slowly the ice jam is breaking up. In 1949 the American Museum of Natural History, long the bulwark of the isolationist school, presented an exhibition of cultural parallelisms between the New World and the Old. The exhibit was prepared by Dr. Gordon F. Ekholm, associate curator of anthropology of the museum, and Dr. Robert Heine-Geldern, research associate. Reviving a thesis of Henri Marchal, these two scholars expressed the opinion that voyagers from the Asiatic mainland—from Indonesia and Indochina—may have crossed the Pacific and discovered America seven hundred years before Columbus. At Chichén Itzá in Yucatán, they pointed out, are columns and balustrades with a serpent motif almost identical with columns and balustrades found in Java. They noted also similarities in types of thrones, in the handling of the lotus motif in India and in Mayan country, and in other traits which have no antecedents in Middle America but resemble traits found in Southeast Asia.[9] Many archaeologists remained unconvinced; and many still do.

Further defections from the citadel of isolation have followed. But in almost every instance, it must be clearly noted, those who expressed credence in pre-Columbian transoceanic contact believed that such contact had occurred by way of the Pacific, not the Atlantic. The archaeological Monroe Doctrine has been modified to this extent: pre-Columbian strangers may be admitted, *provided* they crossed the Pacific.

This is in fact an enormous concession. But what of the transatlantic voyager?

To him the door has been opened a crack. No longer can it be stated, as once it was, that a transatlantic voyage in ancient times was a physical impossibility. When one grants that six men on a raft drifted 4,300 miles across the Pacific, one finds it difficult to deny that Phoenicians, Carthaginians, Greeks, or Romans with better equipment could have sailed with the favoring winds and favoring currents 4,000 miles across the Atlantic to Middle America, there to become the bearded Fair Gods of Middle and South American legend, the Quetzalcoatls and Viracochas.

To be sure, there are many archaeologists who contend that the voyage of the *Kon-Tiki* proved nothing. But they still must account for the transferral of the sweet potato in pre-Columbian times. The only alternative is to grant that Polynesian canoeists found their way across 4,300 miles of Pacific to American shores *and* found their way back to their islands. Having granted this much, again, one can scarcely in logic refer to a voyage of 4,000 miles across the Atlantic, all of it with favoring currents, as "preposterous."

If anything seems preposterous, it is not the putative voyages of Phoenicians a millennium before Christ but voyages even more ancient—voyages which, the findings of botanists indicate, *must* have occurred. Asiatic cotton made its way to the New World in days remote. And so did, according to botanists, the homely gourd.

The bottle gourd or calabash, *Lagenaria siceraria,* with its bulbous end and narrow neck is a bottle sculptured by nature, relatively unimportant as a food plant but enormously useful because its tough rind is so conveniently shaped. The ancient Egyptians found it so; specimens have been recovered from an Egyptian tomb of the fifth Dynasty (*c.* 2680–*c.* 2560 B.C. by recent C-14 dating). Neighboring countries are believed to have adopted the gourd in the third millennium B.C. And the same plant has also turned up in the New World.

Julio C. Tello, excavating at Paracas on the arid South Peruvian coast more than thirty years ago, came upon subterranean communal tombs—possibly family vaults—loaded with archaeological treasure. Here were scores of bodies preserved in the desert sand, their heads artificially deformed and many of them trepanned. Here were well-made textiles, clay Panpines, ornaments made of thin gold but not yet of silver, pottery bearing geometric designs and sometimes a feline motif. And here were numerous gourds of the same genus and species as the Old World variety: *Lagenaria siceraria.*

This was a strange and exciting find, but one yet stranger was presently to be made. Shortly after the end of World War II, Junius Bird was excavating on the northern coast of Peru at Huaca Prieta, which we have noted previously as the first known agricultural site in South America. Here he found cotton identified by botanists an an Asiatic-American hybrid. From a midden at Huaca Prieta he also recovered some intact fruits and thousands of fragments of gourd shells identified as *Lagenaria siceraria.* Bird estimated that the gourds were in use as utensils in potteryless Huaca Prieta at some time between 1000 B.C. and 3000 B.C.

Better perhaps than cotton, the lowly gourd now offers specific clues to at least one incalculably early voyage. Botanists believe that the bottle gourd is probably native to tropical Africa or possibly southern Asia. Could the gourd have floated across an ocean? No, says Carter; the *Lagenaria* would not survive lengthy soaking.[10] If, then, it was necessarily transported across an ocean to the New World by man, which was the ocean?

Earlier, archaeologists saw much to suggest the Pacific. The Peruvian sites where the plant was found lay near the Pacific. The identical plant grew also in Polynesia in pre-Columbian times. But Bird's discovery at Huaca Prieta dealt a heavy blow to the Pacific theory, for at the time when the plant was in use at Huaca Prieta the islands of Polynesia lay empty of people. Moreover, according to present information, the gourd was unknown in southeast Asia until it appeared in China shortly before the Christian era[11]—long after Huaca Prieta was abandoned.

Thus, the Pacific theory now appears to be untenable. And what remains except the Atlantic? Although the superior preservative conditions of the Peruvian climate offer the archaeologist more to work with, the bottle gourd now has been found in early archaeological sites of North America, as well. And until science refutes the botanists' findings, there seems to be no denying at least one very early and as yet unidentified *Atlantic* crossing.

Did the Phoenicians and Carthaginians reach America? Much evidence has yet to be weighed and examined in the light of this possibility. This is a task of stupendous proportions. Consider a few of the complications.

American aborigines turned early to plant domestication in the selfsame areas to which winds and currents would carry a vessel from across the Atlantic. Agriculture, because it brings leisure for creativity, is the queen-mother of civilization, and native cultures developed there *in situ*. One who would determine whether cultural traits imported from the ancient Orient were superimposed on these native American cultures must deal with evidence heaped on evidence and ensnarled in baffling confusion.

And then, when striking parallelisms with Old World products appear, one must render judgment with all the dispassionate wisdom of the godhead. When, in fact, is a parallelism striking? Are "the same eleven working parts" in a loom more than coincidental? How many cultural duplications are needed to constitute positive proof of contact between two worlds? How many similarities become *too* many?

Interpretation of evidence. An archaeologist gazes at a colossal head carved from stone, notes the wide nose, the thick lips, the general Negroid appearance. He notes too that the hand which chiseled the stone was stilled by death some five hundred years before Christ was born. Negroes in America in the pre-Christian era? How could that be? He will call the great head a "Baby-face." And so it is known thenceforth.

A white man crossing the wilds of Peru in the twentieth

century passes a native who is planting with a primitive digging-stick. The white man hears the peasant address him as Viracocha. . . . A sixteenth-century Spanish father converting the pagans of Middle America hears from the lips of a native how once, long ago, a bearded white man had come from over the eastern sea, bringing the arts of civilization. . . . Cortés himself hears it from Montezuma, who grants him the gift of a nation in gratitude. . . . Myth, legend, fable? Yet the infant science of archaeology, little more than a century old, already has vindicated many an ancient author, already has cloaked in measurable fact many a legend that long had passed for fable.

Already, too, this infant science has added chapters to ancient history, writing the story of man in inverse chronology, inscribing history with the trowel instead of the sword. The story that Diodorus Siculus told of a Phoenician ship storm-tossed for many days upon the Atlantic and carried at length to a distant land may one day find space in American history textbooks. The enduring faith of the ancients in a great land westward beyond the Atlantic may soon be traced to its source—perhaps the same source of another enduring faith, the belief of American Indians in a bearded Fair God.

This is a book whose final chapter cannot yet be written. These are not proofs and have not been so represented; rather, they are implications. In fifty years, twenty years, possibly only five years, we shall know more and perhaps even have a positive answer. In the present state of our knowledge, it behooves *no* one to be dogmatic, neither those who believe that adequate proof already exists that a certain people crossed the Atlantic a millennium or two before Columbus nor those who maintain that it *could not have been done*. Least of all the latter.

For man is a fearfully wonderful creature, "infinite in capacity." He creates what he needs and he goes where he wishes, wherever his wits and his curious will may carry him: to the farthest corners of the alien earth, across an uncrossable ocean and homeward again, down to the darkling floor of the sea, into the beckoning void of space, and presently out to the luring moon.

NOTES

CHAPTER 1: MONTEZUMA'S DILEMMA

1. Hernando Cortés, *Five Letters, 1519-1526,* translated by J. Bayard Morris (London, Routledge, 1928), pp. 50-51.
2. Bernal Díaz del Castillo, *The True History of the Conquest of New Spain,* translated by Alfred Percival Maudslay (London, Hakluyt Society, 1910), Vol. II, pp. 39-40.
3. Cortés, *op. cit.,* p. 69.
4. Díaz, *op. cit.,* pp. 43-44.
5. Cortés, *op. cit.,* pp. 70-71.

CHAPTER 2: COLUMBUS CAME LATE

1. Address published only in Norwegian (*Opdagelsenes Nye Århundre* in Norsk Geografisk Tidsskrift, Vol VI, 1936). Translated in part by Geoffrey Bibby in his *The Testimony of the Spade* (New York, Knopf, and London, Collins, 1956), pp. 266-67.
2. Ferdinand Columbus, "History of the Discovery of America by Christopher Columbus," in *A General History and Collection of Voyages of Travel,* edited by Robert Kerr (Edinburgh, Blackwood, 1811), Vol. III, p. 30.
3. Poul Nørlund, *Viking Settlers in Greenland* (London, Cambridge University Press, 1936), pp. 110-25.

CHAPTER 3: ACROSS THE TOP OF THE WORLD

1. Kenneth Macgowan, *Early Man in the New World* (New York, Macmillan, 1950), p. 2.
2. Harold Sterling Gladwin, *Men out of Asia* (New York, Whittlesey House, 1947), pp. 42-43, 62.
3. Earnest A. Hooton, *The Indians of the Pecos Pueblo* (Papers, Phillips Academy Southwestern Expedition, No. 4, 1930), pp. 355-56.

4. Roland B. Dixon, *The Racial History of Man* (New York, Scribner, 1923), p. 402.
5. Earnest A. Hooton, *Up from the Ape* (New York, Macmillan, rev. 1946), p. 650.
6. W. S. Broecker and J. L. Kulp, "The Radiocarbon Method of Age Determination," *American Antiquity*, Vol. 22 (July, 1956), pp. 1-11.
7. Philip S. Smith, "Certain Relations between Northwestern America and Northeastern Asia," in *Early Man*, edited by George Grant MacCurdy (Philadelphia, Lippincott, 1937), p. 86.
8. John Fiske, *The Discovery of America* (Boston, Houghton Mifflin, 1902), Vol. I, p. xii.
9. Macgowan, *op. cit.*, p. 153.
10. H. Marie Wormington, *Ancient Man in North America* (Denver, Denver Museum of Natural History, 3d ed., rev. 1949), p. 158.

CHAPTER 4: MEXICO'S FAIR GOD QUETZALCOATL

1. David Diringer, *The Alphabet* (New York, Philosophical Library, 2d ed., rev. 1953), pp. 129, 133.
2. Christopher Columbus, "Letters on the Fourth Voyage," edited by Edward G. Bourne, in *The Northmen, Columbus and Cabot, 985-1503* (New York, Scribner, 1906), p. 411.
3. Bernardino de Sahagún, *Historia general de las cosas de Neuva España* (Mexico, A. Valdés, 1829-30), Vol. I, pp. iii, vii.
4. *The Song of Quetzalcoatl*, translated from the Aztec by John Hubert Cornyn (Yellow Springs, Ohio, Antioch Press, 2d ed., 1931), pp. 78-85.
5. Juan de Torquemada, *Monarchia indiana*, Vol. I, pp. 254-65, as translated and condensed in Hubert Howe Bancroft, *Myths and Languages*, Vol. III of *The Native Races* (San Francisco, A. L. Bancroft, 1883), p. 258.
6. Juan de Torquemada, *Segunda parte de los veinte i un libros rituales i monarchia indiana* (Madrid, N. Rodriquez Franco, 1723), p. 47.
7. George C. Vaillant, *The Aztecs of Mexico* (Garden City, N. Y., Doubleday, Doran & Company, Inc., American Museum of Natural History Science Series, 1941), p. 184.

CHAPTER 5: PYRAMIDS AND ZIGGURATS

1. William H. Prescott, *History of the Conquest of Mexico* (New York, John W. Lovell Co., [n.d.]), Vol. II, p. 105.
2. C. A. Burland, "Postscript" to Vaillant, *The Aztecs of Mexico* (Harmondsworth, Middlesex, England, Penguin Books, 1950), p. 273.
3. Vaillant, *The Aztecs of Mexico* (Doubleday, Doran, 1941), p. 278.
4. Genesis 11:1-9.

CHAPTER 6: THE MYSTERY OF MONTE ALBÁN

1. Egon Erwin Kisch, *Entdeckungen in Mexiko* (Berlin, Aufbau-Verlag, 1947), pp. 150, 154.

CHAPTER 7: THE REDISCOVERY OF THE MAYAS

1. John L. Stephens, *Incidents of Travel in Central America, Chiapas, and Yucatan* (New York, Harper & Brothers, 1841), Vol. I, p. 102.
2. *Ibid.*, pp. 104-5.
3. *Ibid.*, pp. 126-28.
4. Torquemada, *Monarchia indiana*, Vol. II, p. 52.
5. Frederick A. Peterson, *Ancient Mexico* (New York, G. P. Putnam's Sons; London, George Allen and Unwin, 1959), p. 70.
6. William E. Gates, "Commentary upon the Maya-Tzental Perez Codex," *Papers of the Peabody Museum of American Archaeology and Ethnology, Harvard University*, Vol. 6 (November, 1910), pp. 59-60.
7. *Ibid.*, p. 57.

CHAPTER 9: MEN WITH PETTICOATS

1. Hubert Howe Bancroft, *Myths and Languages*, Vol. III of his *The Native Races* (San Francisco, A. L. Bancroft, 1883), pp. 451-53.
2. Johann Georg Müller, *Geschichte der amerikanischen Urreligionen* (Basel, Schweighauser, 1855), pp. 486-90.
3. Pablo Cabrera, *Teatro critico americano*, in Antonio del Rio, *Description of the Ruins of an Ancient City Discovered near Palenque* (London, H. Berthoud, and Suttaby, Evance and Fox, 1822), pp. 34-36.
4. Lewis Spence, *The Gods of Mexico* (New York, Frederick A. Stokes Company, 1923), p. 135.
5. Sylvanus Griswold Morley, *The Ancient Maya*, rev. by George W. Brainerd (Stanford, California, Stanford University Press, 3d ed., 1956), p. 163.
6. Leviticus 19:27.
7. See Morley, *op. cit.*, pp. 77-78.

CHAPTER 10: THE LORE OF THE JUNGLE SCHOLARS

1. Diringer, *The Alphabet*, p. 527.
2. *Ibid.*, p. 123.
3. C. W. Ceram, *Gods, Graves and Scholars*, translated by E. B. Garside (New York, Alfred A. Knopf, 1952), pp. 318-19.
4. Gregory Mason, *Columbus Came Late* (New York, Century, 1931), p. 159.
5. Morley, *The Ancient Maya*, p. 256.
6. Herbert J. Spinden, "The Reduction of Mayan Dates," *Papers of the Peabody Museum of American Archaeology and Ethnology, Harvard University*, Vol. 6, No. 4 (1924), p. 157.
7. Morley, *op. cit.*, pp. 55, 237, 184.
8. Isaiah 23:8-12.
9. Ezekiel 26:8-12.
10. George Rawlinson, *The Story of Phoenicia* (New York, G. P. Putnam's Sons; London, T. Fisher and Unwin, The Story of Nations Series, 1890), p. 171.

11. Diodorus Siculus, *Bibliotheca historica,* v:19-20.
12. C. Leonard Woolley, *The Sumerians* (Oxford, Clarendon Press [1929]), p. 193. By permission of the Clarendon Press, Oxford.

CHAPTER 11: THE FACE OF THE OLMEC

1. Matthew W. Stirling, "Discovering the New World's Oldest Dated Work of Man," *National Geographic Magazine,* Vol. 76 (August, 1939), pp. 183-218 *passim.*
2. R. J. C. Atkinson, *Stonehenge* (London, Hamish Hamilton, Ltd., 1956), pp. 167-68.
3. Stirling, *loc. cit.*
4. *Cf.* Robert Wauchope, "A Tentative Sequence of Pre-classic Ceramics in Middle America," Tulane University, *Middle American Research Institute,* Publication 15 (1950), p. 238.
5. Matthew W. Stirling, "Great Stone Faces of the Mexican Jungle," *National Geographic Magazine,* Vol. 78 (September, 1940), pp. 314, 310.
6. Désiré Charnay, *Les anciennes villes du nouveau monde* (Paris, Librairie Hachette, 1885), pp. 140-43.
7. Georges Perrot and Charles Chipiez, *History of Art in Phoenicia and Its Dependencies,* translated and edited by Walter Armstrong (London, Chapman and Hall; New York, A. C. Armstrong and Son, 1885), Vol. I, pp. 209-11.
8. Atkinson, *Stonehenge,* p. 108.
9. Stirling, "Great Stone Faces of the Mexican Jungle," p. 317.

CHAPTER 12: OF SHOES AND SHIPS

1. Stirling, "Great Stone Faces of the Mexican Jungle," p. 316.
2. *Ibid.,* pp 326-27.
3. Philip Drucker and Robert F. Heizer, "Gifts for the Jaguar Gods," *National Geographic Magazine,* Vol. 110 (September, 1956), p. 367.
4. Philip Drucker, Robert F. Heizer, and Robert J. Squier, "Radiocarbon Dates from La Venta, Tabasco," *Science,* Vol. 126 (July 12, 1957), pp. 72-73. Reprinted from *Science* by permission.
5. A. E. Cowley, *The Hittites* (London, Oxford University Press, 1926), p. 14.
6. Alexander von Humboldt, *Cosmos* (New York, Harper, 1850-59), Vol. 2, p. 175.
7. A. T. Olmstead, *History of Palestine and Syria* (New York and London, Scribner, 1931), pp. 375-76.

CHAPTER 13: THE DARK RELIGION

1. Genesis 22:2.
2. Atkinson, *Stonehenge,* p. 167.
3. II Kings 17:16-17.

4. Johann Joseph Döllinger, *The Gentile and the Jew in the Courts of the Temple of Christ;* translation of his *Heidenthum und Judenthum* by N. Darnell (London, Longmans, Green, Longmans, Roberts, and Green, 1862), Vol. I, pp. 425-29.

5. Irving Berdine Richman, *The Spanish Conquerors* (New Haven, Yale University Press, 1919), p. 97. From the Chronicles of America. Copyright Yale University Press.

6. Godfrey Higgins, *Celtic Druids* (London, R. Hunter, 1827), p. 126.

7. Stirling, "Great Stone Faces of the Mexican Jungle" (1940), pp. 327-28.

8. Tacitus, *Historiae,* ii:78.

9. Drucker and Heizer, "Gifts for the Jaguar Gods" (1956), p. 367.

10. G. Contenau, *La civilisation phénicienne* (Paris, Payot, 1949), p. 80.

CHAPTER 14: BEARDED, BELOVED, AND BEHEADED

1. George C. Vaillant, "A Bearded Mystery," *Natural History,* Vol. 31 (May-June, 1931), pp. 243-44.

2. *Ibid.,* pp. 245-50, *passim.*

3. *Ibid.,* p. 252.

4. Harold Stirling Gladwin, *Men out of Asia,* (New York, Whittlesey House, 1947), p. 204.

5. Frans Blom, *The Conquest of Yucatan* (Boston and New York, Houghton Mifflin, 1936), p. 136.

6. Désiré Charnay, *The Ancient Cities of the New World,* translated from the French by J. Gonino and Helen S. Conant (New York, Harper, 1887), p. 106.

CHAPTER 15: THE GOLDEN BRONZE AGE

1. Geoffrey Bibby, *The Testimony of the Spade* (New York, Knopf, and London, Collins, 1956), p. 315.

2. Atkinson, *Stonehenge,* p. 163.

CHAPTER 16: THE ENTERPRISING PHOENICIANS

1. Strabo, *The Geography of Strabo,* iii:5:11. English translation by Horace Leonard Jones, The Loeb Classical Library (London, Heinemann, and New York, Putnam, 1923), Vol. II, p. 157.

2. Olmstead, *History of Palestine and Syria,* p. 95.

3. Adolf Erman, *Literature of the Ancient Egyptians* (London, Methuen, 1927), p. 92.

4. Olmstead, *op. cit.,* p. 45.

5. II Chronicles 2:6-7.

6. I Kings 9:12.

7. Sabatino Moscati, *The Face of the Ancient Orient* (Garden City, N. Y., Doubleday & Company, Inc., 1962), p. 215.

8. Strabo (H. L. Jones translation), iii:2:13-14.
9. But see William Culican, "The Sea Peoples of the Levant," in *The Dawn of Civilization,* edited by Stuart Piggott (New York, McGraw-Hill Book Co., [1961]), p. 158.
10. Alan Villiers, *Wild Ocean* (New York, McGraw-Hill, 1957), p. 4. Reprinted with permission of the McGraw-Hill Book Co., Inc. Copyright 1957 by Alan Villiers.
11. E. G. R. Taylor, *The Haven-Finding Art* (London, Hollis & Carter, 1956), pp. 135-36.
12. *Ibid.,* pp. x-xi.
13. Herodotus, *History of Herodotus* iv:42. Edited by George Rawlinson (London, Murray, 1875).
14. Villiers, *op. cit.,* p. 37.
15. Vilhjalmur Stefansson, *Great Advantures and Explorations* (New York, Dial Press, 1947), p. 5. Copyright 1957 by the Dial Press and used with the permission of the publishers.
16. Strabo i:3:2.
17. George Rawlinson, *History of Phoenicia* (London, Longmans, Green, 1889), Chap. 9.
18. Armando Cortesão, *The Nautical Chart of 1424* (Coimbra, Portugal, University of Coimbra, 1954), p. 98.

CHAPTER 17: TESTIMONY OF THE GREEKS

1. Bibby, *Testimony of the Spade,* p. 266.
2. Diodorus Siculus, *Bibliotheca historica,* Bk. V, 19-20. The English translation and the original Greek are to be found in C. H. Oldfather's *Diodorus of Sicily,* The Loeb Classical Library (Cambridge, Harvard University Press, and London, Heinemann, 1939), Vol. III, pp. 145-51.
3. Cortesão, *The Nautical Chart of 1424,* pp. 35, 95.

CHAPTER 18: PHOENICIAN CARTHAGE

1. Herodotus, iv:196.
2. R. Bosworth Smith, *Carthage and the Carthaginians* (London, Longmans Green, 2d ed., 1877), Chap. 1.
3. E. H. Bunbury, *A History of Ancient Geography among the Greeks and Romans* (London, J. Murray, 1879), Vol. I, p. 332.
4. Mungo Park, *Travels in the Interior Districts of Africa* (Philadelphia, James Humphreys, 1800), Chap. 20.
5. *The Periplus of Hanno,* translated from the Greek by Wilfred H. Schoff (Philadelphia, The Commercial Museum, 1912), pp. 3-8.
6. Henry M. Stanley, *In Darkest Africa* (New York, Scribner, 1890), Vol. II, pp. 41-42.
7. Contenau, *La civilisation phénicienne,* p. 232.
8. See C. W. Müller, *Geographi graeci minores* (Paris, 1861), Vol. I, pp. xxi-xxiv.

CHAPTER 19: THE LOST FLEET OF ALEXANDER

1. Gladwin, *Men out of Asia*, p. xv.
2. Atkinson, *Stonehenge*, p. 177.
3. Hooton, *Up from the Ape*, p. 519.
4. Gladwin, *op. cit.*, pp. 232-33.
5. *Ibid.*, p. 270
6. *Ibid.*, p. 273.
7. *Ibid.*, pp. 322-23.
8. Macgowan, *Early Man in the New World*, p. 176.
9. Gladwin, *op. cit.*, pp. 337-39.

CHAPTER 20: STRANGERS IN SOUTH AMERICA

1. Anonymous, *The Conquest of Peru*, as related by a member of the Pizarro expedition. Reproduced from the Seville edition of 1534; translated by Joseph H. Sinclair (New York, New York Public Library, 1929), pp. 37-38.
2. Francisco de Avila, "A Narrative of the Errors, False Gods, and Other Superstitions and Diabolical Rites in Which the Indians of the Province of Huarochiri Lived in Ancient Times" in *Narratives of the Rites and Laws of the Yncas*, translated and edited by Clements R. Markham (London, Hakluyt Society, 1873), Vol. XLVIII, p. 124.
3. Sir Arthur Helps, *The Spanish Conquest in America* (London and New York, John Lane, new ed., 1900-1904), Vol. IV, p. 286.
4. Father Miguel Cabello de Balboa, Miscelánea Antárctica (unpublished manuscript in the New York Public Library), Part III, Chap. xvii, pp. 510-16, translated by Philip Ainsworth Means in his *Ancient Civilizations of the Andes* (New York, Scribner, 1931), p. 51.
5. Philip Ainsworth Means, *Ancient Civilizations of the Andes* (New York, Scribner, 1931), p. 55.
6. Rafael Larco Hoyle, "La escritura mochica sobre pallares," *Revista Geográfica Americana*, Año IX, Vol. 18, pp. 83-100.
7. Harold Osborne, *Indians of the Andes, Aymaras and Quechuas* (London, Routledge and Kegan Paul, 1952), p. 30.
8. Pedro de Cieza de León, *The Travels of Pedro de Cieza de León*, A.D. *1532-1550, contained in the First Part of His Chronicle of Peru*, translated and edited by Clements R. Markham (London, Hakluyt Society, 1864), pp. 374-76.
9. Ronald L. Olson, "Old Empires of the Andes," *Natural History*, Vol. 31 (January-February, 1931), pp. 19-20.

CHAPTER 21: UP FROM SAVAGERY

1. J. Alden Mason, *The Ancient Civilizations of Peru* (Harmondsworth, Middlesex, England, Penguin Books, 1957), p. 28.
2. Bibby, *The Testimony of the Spade*, p. 243.

3. Junius B. Bird, "Preceramic Cultures in Chicama and Virú," in *A Reappraisal of Peruvian Archaeology*, ed. by Wendell C. Bennett (Menasha, Wis., Society for American Archaeology, Memoir No. 4, 1948), p. 25.

4. J. B. Hutchinson, R. A. Silow, and S. G. Stephens, *The Evolution of Gossypium and the Differentiation of the Cultivated Cottons* (London, Oxford University Press, 1947), p. 75.

5. Carl O. Sauer, "Cultivated Plants of South and Central America," in *Handbook of South American Indians*, ed. by J. H. Steward, Vol. VI (Washington, Smithsonian Institution, Bureau of American Ethnology, Bulletin 143 [1950]), p. 537.

6. George F. Carter, "Plant Evidence for Early Contacts with America," *Southwestern Journal of Anthropology*, Vol. VI, No. 2 (Summer, 1950), p. 179.

7. Mason, *op. cit.*, p. 51.

8. Philip Drucker, "La Venta, Tabasco: A Study of Olmec Ceramics and Art," Smithsonian Institution, Bureau of American Ethnology, Bulletin 153 (1952), p. 231.

9. Julian H. Steward, "A Functional-Developmental Classification of American High Civilizations," in *A Reappraisal of Peruvian Archaeology*, ed. Bennett (1948), pp. 103-04.

10. Robert Wauchope, "Implications of Radiocarbon Dates from Middle and South America," *Middle American Research Records*, Vol. II, No. 2 (1954), p. 32.

CHAPTER 22: ENIGMAS OF PERU

1. Victor W. von Hagen, *Realm of the Incas* (New York, New American Library, 1957), p. 72.

2. Ceram, *Gods, Graves, and Scholars*, p. 145.

3. Mason, *The Ancient Civilizations of Peru*, pp. 238-39.

CHAPTER 23: A MUTED RUMBLE

1. Erland Nordenskiöld, "Origin of the Indian Civilizations in South America," in *The American Aborigines, Their Origin and Antiquity*, edited by Diamond Jenness (Toronto, University of Toronto Press, 1933), pp. 262-64.

2. Per Collinder, *A History of Marine Navigation*, translated from the Swedish by Maurice Michael (New York, St Martin's Press, 1955), p. 79.

3. Peter H. Buck, *Vikings of the Sunrise* (New York, Frederick A. Stokes, 1938), p. 314.

4. Edward B. Tylor, *Researches into the Early History of Mankind and the Development of Civilization* (London, J. Murray, 2d ed., 1870), p. 158.

5. J. Macmillan Brown, *Peoples and Problems of the Pacific* (London, T. F. Unwin, 1927), Vol. II, p. 68.

6. Philip Ainsworth Means, "Pre-Spanish Navigation off the Andean Coast," *American Neptune,* Vol. II, No. 2 (April, 1942), p. 125.

7. Thor Heyerdahl, *Kon-Tiki, Across the Pacific by Raft,* translated by F. H. Lyon (Chicago, Rand McNally and Company, 1950), p. 198. Copyright 1950 by Thor Heyerdahl. Published in the U.S. by Rand McNally & Co., and in Great Britain by George Allen & Unwin, Ltd.

8. Thor Heyerdahl, *Aku-Aku* (Chicago, Rand McNally and Company, 1958), p. 373.

9. Robert Heine-Geldern and Gordon F. Ekholm, *Significant Parallels in the Symbolic Arts of Southern Asia and Middle America,* Selected Papers of the XXIXth International Congress of Americanists, Chicago, Vol. II (1951), pp. 299-328. See also Gordon F. Ekholm, "Is American Indian Culture Asiatic?" *Natural History,* Vol. 59 (October, 1950), pp. 344-51. Cf. Robert L. Rands, *The Water Lily in Maya Art: a Complex of Alleged Asiatic Origin,* Smithsonian Institution, Bureau of American Ethnology, Bulletin 151 (1955), pp. 79-153.

10. George F. Carter, "Plant Evidence for Early Contacts with America," *Southwestern Journal of Anthropology,* Vol. VI, No. 2 (Summer, 1950), pp. 166-67.

11. Thor Heyerdahl, *American Indians in the Pacific* (London, George Allen and Unwin, 1952), p. 443.

ACKNOWLEDGMENT
OF SOURCES
OF ILLUSTRATIONS

I am deeply indebted to the following museums, foundations, publishers, authors, artists, and photographers for permission to reprint illustrations contained in this book and wish to acknowledge this obligation with hearty thanks.

FIGURE

1-3. *Codex Florentino.*

4. *Natural History.*

5. Lienzo de Tlaxcala.

6. Miguel Covarrubias, *Mexico South,* Alfred A. Knopf, New York, 1946. Drawing by Miguel Covarrubias. Copyright by The Condé Nast Publications, Inc.

7-10. Désiré Charnay, *The Ancient Cities of the New World,* Harper and Brothers, New York, 1887. Drawings by P. Sellier.

11. Franz Feuchtwanger, *Kunst im alten Mexiko,* Atlantis Verlag, Zürich, 1953. Photograph by Irmgard Groth-Kimball.

12. Paul Westheim, *Arte antiguo de Mexico,* Fondo de Cultura Económica, Mexico, 1950. Photo by Ernest Rathenau. Reproduced by courtesy of Fondo de Cultura Económica.

13. *Arte prehispanico de Mexico,* Instituto Nacional de Antropología e Historia, Mexico, 1946.

14. Ewing Galloway.

15. Feuchtwanger, *op. cit.* Photo by Irmgard Groth-Kimball.

16. Reproduced by permission of G. P. Putnam's Sons from *Ancient Mexico* by Frederick A. Peterson. Copyright 1959 by Frederick A. Peterson.

17. Reproduced from *Gods, Graves, and Scholars* by C. W. Ceram, by permission of Alfred A. Knopf, Inc. Copyright 1951 by Alfred A. Knopf, Inc.

18. A. T. Olmstead, *History of Assyria,* Charles Scribner's Sons, New York, 1923.

FIGURE

19. Feuchtwanger, *op. cit.* Photo by Irmgard Groth-Kimball.

20. Egon Edwin Kisch, *Entdeckungen in Mexiko,* Progress-Verlag Johann Fladung, Düsseldorf, 1952. Drawing by Gisela Kuske.

21. Leopoldo Batres, *Exploraciones de Monte Albán,* Casa editorial Gante, Mexico, 1902.

22. Feuchtwanger, *op. cit.* Photo by Irmgard Groth-Kimball.

23. Paul Westheim, *La Escultura del Mexico antiguo,* Universidad Nacional Autónoma de Mexico, Mexico, 1956. Photo by Ernest Rathenau. Reproduced by courtesy of the Dirección General de Publicaciones de la U.N.A.M.

24. John L. Stephens, *Incidents of Travel in Central America, Chiapas, and Yucatan,* Vol. I, Harper and Brothers, New York, 1841. Drawing by Frederick Catherwood.

25. Reproduced from *Gods, Graves, and Scholars* by C. W. Ceram, by permission of Alfred A. Knopf, Inc. Copyright 1951 by Alfred A. Knopf, Inc. Reconstruction drawing by Tatiana Proskouriakoff.

26. *Natural History.*

27. Feuchtwanger, *op. cit.* Photo by Irmgard Groth-Kimball.

28. American Museum of Natural History.

29. Charnay, *op. cit.*

30. S. Greco.

31. Alberto Ruz Lhuillier.

32. Paul Rivet, *Cités Maya,* in "Les Hauts Lieux de l'Histoire," ed. by Albert Champdor. Albert Guillot. Paris, 1954. Photo by Alberto Ruz Lhuillier.

33-35. Alberto Ruz Lhuillier.

36. *Pemex Travel Club Bulletin,* Mexico, September 1, 1956.

37. John L. Stephens, *Incidents of Travel in Central America, Chiapas, and Yucatan,* Vol. II, Harper and Brothers, New York, 1841. Drawing by Frederick Catherwood.

38. Instituto Nacional de Antropología e Historia, Mexico.

39. *Arte prehispanico de Mexico,* Instituto Nacional de Antropología e Historia, Mexico, 1946.

40. Charnay, *op. cit.*

41. Reproduced by permission of G. P. Putnam's Sons from *Ancient Mexico* by Frederick A. Peterson. Copyright 1959 by Frederick A. Peterson.

42. Georges Perrot and Charles Chipiez, *History of Art in Phoenicia and Its Dependencies,* Chapman and Hall, London; A. C. Armstrong and Son, New York, 1885, Vol. I.

43. Harold Sterling Gladwin, *Men out of Asia,* McGraw-Hill Book Company, New York, 1947. Drawing by Campbell Grant.

44. Paul Westheim, *Arte antiguo de Mexico,* Fondo de Cultura Económica, Mexico, 1950. Photo by Arnold Deutsch. Reproduced by courtesy of of Fondo de Cultura Económica.

FIGURE

45. Paul Westheim, *Ideas fundamentales del arte prehispanico en Mexico,* Fondo de Cultura Económica, Mexico, 1957. Photo by Ruth Deutsch. Reproduced by courtesy of Fondo de Cultura Económica.

46. Paul Westheim, *La Escultura del Mexico antiguo,* Universidad Nacional Autónoma de Mexico, Mexico, 1956. Photo by Ruth Deutsch. Reproduced by courtesy of the Dirección General de Publicaciones de la U.N.A.M.

47. Courtesy, Trustees of the British Museum.

48. A. E. Cowley, *The Hittites,* Oxford University Press for the British Academy, 1926.

49. Leopoldo Batres, *La Lapida arqueología de Tepatlaxco,* Orizaba, Mexico, 1905.

50. John Garstang, *The Hittite Empire,* Constable and Company, London, 1929.

51. A. Martello.

52. Perrot and Chipiez, *op. cit.,* Vol. II.

53. Pierre Montet, *Byblos et l'Egypte,* Paul Geuthner, Paris, 1928-29.

54. Perrot and Chipiez, *op. cit., Vol. I.*

55. Courtesy, Trustees of the British Museum.

56-67. Charnay, *op. cit.*

58. *Natural History.* Original in the American Museum of Natural History.

59. Perrot and Chipiez, *op. cit.,* Vol. II.

60. Original in the De Sosa collection.

61-62. American Museum of Natural History.

63. Paul Rivet, *Cités Maya,* in "Les Hauts Lieux de l'Histoire," ed. by Albert Champdor. Albert Guillot, Paris, 1954. Photo, Musée de l'Homme.

64. American Museum of Natural History.

65. Charnay, *op. cit.*

66. Paul Rivet, *Cités Maya,* in "Les Hauts Lieux de l'Histoire," ed. by Albert Champdor. Albert Guillot, Paris, 1954. Photo by Jesus Núñez Chinchilla.

67. Ernst Sellin, *Tell Ta'annek,* C. Gerold's Sohn, Vienna, 1904.

68. Perrot and Chipiez, *op. cit., Vol. II.*

69-70. Reproduced from *Gods, Graves, and Scholars* by C. W. Ceram, by permission of Alfred A. Knopf, Inc. Copyright 1951 by Alfred A. Knopf, Inc.

71. G. Contenau, *La civilisation phénicienne,* Payot, Paris, 1926.

72. C. C. Torrey, *Annual,* American Schools of Oriental Research, Vol. I, 1919. Courtesy, American Schools of Oriental Research.

73. Perrot and Chipiez, *op. cit.,* Vol. II.

74. Perrot and Chipiez, *op. cit.,* Vol. I.

75. Courtesy, The Commercial Museum of Philadelphia.

76. Perrot and Chipiez, *op. cit.,* Vol. II.

77. Kenneth Macgowan, *Early Man in the New World,* Macmillan Company, New York, 1950.

INDEX

ABOUT THE AUTHOR

Constance Irwin's interests extend from archaeology to history, literature, travel, and sports. She has written a study of the dramatic criticism of George Jean Nathan, four teen-age fiction books with sporting backgrounds, and a children's picture book. After graduating from Indiana University, where she was a member of Phi Beta Kappa, she received an M.A. from Indiana and a B.S. from Columbia University. At present she is an instructor in Library Science at the University of Iowa.

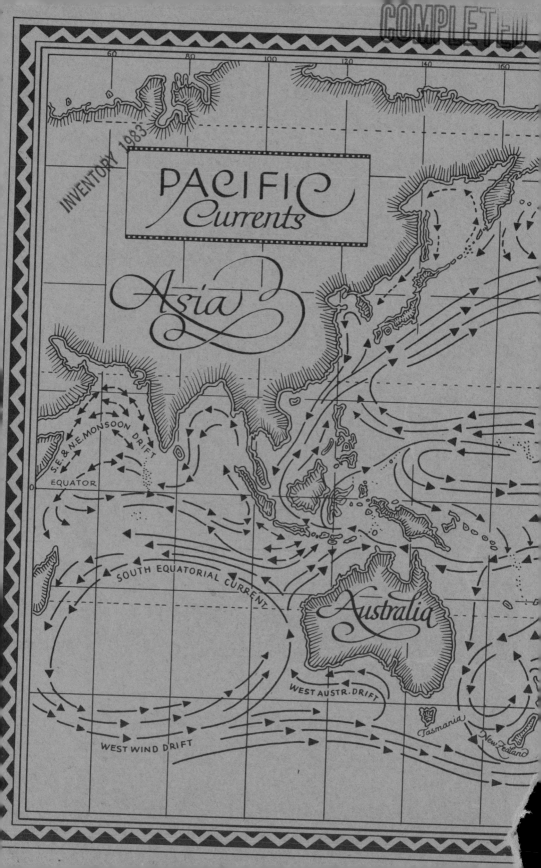